THE STATE OF THE REAL

THE
STATE
OF THE
REAL

AESTHETICS
IN THE
DIGITAL AGE

edited by
Damian Sutton
Susan Brind
Ray McKenzie

I.B. TAURIS

LONDON · NEW YORK

Published in 2007 by I.B. Tauris & Co Ltd
6 Salem Road, London W2 4BU
175 Fifth Avenue, New York NY 10010
www.ibtauris.com

In the United States and Canada distributed by Palgrave Macmillan,
a division of St. Martin's Press, 175 Fifth Avenue, New York NY 10010

ISBN: 978 1 84511 077 2

A full CIP record for this book is available from the British Library
A full CIP record for this book is available from the Library of Congress
Library of Congress catalog card: available

Typeset in Palatino by Dexter Haven Associates Ltd, London
Printed and bound in Great Britain by TJ International, Padstow

Contents

List of Illustrations

Plate section

Notes on Contributors

Susan Brind is a lecturer in the Department of Sculpture & Environmental Art at Glasgow School of Art. She has exhibited widely in the UK and Europe and she has also received a number of awards and commissions, including, in 2001, a permanent commission for the London School of Hygiene & Tropical Medicine's Keppel Street building. Previous published writing includes *Curious: Artists' research within expert culture* (Glasgow: Visual Arts Projects, 1999).

James Coupe is an artist who draws upon computer science, bio-engineering and nanotechnology to build art systems that are self-organising, interconnected encounters. His work has been exhibited online and offline throughout the world and he has been the recipient of several prestigious awards, grants and commissions. Documentation is available at http://www.ctrl.me.uk. Originally from the UK, he now lives in Seattle, where he is a Research Fellow at DXARTS, University of Washington.

Alan Dunning is Chair of Media Arts & Digital Technologies at Alberta College of Art in Calgary, Canada. He has received major awards from Canada Council, La fondation Daniel Langlois, the Social Sciences and Humanities Research Council and the Association of Commonwealth Universities. His work is included in collections at the National Gallery of Canada and MoMA, New York.

Andrew Lee studied Fine Art Photography at Glasgow School of Art, graduating in 1996. He is currently a photographer, artist and occasional lecturer based in Glasgow

Neil Matheson is Senior Lecturer in Theory and Criticism of Photography at the University of Westminster. He is editor of the collection *The Sources of Surrealism* and has written on surrealism in England and on the Belgian surrealist E.L.T. Mesens. His recent work has focused on the role of photography in relation to cultural memory.

Elizabeth K. Menon is Assistant Professor of Contemporary Art History at Purdue University, West Lafayette, Indiana. Professor Menon's current research, entitled Cyborg Art History, seeks to integrate new media and technology-driven art into the art history canon. Recent publications include 'Ut Pixel Poesis', in *Turning Trees: Selected Readings of the International Visual Literacy Association*, edited by Robert Griffin (Rochester, NY: IVLA, 2003).

Ray McKenzie is Senior Lecturer in the Department of Historical and Critical Studies, Glasgow School of Art, where he teaches mainly the history of photography and sculpture. His publications include *Photography 1900* (1994), *Dangerous Ground: Sculpture in the City* (1999) and *Public Sculpture of Glasgow* (2002), which won the Saltire Society's Research Book of the Year award in 2002.

Jenna Ng is a PhD candidate in Film Studies at University College, London. She is writing her dissertation on digital cinema.

Lennaart van Oldenborgh is a London-based documentary filmmaker and broadcast video editor. He received an MA in Screen Documentary from Goldsmiths College, London, in 2004. He has recently formed a partnership with Adnan Hadzi under the name H+O Films, specialising in documentaries that explore political and historical issues through individual stories. Van Oldenborgh previously studied at the Rijksakademie in Amsterdam, and at Hampshire College in Amherst, Massachussetts.

Kate Robinson is a sculptor. She has exhibited work, and completed public commissions, throughout Britain and abroad. A recipient of a Guardian/Modern Painters' Prize for Writing on Art in 2004, her book *A Search for the Source of the Whirlpool of Artifice* was published by Dunedin Academic Press in 2006.

Susanne Østby Sæther is Research Fellow at the Department of Media and Communication, University of Oslo, Norway, where she is currently completing a doctoral thesis on the aesthetics of sampling in contemporary video art. She was Curatorial Fellow in the Whitney Independent Study Program at the Whitney Museum, New York, in 2005–2006, and is a regular media commentator in Norwegian newspapers.

Michael Smyth is a Senior Lecturer in the School of Computing, Napier University, Edinburgh. His principal research activities are in the areas of Human Computer Interaction, the Support of Design Exploration, Metaphors in Interface Design and Interaction Design. He has published over 30 papers in academic journals and conferences.

Damian Sutton is a Lecturer in Historical and Critical Studies at the Glasgow School of Art. He has published in journals on photography, cinema and television, and is the author of *Photography, Cinema, Time*, forthcoming from University of Minnesota Press.

Jane Tormey lectures in Critical & Historical Studies at Loughborough University School of Art & Design. Her research interests focus on the ways in which photographic practices can disturb conceptual and aesthetic traditions and reference a range of work from Walker Evans's late Polaroid portraits to Allan Sekula's critical realism. She co-edits the electronic journal *Tracey – Contemporary Drawing* and has had work published in *Masquerade: Women's Contemporary Portrait Photography* (Ffotogallery, 2003), *IJADE* and *AfterImage*.

Jennifer Willet and **Shawn Bailey** have worked collaboratively on BIOTEKNICA (www.bioteknica.org) for five years. Shawn Bailey is a practising artist, an Associate Professor at Concordia University, Montreal, in Studio Arts (Print Media) and an artist-researcher with the Hexagram Institute, Montreal. His work has been presented in exhibitions, publications, public lectures and multimedia/web projects across Canada and internationally. Jennifer Willet is a professional artist and a faculty member in Studio Arts at Concordia University. Her work explores notions of self and subjectivity in relation to biomedical, bioinformatic and digital technologies, with an emphasis on social and political criticism. She exhibits, lectures and publishes across Canada and internationally.

Paul Woodrow is Professor of Art at the University of Calgary. He has been involved in a variety of interdisciplinary activities since the late 1960s, including performance art, installation, video, painting and improvised music and jazz. He has exhibited extensively in Japan, France, Italy, Sweden, England, Argentina and the United States, including at the Museum of Modern Art, Stockholm, and the Tate Gallery, London. He has received major awards from the Canada Council and the Social Sciences and Humanities Research Council.

Slavoj Žižek is Senior Researcher at the Institute for Social Sciences in Ljubljana, Slovenia. His books include *The Sublime Object of Ideology*, *Everything you always wanted to know about Lacan (but were afraid to ask Hitchcock)*, *The Plague of Fantasies*, *The Fragile Absolute*, *Iraq: The Borrowed Kettle* and *Interrogating the Real*.

Preface

This book provides an overview of the key issues that have come in recent years to dominate the critical discussion of the concept of the real, and assesses the impact these are having on current practices in visual culture. It brings together contributions from authors working in a wide range of disciplines, including fine art and design history, film and media studies and critical theory, as well as from practitioners working at the front line of art and design itself. It makes no claim to be the last or most definitive word on its subject; indeed, a central part of its purpose is to raise new questions and open up fresh lines of investigation. All the same, we do believe that the particular combination of interests gathered together here provides a reliable cross-section of the most innovative and provocative research currently being pursued under the general rubric of 'the state of the real'.

The production of this publication was preceded by a conference with the same title that took place at Glasgow School of Art in November 2003, and it was largely as a result of this international gathering that the need for a more in-depth investigation became evident. It is important to state, however, that the result is not intended as a volume of conference 'proceedings' in the conventional sense. While most of the texts collected here have been derived from papers delivered on that occasion, and so may be said to stand as a partial record of the event, no attempt has been made to document the conference as it actually occurred. The intention, rather, has been to develop the main areas of concern that emerged from the live presentations and to recast them in a form more appropriate to self-standing publication.

By its nature, the discussion generated by a concept as fundamental as the real lends itself to a wide variety of editorial approaches. The strategy adopted here has been to assemble the contributions in a way that will allow ease of navigation for the reader, and to achieve this it has been found helpful to divide the anthology into three broad themes. At the centre of the debate, and forming the middle section of the book, is the work of a number of contemporary artists who have chosen to address, either directly or from a more oblique perspective, the way in which recent technological innovations have begun to penetrate our perception of reality. In addition to the four chapters that explore this issue discursively, 'Realism in practice' also includes a photographic essay by the artist Andrew Lee, whose seductive views of the interiors of call centres provide a tellingly understated visual complement to the critical discussion flowing through the entire book. Rigorously dispassionate, but replete with haunting detail, these images resonate with the contradictions of a culture that has allowed itself to become dependent xiv / THE STATE OF THE REAL

on the instantaneous transmission of information by electronic means. They are reproduced here with no text and no interpretative gloss – a mode of presentation precisely analogous to the mute eloquence of the office hardware on display within them.

The middle section is framed by groups of contributions that context-ualise the discussion in two principal ways. In 'Realism reinvented' the issues dominating the current debate are shown to have their roots in critical practices that have been evolving steadily throughout the post-war period, chiefly in photography but also in certain aspects of painting. In the final section, 'How real is the Real?', the discussion leads naturally into the terrain of virtuality and other branches of advanced technology, bringing together a range of new insights into the task of interpreting their role within contemporary visual culture and the way in which we engage with it. This section, and the book as a whole, concludes with Professor Žižek's magisterial synthesis of the political, philosophical and scientific issues that remain embedded within the discourse of the real, however dramatically it might appear to have changed in recent years.

In preparing this anthology the editors have been assisted by many people in many different ways. Thanks are due, first and foremost, to the staff of the Department of Historical and Critical Studies and other colleagues elsewhere in Glasgow School of Art for their support during the 2003 conference: Jane Allan, Elaine Boyle, Ross Birrell, John Calcutt, Tanya Eccleston, Patsy Ford, Gordon Hush, Antonia Malcolm, Lyn McLaughlin, Nicholas Oddy, Bruce Peter, Frances Robertson, Sarah Smith, Jim Ward and Elizabeth Biedler. Acknowledgement is made to the Research Committees of the Schools of Fine Art and Design for their generous financial support for the conference and publication. Special thanks must go to the contributors for their patience during the drawn-out process of bringing the text to completion, and to the editorial team at I.B.Tauris for their helpful advice throughout. Grateful thanks are also extended to the following: Linda Nochlin, Simon Gough, Kerry McKenzie, Peter Seddon.

INTRODUCTION
The State of the Real

Damian Sutton, Susan Brind,
Ray McKenzie

The Twenty-First-Century Real: some working assumptions

Finding a point of entry into a debate as multi-layered as the one being
addressed here was never going to a simple or straightforward matter,
and as a result it has been necessary to take as given many aspects of it
that might rightly be viewed as in themselves open to contestation. In
particular, there are two central assumptions that provide what might
be described as the book's animating motive, and it is important that
these are made clear at the outset. The first is that the period within
which the arguments articulated in this book have been formed is one
in which a major process of cultural transformation is taking place, with
potentially far-reaching implications for the way in which we might soon
come to experience the 'real world'. The second is that visual practices,
far from having a merely reflexive or contingent role in this process, are
among the most important agents through which that transformation is
being brought about.

   With regard to the first of these assumptions, there is certainly an
abundance of evidence to support such a view, so much so that it is
tempting to suggest that in the transition we have recently made from
the twentieth century to the twenty-first it was more than just the page of
a calendar that was turned. In almost every area of cultural endeavour
we care to look at – in science, in art and design, in the popular media,
but above all in the field of information and communication technology
– recent developments have been so rapid, and the qualitative impact
they have made on our lives so decisive, that it seems almost perverse
to deny that a more or less major process of change is now under way.
A sea change, a step change, a tipping point, a paradigm shift – it is

difficult to know which metaphor most closely characterises the historical moment we are now living through, but there is little doubt that the onset of a new world of some kind, brave or otherwise, has accompanied the arrival of the new millennium.

Evaluating the dynamics of historical change, and identifying those factors that signify structural rather than merely incidental alterations in our cultural landscape, is a notoriously hazardous undertaking, and it may well be that the process of transformation that is being posited here will be shown in time to have been more apparent than real. All the same, it is worth noting that there are many other areas of intellectual practice in which the relevance of inherited or 'common-sense' notions of the real are now being re-examined. One example (and there are many others) from within science is Susan Greenfield's *Tomorrow's People*, a speculative analysis of what developments in technology might bring us over the next half-century.[1] Her concern here is not just to outline the practical advantages that new gadgets and techniques are likely to deliver, but rather to identify the phenomenological changes they will bring with them and which will in turn force us to redefine 'what we see as reality'. The book is not, she insists, 'a catalogue of "wow" phenomena and inventions, but rather the beginning of understanding how we might think about ourselves in a rather different way, and how the boundary between ourselves and the outside world might start to blur'.[2]

How much of what we think of today as the 'human condition' will survive this blurring process remains to be seen. In the meantime, the question of what reality might begin to *feel* like in the future has already become a familiar concern within what can still just be recognised as traditional fine art practice. Typical of many forays into this area of creative speculation is the 2005 exhibition at the Norwich Gallery by the former BANK member John Russell, the 'dead son of bourgeois mysticism'. Entitled *Geniess*, it consisted of a '28 x 8 ft *image-object*' incorporating 'blood, entrails [and] internal organs' as well as 'ecstatic uses of flesh such as childbirth'. The result, it was promised, constituted an event space that would enable those who viewed it to 'experience new modalities of subjectivity'.[3]

The claim that the world is indeed changing and, more crucially, that *we* are changing with it, seems to be sufficiently in tune with current critical thinking, and sufficiently likely to generate usable insights into the nature of contemporary experience, to be worth adopting as a working hypothesis. It is on this basis that the current anthology has been produced.

Words and Things: the appearance of the real

Any attempt to define what constitutes the real, and how it is perceived at any particular historical juncture, involves more than merely identifying the relevant cultural forces in play at the time; a number of more abstract theoretical issues also need to be addressed. In this regard it might be useful to consider the expression 'more apparent than real', which has just been used in connection with the alleged cultural transformation taking place around us. What questions are begged by formulating the problem in this way? To begin with, the antithesis between the real and the apparent derives whatever force it has in this context from its implied association with the cognate binarism of the true and the false. In normal usage, it is understood that, if what we perceive is only apparently the case, then we must in some sense be mistaken – we have failed to grasp what is really, and therefore truly, the correct state of affairs. Such an elision between the real and the true is dubious at the best of times, but in a context that concerns itself primarily with representation – as is the case with this book – the problems it raises are particularly acute and need to be scrutinised with some care. Representational practices occur within an economy of meaning in which appearances are themselves the principal medium of exchange. How, then, is the notion of appearance to be understood here? We cannot begin to answer this question until we have looked a little more closely at the concept of the real, and more specifically at that uniquely troublesome entity, the word 'real' itself.

A little-known but in this context very pertinent analysis of the word can be found in J.L. Austin's *Sense and Sensibilia*, a series of essays based on notes for a lecture course first delivered in Oxford in 1947, but not achieving their definitive form until 1959.[4] As a linguistic philosopher, Austin was less concerned with explaining what words mean – that, after all, is the job of a dictionary – as with investigating how their behaviour is determined by the semantic field in which they occur, and it is by this strategy that he is able to demonstrate that many of the so-called 'problems of philosophy' are not really problems at all, but obfuscations stemming from a confused use of language. The target of his critique in this case is *The Foundations of Empirical Knowledge*, A.J. Ayer's influential exposition of the then fashionable empiricist doctrine that we do not experience the real world directly, but only through the mediation of mental events known as 'sense data'.[5] The central proposition of this doctrine is the 'argument from illusion', which Ayer illustrates by citing the familiar optical phenomenon in which a stick that is partially immersed in water appears to be crooked. For Ayer and his empiricist colleagues, the fact that there is such a pronounced difference between what we see (an illusory crooked stick) and what is actually in front of us (a real straight stick) casts doubt on the reliability of the entire process of sense perception, and confirms the belief that we can never, by definition, know the world 'as it really is'. But various questions immediately arise. In what sense is the straight stick more real than the crooked one? Precisely what sort of unreality characterises its existence when it is in the water as opposed to when it is on dry land? And what if the stick were slowly withdrawn from the water – are we to say that it gradually becomes more real in the process? The questions are nonsensical, of course. For Austin, however, they provide a salutary reminder of the absurdities that can occur when we try to deduce epistemological generalisations from terms that have not been properly examined.

The root of the problem here is the fact that the word 'real' is, at least in Austin's analysis, one of the most profoundly complex monosyllables in the entire English language, its behaviour so volatile that it must be handled with the linguistic equivalent of radiation-protection gloves. It belongs to a small but semantically treacherous group of expressions that he describes as 'substantive-hungry' – expressions, that is to say, that signify nothing in isolation, but derive their meaning entirely from the context in which they are deployed.[6] In an even more colourful formulation of this view (though one that is unlikely to win many admirers today), he goes on to describe 'real' as 'what we may call a *trouser-word*'. It is, he says,

> usually thought, and I dare say usually rightly thought, that what one might call the affirmative use of a term is basic – that to understand '*x*', we need to know what it is to be *x*, or to be an *x*, and that knowing this apprises us of what it is *not* to be *x*, not to be an *x*. But with 'real'…it is the *negative* that wears the trousers. That is, a definite sense attaches to the assertion that something is real, a real such-and-such, only in the light of a specific way in which it might be, or might have been, *not* real.[7]

Thus the statement 'this is a real duck' is, for all practical purposes, a meaningless assertion unless it is made clear from the context precisely what kind of non-real duck the speaker intends to exclude – a decoy used to attract larger waterfowl; an ornament on a chimney breast; a toy floating in a bathtub – all of which may be perfectly real in all sorts of other ways. The range of options is sufficiently wide for Austin to be able to draw the general conclusion that

> the attempt to find a characteristic common to all things that are or could be called 'real' is doomed to failure; the function of 'real' is not to contribute positively to the characterisation of anything, but to exclude possible ways of being *not* real – and these ways are both numerous for particular kinds of things, and liable to be quite different for different kinds of things.[8]

We can see now that the semantic bracketing with which we began – real versus apparent – is only one of a much larger network of binary oppositions within which the concept of the real is free to roam. In addition to the different forms of non-real ducks we have already encountered, a provisional list of answers that might be given to the question 'real as opposed to what?' would include the following: an hallucination; a mirage; an illusion; a dream; a copy; a hoax; a pretence; a fake; an allegory; a mirror image; a representation (a painting, a sculpture, a video and so on). Nor should we ignore the various adjectival expressions that are commonly used to signify a non-real status, such as artificial ('astroturf is not real grass'), phoney ('he's not a real punk') and ideal ('in an ideal world…'). The latter opposition is one that needs to be treated with particular caution. To assert that something exists not in the real world but in the realm of ideas can signify many things, ranging from the intellectual austerity of the Platonic universal to the wish fulfilment peddled by magazines such as *Ideal Homes*.

Doubtless the analysis could be usefully extended from the noun 'real' to the various adjacent terms derived from it, such as 'really', 'reality', 'realistic, 'realism' and so on, but enough has been said to confirm the general insight that emerges from Austin's discussion.[9] However much our everyday linguistic habits might suggest otherwise, there is in fact no one property that is being ascribed to things when we designate them as real. This is true regardless of whether we are dealing with simple objects or a more general notion of the 'real world', understood in either its colloquial or philosophical sense. The meaning of the word is dispersed across a vast and complex pattern of linguistic possibilities, performative contexts and private intentions. Though this does not in itself rule out the possibility of deducing a reified Platonic entity designated as 'the Real', it clearly signals the caution that must be exercised in performing such a precarious philosophical manoeuvre. It also exposes the bizarre conclusions we are led to when we try to erect an epistemological system on the basis of something as insecure as an optical illusion.

The Visual Real

Among the various binary possibilities generated by the linguistic functions of the real, the most relevant to the visual arts is, as has already been hinted, that in which it is opposed to appearances. Indeed, one might go so far as to say that in this context the real and the apparent are locked together in a relationship of mutual semantic dependency. Even here, however, the concept of appearance cannot be regarded as philosophically (or, indeed, morally) neutral; the suspicion that some form of deception is being worked is never very far away. One of the founding myths of European art history is the story of Zeuxis, who is alleged to have produced a painting of a bowl of fruit so visually convincing that flies settled on it in the mistaken belief that the fruit was real. The entire tradition of *trompe l'oeil* painting stems from this example, and, although this never achieved more than a marginal status in mainstream European art, it was for a long time regarded as a touchstone for what could be achieved in the field of mimesis – the technical mastery of how things in the world actually look.

The belief that in painting reality and appearances are theoretically interchangeable was to acquire a particular urgency in the context of the Italian Renaissance, partly because of the generally more 'scientific' approach to representation that developed at that time, but more specifically because of the invention of single-point perspective. The relevance of perspective to the main theme of this book, however, is not simply the fact that it provides a powerful historical model for how the real can operate in the context of a particular visual practice; it anticipates an aspect of the contemporary critical debate in a much more precise way. One of the central issues raised by the transition from analogue to digital photography is the realisation that in the production of a digital image it is not necessary for the 'subject' of the photograph to refer to a pre-existing 'object' in the world, that there is nothing outside the representational process that might be thought to function as its prototype. Whereas in conventional photography an independent entity of some kind – a person, a landscape, a building – is normally thought to be necessary as a causal precondition for the production of its pictorial representation, in the digital system this need not be the case. The various dilemmas, moral and otherwise, that are raised by this are familiar enough by now, and some of the problems associated with this issue are touched upon in later pages in this book. But the question also arises: is this such a new predicament?

Linear perspective was invented in the early fifteenth century, but, as with the introduction of photography four hundred years later, it took more than one form. It is generally assumed that the first systematic application of the laws of linear perspective to the task of picture-making was the experimental painting of the Florence Baptistry, produced some time between 1410 and 1415 by the architect Filippo Brunelleschi (1377–1446). Painted on a wooden panel, this image of the building was captured with such fidelity to the laws of perspectival recession that the result struck his contemporaries as looking 'absolutely real'.[10] We know from an account of the process by the artist's biographer Antonio Manetti that Brunelleschi's intention was that the image on the panel should correspond exactly to the appearance of the baptistry when it was viewed from a pre-determined spot, and that to achieve this he contrived a method of controlling the viewing position using a peephole drilled into the rear of the panel and a mirror held in front. The illusion was completed by the application of burnished silver in the area representing the sky, so that clouds could be seen reflected in it from the real sky above. Although Manetti does not go into any detail here, it is evident that a complex process of geometric calculation was used in reducing the building's structural relations, and all the perspectival diminution involved in viewing it from a distance, to the miniature scale of the panel. But the important point is that the picture had a subject – it was a visual replication of an independently existing structure.[11]

Some twenty years later Leon Battista Alberti was to write his seminal treatise, *On Painting*, in which he outlined his own approach to the creation of perspectival images.[12] In this case, however, no buildings or any other physical objects were needed to achieve the goal of a realistic representation. The procedure is described in Book One, which Alberti himself acknowledges as being 'all mathematics', and involves the step-by-step construction of an illusionistic space with nothing except a pencil, a ruler and a pair of dividers.[13] Although Alberti tellingly refers to the picture plane as something that is 'considered to be a window through which I see what I want to paint', it is clear that this is only a metaphor, and that no actual window with a view onto the outside world is required.[14] The pictorial space is generated entirely from within the theoretical structure of the system itself, with buildings and figures distributed at will within the pattern of internal relations established by the vanishing point and the network of transversals and orthogonals that flow logically from it. Alberti's experiments with the idiom, like Brunelleschi's panel, have been lost, but an image such as the celebrated panel entitled *Ideal Town* in the Palazzo Ducale, Urbino, dating from c.1450, probably gives us a reasonable idea of the results he produced: a perfectly convincing representation of an urban scene, but for which no existing town served as a model.[15] If such an image can be said to 'represent' the world, it clearly does so in a very different way from Brunelleschi's panel. It is in fact closer to the contemporary notion of the 'simulacrum', defined as 'a copy without an original'.

The pattern of dialectical relations involved in this process, with the concept of representation acting as a middle term between reality and appearance, was to remain central to the discourse of visual art throughout the whole post-Renaissance period, and was still a relevant concern when the historical movement we nowadays refer to as Realism began to emerge in the early nineteenth century. At this point, however, a number of new complications enter the debate. For one thing, photography itself had by now made an appearance, enabling artists to achieve by purely mechanical means the kind of replication of spatial experience that Brunelleschi could produce only with the aid of mirrors, burnished silver, wood-boring tools and a laborious process of calculation. But the introduction of photography was only one part of a much broader process of historical change taking place at this time, largely precipitated by the triumph of Positivism in the physical sciences, the penetration of industrial capital into the economic sphere and the creation of a politicised urban working class. Of major historical importance at this time also was the establishment of the various socio-political forces – such as Chartism and the trade union movement – that were linked to the demand for democratic accountability. Against a background such as this it is hardly surprising that the critical discussion of Realism was to open up on a number of new fronts, with questions of visual style giving way to the more urgent concern to define the function of the artist in relation to the social, moral and political issues of the day. In purely optical terms, the *grandes machines* of the Salon and Academy painters of the Victorian period are no less 'realistic' than the paintings of near-destitute agricultural workers by Gustave Courbet and Jean-François Millet. Indeed, the historical costume dramas of artists such as Lawrence Alma-Tadema, who borrowed heavily from photographs, are arguably more so. What gives a work such as Courbet's *The Stonebreakers* (1849) its relevance to specifically nineteenth-century conceptions of Realism is nothing to do with the illusionistic efficacy or otherwise of its surface treatment but the provocative frankness with which it confronts an uncomfortable political truth. Here the opposition between reality and appearance does indeed begin to elide with the true and the false, with the notion of historical authenticity played off against the sanitised idealism of establishment art.

Nor is it just in the visual arts that such a view is to be found. Much of the critical literature of the period is permeated by the same desire to invert the age-old subordination of the real to the ideal, the same privileging of the quotidian and the same imperative to pit the actuality of the world as it is against everything that is false and inauthentic. The English critic G.E. Lewes, for example, is quite blunt in his assertion:

Gustave Courbet, 'The Stonebreakers', 1849 (destroyed).

'Realism is the basis of all art, and its antithesis is not Idealism, but Falsism.'[16] But the true spirit of the debate is nowhere more memorably expressed than in the words of Henry Thoreau, when, in a striking passage in *Walden*, he enjoins us to 'settle ourselves, and work and wedge our feet downward through the mud and slush of opinion, and prejudice, and tradition, and delusion, and appearance...till we come to a hard bottom and rocks in place, which we can call *reality*...Be it life or death, we crave only reality.'[17]

Exasperated by the persistence of the old ways of thinking, Thoreau was clearly a man of his time. Indeed it is difficult to imagine a leading intellectual placing such uncritical faith in the world as we find it – in the value of ordinary things perceived for what they are – except in an historical context in which scientific discourse was dominated by the philosophy of Positivism and in which the paradigm of visual representation had shifted so decisively from the painting to the photograph.

Penetrating the Visual Real

Perhaps the most celebrated example of the impact of photography is the story of Paul Delaroche seeing a daguerreotype for the first time and exclaiming: 'From today painting is dead'.[18] Yet Delaroche was already painting the kind of frozen moment that would later, in the twentieth century, become the peculiar ellipsis of time expected of the photograph. In fact, Delaroche's *The Execution of Lady Jane Grey* (1833) owes more in its representation of time to Michelangelo than it can ever be understood to presage Henri Cartier-Bresson's description of the photograph's 'decisive moment'. Jane's hand, stretching desperately for the executioner's block, echoes Adam's hand reaching to God's in Michelangelo's Sistine ceiling (1509–1512). The birth of man as the maker's final triumph is mirrored by woman's fall. Jane Grey, of course, was overthrown by the agency of Mary I, but the composition of the *Execution* has the headsman and sergeant of the tower looming over her in a similar manner to Michelangelo's Creator. Delaroche's exclamation cannot readily be understood as a prescience of photography's ability to divide time in such an excruciating manner. Photographic technology would take a number of decades to achieve the kind of instantaneity required to achieve this, and may even have been developed partly as an attempt to do with photography what painting had already achieved. Yet, if this is the case, to what was Delaroche's (possibly apocryphal) statement referring?

The answer, perhaps, lies in Courbet's brutal composition for *The Stonebreakers*, which suggests not only the moment of the photograph (in the tired swing of the hammer, in the teetering basket of rocks) but the *view* of photography. Not only does the point of perspective identify the viewer in a position above and distanced from the workers (thus visually referring to the class divide; an earthier, more pragmatic divide than that suggested in Delaroche's *Execution*), but the awkwardness of their looking away from the viewer echoes the peculiarly indiscriminate nature of so much candid photography. The composition is used by Courbet as if to suggest an incontrovertible relation between reality and the painting's viewer; an entrapment in the real, rather than a penetration of space by the objective eye. Delaroche's prediction that 'painting is dead' may not then have referred to the representation of reality that had been painting's charge since the Renaissance, but instead this unique ability to trap the spectator in the real; not just to penetrate space but to maroon the spectator within it. Just as one is trapped in this painful moment of toil, one is trapped in the awful circumstances that brought the situation about. Courbet's painting therefore emphasises a 'truth' (of the power relation between viewer and scene) through what the perspectival viewpoint cannot show us, rather than through what it records referentially – the often-assumed power of the photograph.

The Stonebreakers, with all the attendant mechanical problems of the camera eye though *painted* rather than photographed, therefore illustrates André Bazin's suggestion that photography took over the Renaissance project of representing the world as it is seen.[19] It should come as no surprise that photography forms a key disciplinary discussion in this book. Bazin's ontological argument of the interpenetration of photograph and object is just one theoretical approach to the privileged relation of photography with the real. Instrumental to its early experimenters, such a relation had also been a part of its phenomenal success after its invention, in both portraiture as well as the earliest photographic survey movements.

It is no less a truism, furthermore, to say that it is in photography's privileged relation to the real, advertised by the very public discussion of the science of photography that attended many of its stages of invention, that the 'real' began to be equated with 'truth'. By the end of the nineteenth century, police practices of surveillance, such as the anthropometric technique of 'Bertillonage', succinctly did away with any debate over the photographic 'real', with the photograph providing silent evidence of identity. What marked it out as different from previous examples of inmate photographs, landscape surveys or even the earliest photographic inventories, such as those made in the 1840s by William Fox Talbot of his possessions, was Bertillonage's archiving of the indiscriminate and the aleatory in order to rationalise the real. The process relied not on representing the likeness of the sitter or the object, nor even the fact that so many criminals looked 'alike', but that the archive would demonstrate how the real defied generalisation, as a scar or a birthmark would ensure that a criminal could not disappear into the generality of the crowd.[20]

The snapshot, which emerged after 1888, extended the photograph's link to reality only insofar as it placed the means of photography in the hands of the public. This appearance of reality, which exercised Roland Barthes enough to write his famous *Camera Lucida*, is as evident in the 'that has been' of any 1840 daguerreotype as it is in any snapshot taken in the twentieth century.[21] Yet many of Barthes' illustrations are from the emergent genre of photojournalism – Matthew Brady, James Van Der Zee, William Klein – and it was in this genre that the notion of 'truth' would first really test the photograph's connection to the real. Lewis Hine's acknowledgement in the 1920s of the power invested in the photographer – '[whilst] photographs may not lie, liars may photograph' – began a debate that always rested in the 'trust' that can or cannot be placed in the photographer.[22] When the photograph is described as objective, or indeed part of the object itself as in Bazin, it is necessarily separated from subjectivity. After Hine, photographers in the Soviet, German and American schools would embrace 'straight photography' in an effort to purge the image of anything that might betray the subjectivity of the photographer – in particular those signs of manipulation that had come to be tainted with the bourgeois notion of the picturesque. Serious critical approaches to the technology of photography as implicated in a contest of truth are few and far between until the advent of digital photography in the late 1980s, despite the medium having a long and healthy 'history' of manipulation. Such a history includes retouched images of China's 'gang of four' or of Stalin's former supporters, each removed as they were assassinated. It goes further back to photographs of fairies, staged battle photographs from the Crimea or the Civil War in America, and has its parallel in the selective composition of elements in the pictorialist images of Oscar Rejlander and Henry Peach Robinson in the 1860s.[23] In fact it had to wait until the period after Bazin, when the notion of 'truth' came under the greatest assault from postmodern theory, for this debate to take on a full life in the academy. Yet the most severe attacks on 'truth' were directed towards the photographer as author, in accusing works by Sherrie Levine, for example, or in the writing and photography of Martha Rosler. In contemporary times, the apparent ease with which digital photographs can be altered appears to put under strain the accepted notions of truth, evidence and the 'real' which we have popularly taken for granted. Yet this picture of our reliance on photography being broken by digitality – a picture given shape by the flourishing of new academic writing on the digital image in the mid-1990s – is woefully inadequate to illustrate the complex relationship that photography has always had with the real.[24] Hence this book contains no fewer than four essays that explicitly deal with such an elemental debate.

So where did this sudden acknowledgement of the *unreliability* of photography's relation to truth come from? The advances made in computer-generated imagery (CGI) in cinema, in the development of real-time computer image simulation, as well as in digital manipulation in photography, were concomitant. It is no accident that blockbuster cinema of the 1990s developed storylines that exploited anxieties of virtual reality simulation – *Lawnmower Man* (US, Brett Leonard, New Line Cinema, 1992), *Disclosure* (US, Barry Levinson, Warner Bros, 1994), *eXistenZ* (Can/UK/Fr, David Cronenberg, Columbia/Alliance Atlantis, 1999) – or which questioned the reality effect of digital simulation by using it to create virtual worlds through computer-generated effects and imagery – *The Matrix* (US, Andy and Larry Wachowski, Warner Bros, 1999). Throughout the 1990s the discussion of the 'real' circulated around the separation of the real from simulation, subjectivity and virtuality. If there is a technological fulcrum around which this debate swings, it is most certainly the development of, and hype surrounding, virtual reality (VR) in art and design practice, emerging from both military and commercial videogame applications. The notion of VR itself – a computer-generated environment into which a disembodied spectator/user is immersed – re-stimulated the binarism of the real by collapsing the semantic dualism inherent in the proposition of a 'virtual' reality. Largely based on VR's simulation of the real, cinema's depiction of VR illustrated a technology of extraordinary complexity for sheer spectacle (*Disclosure*), to suggest enlightenment (*Lawnmower Man*), or to illustrate a breakdown of the comprehensible difference between reality and simulation to the point of confusion (*The Matrix*, *eXistenZ*). The seeming effect of VR was to turn the notion of Platonic mimesis on its head. A bed produced in the cinematic vision of VR was not an image removed from reality, as Plato's example of a painting of a bed was.[25] In the cinema's depictions of VR one could *really* lie on an image of a bed, really create new objects that were only images but nonetheless could be manipulated and 'dealt with' as corporeal objects. Indeed, on this principle, the 'holodeck' became an enduringly popular aspect of the television series *Star Trek: The Next Generation* (US, Paramount, 1987–1994).

The anxieties of simulation – to wake up realising that one has been imagining the world, or to not know when one is playing in virtual reality or in 'real' reality – expressed in films such as *The Matrix* and *eXistenZ* relied upon the assumption that one day, if not today, the simulation of reality would be photographically real. VR in the 1990s was, and largely remains, far short of such complexity, for the most part due to the processing power required of computers to render the artificially created world in real time. Where cinema production allows for large amounts of time, and often *thousands* of 'farmed' processors, to render images for computer-generated animation, real-time applications such as VR or videogames fall far short of the imagined complexity of simulation often depicted in those same films.

'Healing' the Real

The fissure between what was expected of the simulation of 'another reality' and the abstractness created by current technology was demonstrated in large-scale artistic applications of VR, of which Char Davies' *Osmose* (1995) is perhaps the most famous. Immersing oneself in *Osmose* involved being strapped into an apparatus that reacted to deep breathing to allow up and down movement: weightlessness encouraged by deep inhalation, relaxation encouraged by exhalation. Such subtle movement offset the clumsiness of the headset, which showed the three-dimensional virtual world into which the 'immersant' passed.[26] The world itself was organised around levels that represented actual space (a pond) as well as abstract space (free-floating though data and text), thus combining the approximate and realisable abilities of VR environments. However, with an expected euphoric and affective response to the environment, *Osmose* can hardly be seen as a simple attempt at mimesis designed to fool the eye as *trompe-l'oeil* (and later nineteenth-century dioramas) had been. Instead, *Osmose* and its later manifestation *Ephémère* (1998) were, for Davies herself, clear attempts to provide an artistic *and* cognitive solution to the binarism inherent in the self/other equation of mind and matter.

> Osmose is about our relationship with Nature in its most primary sense...Osmosis: a biological process involving passage from one side of a membrane to another. Osmosis as a metaphor: transcendence of difference through mutual absorption, dissolution of boundaries between inner and outer, inter-mingling of self and world, longing for the Other. Osmose as an artwork seeks to heal the rational Cartesian mind/body subject/object split which has shaped so many of our cultural values, especially towards nature.[27]

Thus the ultimate aim of Davies' project was for the mind to penetrate the Euclidean space suggested in the image by both passing through a mimesis (pond) as well as dissolving extensity itself (data/text). It tried to 'heal', yet ultimately relied upon, a philosophical, dualistic appreciation of reality and the mind following Descartes and others.

In fact, in another etymological twist, the term 'virtual' had already been used in the phenomenological sense to refer to quite the opposite state of affairs to those seen in VR, and it is this that becomes more useful for understanding the 'state of the (technological) real'. 'Virtual', in an explanation by Gilles Deleuze, is opposed to the 'actual' of the optical image. For Deleuze, the actual image on screen in film – as dreams, recollections, memories – is always surrounded by a virtual, pure recollection that is always in a mutual relationship with it. 'The actual is always objective,' Deleuze confirms, 'but the virtual is subjective'.[28] Thus the film is an actualisation of so many dreams, recollections and memories

which are drawn from the virtual. Could it not be the case for all photographic images? Perhaps more fundamental is that such a reversal of what has come to be accepted as the 'actual/virtual' asks us to relocate the 'real' within it. Whilst the photographic image may be actual, what are real are the 'virtual' images which inform it. This has further resonance as the hubbub surrounding VR has subsided and other technological issues have questioned our acceptance of the real.

As an example of this, the problem of 'truth' in the photographic image, as illustrated in a reality rendered entirely artificially (VR, computer-generated cinema), has given way to anxieties of manipulation. Despite being the subject of intense debate for many decades, stories of the manipulation of photographs regularly hit the news-stands. More recently these have included staged photographs, such as the *Daily Mirror*'s controversial use of faked images of prisoner abuse in Iraq in 2004, as well as digitally manipulated images, such as the combination image of Jane Fonda and US presidential candidate John Kerry appearing together at a Vietnam rally in the 1970s. Many of the *real* pictures of prisoner abuse in Iraq, which emanated from the Abu Ghraib prison in 2004, were taken and circulated digitally, suggesting once again that photography's relationship to real events is one based on trust, rather than truth, and that the digitisation of photography has altered this rather less than might be expected.

Virtual reality environments continue to be used and refined in industrial and architectural design, amongst other uses, and the level of rendering quality in these applications continues to improve. Yet such applications continue down a path of photographic realisation that relies heavily on visual immersion into a virtual environment. The primacy of visuality in these uses has led to calls for a return to 'tangible' design methods, some of which are discussed in this book – calls that echo in a broader debate over the loss of the object in art practice and criticism. Technologies of virtualisation have, in this sense, replaced the corporeal or 'hard' world with an objectless or 'soft' one. The technology of virtuality in this case is the rapid expansion of the Internet since the late 1990s, taking VR's place as the dynamo of a dissolving social world. The discussion surrounding the art object on the net is just one example of a wider social change occurring through technologies of mobility – so called because they are often mobile in themselves (the laptop, the cellphone) or they promote a mobile life in place of a static one (webmail, weblogging).

The move towards a mobile society, as studied by groups such as CeMoRe – Lancaster University's Centre for Mobility Research – has seen the dissolution of many social and cultural institutions in favour of more accessible versions available on the Internet and via mobile devices. Websites such as Amazon and eBay have been instrumental in the evolution of a virtual shopping mall, whilst most banks now have Internet banking. For John Urry and Mimi Sheller, researchers at CeMoRe, this increased mobility is a dominant change in society, reflected in persons that cease to be embodied in a particular time, space (or even body), and who instead leave 'traces of their selves in informational space' to be accessed from a-centred locations.[29] A defining action for such persons is the daily 'self-retrieval' (of email, of interesting news items, of sports results) carried out in front of a screen that reflects their life back to them.

The Desire for the Real

No doubt it is the spectacle of our progressively 'dissolving social world', together with the need for us to learn to live an increasingly 'mobile life', that explains the apparent drive to reassess what can be verified. We need to find some fixed point(s) by which to orient ourselves in the postmodern world, or at least some constant with which to identify in order to navigate a way through the collective schizophrenia that could be said to characterise our condition today.[30] Psychoanalytic theory, the body of knowledge established and developed in the twentieth century (which was itself the age that gave rise to our increasing sense of individualism), has proved an indispensable guide to the contemporary interpretation of what the Real might be.

Psychoanalytic theory is a rational and secular discourse that attempts to define reality as experienced by the subjective individual, and the key theorists in this field whose work is most relevant to the debate here are Sigmund Freud and Jacques Lacan. Freud developed many theories that illuminate the concerns of this book, not least his identification of the significance of the unconscious in the formation of identity and the expression of repressed desire. But he also made an observation that is of particular importance to the present discussion. He was the first to point out that the real object we desire is the mother's breast, which he described as 'the "always already lost" object that may be thought of as the idyllic union with the mother that actually never was but which the subject nonetheless presumes that it had and seeks indefatigably to retrieve'.[31]

Lacan subsequently pushed Freud's theories about the desired object further by asserting that the object was lost with the entry into language.[32] During the Oedipal phase the infant has no consciousness of anything outside itself and the breast to which it is attached. In the 'mirror stage', Lacan believed, the infant becomes aware of difference (between self and other) and subsequently functions in the world through the operations of the 'symbolic order' – that is through image and language. With the awareness of separation, the connection with the *real* object is, Lacan argues, always eluding us and can never be fully described. Both image and language, then, are always a substitute for the thing itself. 'Just as language can never fully seize on meaning, so desire, for Lacan, is a driving force with no ultimate satisfaction.'[33] Thus the Real is 'the essential object which is not an object any longer, but is something where all words cease and all categories fail, the object of anxiety *par excellence*'.[34]

Our endless return to the mirror stage is an attempt to satisfy our desiring selves, a process by which identity is vested in the self and the world is perceived as 'other'. The image and text made of light that emanates from the computer screen might, indeed, be one such return. Essentially, though, this permeable surface is a complicated kind of mirror: one that reveals to us not only our desires and our lack, but one that may also contain the potential cause of our neurosis. Whereas the reflection that we see in a static mirror (or image) allows time for deep inner reflection, the information about ourselves embedded in the image within the screen is constantly changing. The diaphanous mobile screen of the PDA, cellphone or computer is thus the new Lacanian mirror.

With the growing penetration of virtual technology into our lives, we have become more urgently aware than ever of the need to make sense of a world in which nothing is fixed and in which our sense of what we are is always defined in relation to something other than ourselves; a world, as described by Karl Marx in his Communist Manifesto, in which 'all that is solid melts into air'. Postmodern discourse has created the impression that this condition is unique to the contemporary world but an examination of the historic concerns of philosophers suggests other-wise. Here it might be useful to invoke the writings of Bertrand Russell. In his analysis, for example, of how knowledge and perception were understood by Plato – whom he regards as both a philosopher and a mystic – Russell identifies three interconnected theses that have been central to Western thought since the days of the pre-Socratic philo-sophers. These are:

(1) knowledge is perception;
(2) Man is the measure of all things;
(3) everything is in a state of flux.[35]

It would seem, then, that nothing much has changed except the nature of the context that surrounds us. We still live in the world of appearances, precisely as described in Plato's simile of the cave.[36] The only difference now is that the apparent reality we see is not projected by the light of the fire but created by the light of the flickering impulse controlled by binary code – a kind of digital mirage that, as it pulses on and off, appears and disappears in rapid succession. In our renewed quest for the Real in the digital age, we are thus logically drawn towards Bertrand Russell's three 'Laws of Thought', the last of which, known as 'the law of excluded middle', states that *everything must either be or not be*.[37] A one or a zero – there is no middle term. We thus define ourselves by looking for things, or images, that either affirm what we are or confirm what we are not. It is by this means that we identify what we want to become. Freud, it is significant to note here, made an additional point about our ultimate state of desire. In *Beyond the Pleasure Principle* he asserted that 'human beings possess a death instinct, a built-in self-destructive wish to die, to revert to the inanimate state'.[38] This, he asserted, is our *real* desire.

It has since become a commonplace to say that the only real events about which we can have no doubt are our birth and our death: in the absence of all other certainties about what is real, these are the two hard facts that define our existence. And yet it is remarkable how many diverse interpretations this simple truth has generated. A Freudian, for example, would explain this as the death-drive – the compulsion that carries us from sex to our demise. A philosopher such as Leibniz, on the other hand, would discuss it in terms of the question of existence and non-existence.[39] In contrast to both of these, a Sufi mystic would, echoing Plato, express it as the journey of transformation – from the 'first stage of the self'[40] towards annihilation; becoming 'extinguished' in an 'infinite Reality'.[41] Be it through psychoanalytic theory, philosophy or mysticism, the common aim is to identify the point at which Russell's second 'Law of Thought' – *nothing can both be and not be* – is true. We long to reach the state where our desires have been met, where being and nothingness are both discrete and concrete, where union is achieved and 'nothing' (or 'existence Beyond-Being') might be an absolute reality.[42] By whichever means, until we arrive at that point of completion, all events between the two extremes of birth and death are either traces of the trauma of the approaching void, or the process of being, or the journey of becoming.

What do we make of this process and how can we learn from it? However inadequate Lacan's realm of 'the symbolic' might be, the fact remains that language and image are the only means we have at our disposal here: we simply have no alternative but to speak from our own position and to create for ourselves some kind of tolerable reality, however partial. However, with everything in flux in the world around us, it becomes all the more crucial to be sure of our own position in relation to things outside ourselves, and to attempt to find some sense of an objective reality for ourselves, should such a state exist. This requires consciousness – the attribute that, philosophers tell us, distinguishes us from all other creatures. It is our responsibility to use our consciousness – and our ability to reflect – in order to interpret the reality that we find ourselves occupying and to be sure that we contribute to living the reality that we wish to experience. Certainly we can use psychoanalysis and recent critical theory to understand how to achieve presence through the process of reflection. As Victor Burgin reminds us:

> Forward movement in life is achieved through a backward move-
> ment in memory, but one that is more than a simple temporal
> regression. In place of the blocked nostalgia or nausea of the perpetual
> return, the past is transformed in such processes as 'working through'
> and 'deferred action'.[43]

If we do not act there can be no change, and we will be destined to
remain in the endless cycle of our neurosis. We can reflect and move on,
as Victor Burgin tells us, and we know from Plato that consciousness
enables us to speak with integrity and to see with clarity.[44] So how are
we using the resources of knowledge and consciousness at our disposal
to help us better understand not our fantasies but our lived reality?

Through engaging in philosophical and political discourse, as well as
through science and art, we can reflect on life and consciousness. To do
so is not to indulge in mere navel-gazing introspection, but to confront
the world as it presents itself to us, and to examine how our own moral
conduct operates within the economic and other power structures at
work around us. Artists now employ any media and means at their
disposal to re-present to us the world as they see it – or rather as *we* see it,
since increasingly these media include embracing the viewer's subjective
experience as an integral element of the work. The integration of each
viewer acts as a way of creating many unique meanings but also, in the
case of installation art, as a device to call the viewer to consciousness,
physically as well as mentally – to be 'present' with and through the
work. Such an experience with any work of art that aims to address the
instability and danger of the world can, however, never give a complete
representation of reality, nor an act of closure. Indeed it is precisely the
opposite. It is 'an encounter with this [as an] impossibility'.[45] The potential
of such art is to open our senses to the enormity of our dislocation from
the Real in everyday life by confronting us with an authentic experience:
one that cannot be circumscribed. This is what Julia Kristeva calls the
'True-Real'; an experience with art that might bring about change within
ourselves.[46]

Telling Truths and Tasting the Real

It is arguable that in the West we are beginning to realise that the
attempt to fulfil our desires and construct our identities through the
consumption of commodities does not bring us any closer to knowing
our real selves.[47] And as we become aware of the impact that this type
of lifestyle and the values associated with it have on communities on
the other side of the globe, as well as on our own environment, it is
increasingly clear that consumer capitalism is rapidly losing whatever
allure it may have had in the late twentieth century.[48] In Europe in the

twenty-first century we may no longer be breaking stones by hand but we can now see that others elsewhere have paid the price for our progress. We have begun to see that our desire to consume, either in the real shopping mall or in the virtual store, is no more than a veil between ourselves and a range of more important political, social and (some would argue) metaphysical debates. We have begun to have to look elsewhere in our attempt to experience something *really* meaningful, by means of which we might see more clearly who and what we are.

Apart from of our consumer identities but still within the public realm, where better to see a true reflection of who and what we are than via documentary footage? Russell tells us, in the first of his 'Laws of Thought' – 'the law of identity' – that *whatever is, is*.[49] Logically, then, if we have seen that something occurred, it must be *true*. Although, as stated earlier, we know that some images are manipulated and may therefore not be true. But, to complicate matters further, things hard to believe have really happened, *have* happened. We have seen mice with human ears on their backs and we have witnessed 9/11. We have seen it all on the news, so in some sense it must have happened, must therefore have been. Weirder than any straight stick that appears to be crooked, these are the facts that can be verified and we have the images to prove it. The trauma of these 'live' video images of death is that they look almost *too real to be real*. We struggle to absorb and comprehend them. Ultimately, the moment of rupture contained within them becomes embodied within us, but all they can actually *prove* to us at the time is that it is not we who are dead. Individually and collectively, we still are left to deal with the moral and ethical implications contained, however, within such images.

We try to use scientific facts and medical ethics to verify at least what it means for the body to be alive. With the technology of positron emission tomography (PET) we can now 'prove' what happens in the brain when the body moves: that old question that Descartes posed and never really managed to answer. Using a virtual 'cone of vision' instead of Brunelleschi's mirror, science now permits us to see precisely what is going on in the brain when the body attached to it is experiencing sexual pleasure. Science can now reveal, to anyone who requires the proof, whether an orgasm is real or whether it is being faked.[50] We have truly entered the space of desire!

Whatever the motivation for imaging the orgasm, however, PET can explain only the mechanics of sex. This is the kind of scientific objectivity that brings us full circle in trying to see what lies between sex and death. It provides the visual evidence of how connections are made between the body and the brain, but tells us nothing about the pleasure of submission and abandon, or the experiential content of the bliss engendered by the act of sexual union.

But, as Slavoj Žižek points out in his essay in this volume, what about when one feels that one is 'passionately in love'? How can we prove that love really exists? Not through language, and certainly not through images, but through *tasting*: by knowing through the body and the heart; by feeling as well as thinking. Descartes may have been responsible for separating the mind from the body (as vessel), but even he was still trying ultimately to comprehend the individual being as a unified whole. To that end he tried to understand the role of the heart. It is necessary, he claimed, 'to know that although the soul is joined to the whole body, there is yet a certain part in which it exercises its functions more particularly than in all the others; and it is usually believed that this part is the brain, or possibly the heart'.[51]

Indeed, he tried to ascertain the point of interaction, the soul, precisely in that space he saw between the heart and the mind. He found it, he thought, in a part of the brain he called the 'gland', which he defined as 'the most inward of all its parts…a certain very small gland which is situated in the middle of its substance and which is so suspended above the duct whereby the animal spirits in its anterior cavities have communication with those in the posterior'.[52]

Whereas Descartes was trying to find a physiological home for the soul, approximately two centuries later, in his celebrated analysis of human anatomy, Henry Gray informed us that the 'gland', named the pineal gland, is actually no more than a

> small reddish gray body, conical in shape…[that]…consists of a number of follicles, lined by epithelium, and connected together by ingrowths of connective tissue. The follicles contain a transparent viscid fluid and a quantity of sabulous matter named *acervulus cerebri*, composed of phosphate and carbonate of lime, phosphate of magnesia and ammonia, with a little animal matter.[53]

Again, we can say that these are the facts, but they still do not explain what it feels like to fall in love, when we are consumed by love *body and soul*.

If we were to close the gap opened up by followers of Descartes – and thereby reunify the mind and the body through reinstating the notion of the soul, as Julia Kristeva suggests might be possible – we might be able to experience love, consciousness *and* reality through the simultaneous use of all the knowledge that we have at our disposal: with the mind, the pineal gland and the heart working together as a unified experiential agent.[54] Might we then be better able to understand what lies at the heart of our *real* sense of lack? This was a familiar enough prospect to both the early Christian and Sufi mystics, who believed that if the 'mirror of the heart' were polished sufficiently to reflect the Divine Other within us, a much clearer perception of reality would be achieved than when the brain is busy with purely intellectual analysis, or the ego preoccupied solely with itself.

As the images that surround us proliferate, and as our belief in the truth of them becomes less secure, the world we inhabit begins to look more and more like the world of light and appearance posited by Plato. This is a place in which the 'law of contradiction' – the second of Russell's 'Laws of Thought' in which *nothing can both be and not be* – is the rule.[55] It is also a place where the only true Real is that which exists in the space between ourselves and that which can *never* be defined, either through language or the visual image. The irony, as this book testifies, is that our condition as humans – our existential state – means that we never stop trying to define it.

We know from ancient literature and philosophy that the desire to ask questions of, and reflect upon, the nature of our existence is something Man has wrestled with for centuries. Psychoanalytic theory has replaced spirituality as the central focus in defining the Real, and it is no coincidence that this occurred at the point when the Church began to lose control over Western society. It is because our desire to define reality is so deep-rooted that psychoanalytic theory became such a dominant influence on twentieth-century thought, and why visual art has such a crucial part to play within any discourse on the representation of reality.

Whether we approach it through rational thought or subjective experience, through psychoanalysis, political action, spiritual belief or purely through its re-presentation in art, it would appear that our experience of the Real can never be more than partial. This is the challenge taken up by the essays in this compilation in their attempt to map the contemporary debate. The book does not profess to be a definitive text on either philosophy or psychoanalytic theory. What it does demonstrate is the significance of those disciplines to artists, art historians and cultural theorists alike in their endeavour to illuminate our understanding of the Real, and to help us think about what is *good* on the basis of consciousness rather than appearances.

I / REALISM REINVENTED

Introduction

No discussion of realism can begin in earnest without acknowledging the degree to which our understanding of it is conditioned by the cultural circumstances in which we, and it, are embedded, and by extension the degree to which the concept has evolved and mutated over time. Whether we choose to focus on Realism (an art historical category) or 'the Real' (a philosophical construct), it is evident from what has been discussed already that neither is going to oblige us by falling tidily into a unified or stable definition. They are both inventions that have already been reinvented many times over. The first task, then, is to determine how realism is to be defined *for us,* and how the critical debate associated with this endlessly contested term can be best adapted to suit the particular historical juncture in which we find ourselves today.

The texts brought together in this first section offer four alternative takes on how this might be done, in the process laying the groundwork for many of the more specialised debates that will be developed later. Even at this early stage, however, it is clear that the issues encompassed by this debate are both complex and varied, ranging from visual aesthetics to the sociology of broadcasting, with various major critical systems such as semiotics and deconstruction invoked along the way. For all their diversity, the four contributions here are nevertheless underpinned by a number of common concerns, some of them overt, others less so, but all of them confirming the relevance of the real as a major critical issue within contemporary visual culture.

The first and most obvious shared concern is the problematic status of photography, understood broadly to include any process in which a form of camera technology has been used to relay visual representations, either moving or still. Among the more specific issues identified here as requiring special consideration is the question of the medium's 'index-icality' – the fact that a photographic image has a causal relationship with the objects it represents. This is the central conundrum from which any investigation of the uniqueness of photography must proceed, and to which it will always sooner or later return. Many key aspects of its ontology – to say nothing of its behaviour as a cultural practice – may be explained by reference to this fundamental characteristic, from its status as a paradigm of documentary reliability to the naïve wonderment it allegedly provokes in us all. The work of various distinguished theorists has proved to be enduringly helpful in the exploration of this issue, and the writers in this section are unequivocal in acknowledging their debt to, among others, Walter Benjamin, Jacques Lacan, Jacques Derrida and Roland Barthes in formulating their responses. There is no doubt, however, that the commentator whose ideas have done most to determine the character and direction of this debate is Jean Baudrillard. It is in his assertion that the real has become a 'copy of itself' that we find the most radical statement of the post-structuralist position on photography as a signifying process, and the most provocative challenge to conventional notions of how our perception of the world is mediated through images. Implicit in any debate about the reinvention of the real is the question: how does one continue to make meaningful pictures of the world – whether in photography, video or film – when the world itself is no more 'real' than the images that claim to represent it?

Various answers are posited here. The two writers who concentrate on the still image are both agreed that the aesthetic regime that dominated fine art photography throughout the ascendancy of Modernism – with its striving for the privileged moment 'captured' in a meaningful pictorial structure – is no longer either relevant or viable. But where Jane Tormey sees the alternative in the brutal subjectivity of Boris Mikhailov and Richard Billingham, Neil Matheson locates the debate within a more expansive historical framework, substituting an allegorical function for the medium's traditional documentary role. The upshot, however, is much the same. By steering photographic meaning into a territory that is neither real nor unreal, Tormey and Matheson both identify a cultural space where the project of photography can indeed continue, unencumbered by the various entrenched 'myths' by which it was burdened in the past.

The issue of indexicality is no less relevant for Susanne Sæther and Lennaart van Oldenborgh, who use their essays to explore the most recent manifestations of postmodern practice in the context of the moving image. It is here that the implications of Baudrillard's thinking – most notably his concept of 'hyperreality' – come most fully into play, and where the difficulties of negotiating meaning in a world apparently overwhelmed by 'simulacra' achieve their most insistent form. In their analysis of the various ways in which the documentary imperative of photography has been reconfigured through film and TV, respectively, Sæther and Oldenborgh present a picture of the world we inhabit today that would scarcely have seemed credible to the artists and commentators concerned with the real in the heyday of Modernism. It is a world in which what we once believed to be the private, unitary 'self' really does begin to behave like a postmodern fiction, dispersed across a pattern of social relations that have, in turn, become nothing more than kaleidoscopic reflections in an endless hall of mirrors. It is a world where history, reduced to little more than a vast random-access memory bank, can be dialled up on a mobile phone and where reality itself has become, in Oldenborgh's memorable formulation, just another 'special effect'.

It is not, however, the concern for the ontological status of the mechanically reproduced image that provides the only unifying thread between the chapters in this section: equally telling is their identification of violence as an issue that has come to dominate the contemporary discourse of the real. We first encounter it in Jane Tormey's reminder of how Roland Barthes tried to formulate a general theory of photographic meaning by invoking the concept of the *punctum*, the act of pricking through which the overt content of a photographic image is opened up to provide a glimpse of another, ostensibly more 'authentic', reality. This is a very benign form of violence, to be sure; but the stakes soon begin to climb. In their attempts to isolate the concept of the real we find the authors here repeatedly resorting to metaphors of violation, as if the real can be accessed only through an act of rupturing, or piercing or tearing away. The most immediate reference point for this aspect of the current debate – and by far the most frequently cited source – is Hal Foster's positing of trauma as the precondition of the current 'return of the real'. Where it has returned from – and quite why it ever went away – are matters that still perhaps need to be explained. There is no question, however, that in the context of contemporary critical discourse the concept of 'real' has re-established itself as a central concern. This is the process of reinvention that is now under way, and it is this that the first section of this book seeks to address.

1 Photographic Practice, Postmodernism and the 'Irreal'[1]

Jane Tormey

Looking at depictions of people in contemporary 'art photography', a pattern can be seen to emerge that is unstated but evident in the concerns and the methods used. Focusing particularly on the moment of taking the photograph and the interaction between photographer and subject, this chapter considers the demonstration of postmodern notions of the 'real' reflected in photography and the assumptions that drive such practice. In this context, the understanding of 'postmodernism' is not of a now 'faded' era,[2] but of a consistently dislocated relation to the world,[3] where response to a radically altered consciousness has long since assimilated the inauthenticity of the real. Following this reasoning, successive reactions to experience test the rules of existing aesthetic practice, provoking successive conceptions of the real in a series of 'anti-aesthetics'.[4] Currently, aspects of a photographic aesthetic can be located in conceptual shifts of understanding and in assumptions with regard to the positions of authenticity, authorship and meaning. Photography has facilitated, and to a large degree defined, many of the familiar aspects of what is commonly termed 'postmodern' practice. But issues of authenticity and authorship have had a more elusive and profound influence on meaning than the oft-cited, literal artificiality of depicting false identity, false origin and false reality, evident for example in the works of Cindy Sherman, Sherrie Levine and Jeff Wall. A more pervasive effect is suggested than mere quotation. Photographers, in a 'panic-stricken'[5] search for the real, circumvent the impossible task of making definitive photographic statements by assuming methods that avoid expression and 'meaning' and deflect directorial subjectivity. A quiet reformation is manifested in the way that photographers avoid decision and technical control by embracing 'amateurish things'[6] and the 'non-moment',[7] use strategies that are ambivalent and non-determinate, or adopt a crude form of realism.

In responding to Baudrillard's invitation to play with his ideas,[8] and applying them to photographic practice, I am assuming his notion of 'successive phases of the image': in the reflection of a basic reality; in masking and perverting a basic reality; in masking the absence of a basic reality; and finally 'in bearing no relation to any reality at all'.[9] The tradition of modernist photography could be said to equate with Baudrillard's first phase, of reflection – but with the additional requirement that a 'good photograph' must reveal a more meaningful 'real' behind appearance, transcending the real. We are familiar with Baudrillard's discussion of representation – that of a reality constructed by the image, where we can no longer distinguish between original and copy, between real and imaginary. Thus in subsequent phases of the image, photographers, recognising both our desire for representation of what is 'real' and the impossibility of its depiction, respond by playing with qualities reflecting an ironic, false reality. Because the indexical property of photographs has led us to believe that presentation is possible, that what is presented is real, photographs can easily misrepresent, disguise or bear no relation to reality at all and can be entirely fabricated.

Given that photography confirms 'seeing' as being intrinsic to our understanding of reality, it is its own contradiction in that it must always, by its very nature, reflect appearance. Thus appearance, and its counterpart, the 'real' behind appearance, are central to the irony of the photograph and its meaning; the equivocal role of photographs is key in the evolution of aesthetic strategy. The peculiar condition of the photograph's authenticity thus simultaneously presents the opposition of truth and falsehood, as it invites both a literal (due to its indexical nature) and a figurative (due to the power of metonymy) interpretation. In the contemporary context we have come to expect photographic fiction. Instead of constructing an interpretation that conforms to conditions in the actual world, we suspend reference and project ourselves into a fictional world where anything is believable. However, the concept of the non-literal in photography is contradictory because we *see* the literal reference and the indicative content will always refer outside itself, caught as it is in the inevitable cycle of cause and effect and metaphor. The very literalness of Annelies Strba's *Shades of Time*,[10] for example, implies a multitude of conceptual associations other than the literal, whilst the content remains ultimately banal.

The now customary questioning of authorial 'objectivity' can provoke deliberately contrived manipulations of the photographic encounter, where, for example, subjects whilst being photographed may be instructed to hold their breath or be hypnotised.[11] And a shift in attitude regarding the supremacy of the author provokes either an abdication of the photographer's subjectivity and an avoidance of involvement altogether (as with Shizuka Yokomizo or Beat Streuli, for example[12]) or an interdependence of subjects – photographer and photographed – in an intimate exchange that confounds objectivity, as in the work of Nan Goldin or, more recently, in the manufactured intimacy of Nikki S. Lee.[13] Photographers, no longer having the certainty of their own authority or that of objective vision, and self-consciously aware of this disrupted authorship, have adopted methods that divert authorial interpretation. They carefully present us with documentation without intervention, with appearance only, disallowing any attempt to reveal 'reality' behind

Annelies Strba, 'Sonja with a Glass', from the series *Shades of Time*, 1991. Courtesy of the Frith Street Gallery.

Shizuka Yokomizo, 'Stranger, No. 10', 1999. Courtesy of the Approach Gallery.

the 'mask', presenting instead non-event and an indifference of seeing. The premise of non-determinacy underlines a new kind of 'dis-interested-ness' apparent in photographic practice.

Baudrillard radically challenges the order of the subject and the power of subjectivity and uses his reference to photography to confirm his theories and his idealism regarding lack of communication and significance.[14] In his writing on photography specifically, he proposes an un-definition of what is real.[15] If the central tenet that there is an authentic truth to be found through endeavour is no longer viable, then it becomes meaningless to pursue it and logically one should actively abandon the attempt. Baudrillard describes photography as 'irreal' – empty, a kind of untruth, an absence, a toppling over into the unreal. He challenges the photographer to 'disappear', to 'give up representation', not 'seek an image', not depict reality, 'essence' or universal quality, but present the 'mask' instead – present raw, unmediated appearance, approaching a non-aesthetic.[16] He advocates that the activity of taking the photograph itself be pivotal, be kept careless and uncontrolled, as an 'objective meditation', 'a mental process', replacing the prospect of the anticipated image.[17] He promotes an authenticity mediated by the reader, a 'real' that is not the author's constructed idea of the subject but a disappearance of the photographer as interpreter. Uprooting the photographer's primary role as translator, Baudrillard proposes, and many photographers assume, a lack of control or purpose, allowing meaning to assert itself by way of the insignificant and ordinary in the image. In the face of simulacral confusion, he promotes an oblique re-emergence of the real – decentred, less complete, less focused.

Strba closes her eyes as she presses the shutter and immerses herself in the context of indiscriminate ordinariness and the insignificant whereby nothing is translated for us. Ulf Lundin hides from his subjects, and the series *Pictures of a Family* presents what is incidental and irrelevant.[18] If there is purpose in these series, it is for the a-special moment and the retention of particularity, without irony or cute reference. Metaphoric reference is minimal or indistinguishable. Recognising that an accidental or unassuming image can be equally eloquent leaves the photographer with the ironic possibility that artifice or lack of artifice may be equally deceptive or meaningful. Benjamin Buchloh has used the terms 'carefully careless', 'de-skilling' and 'de-seeing' to describe the prevalence of photographs that are neither crafted nor remarkable.[19] What is 'real' need no longer be elevated or made beautiful and much recent work has embraced this absence by deliberately looking chaotic and uncalculated or distinctly banal – to the point of being super-banal. The assimilation of the snapshot as a genre disrupts the seriousness of photography, as it does not conform to the ethic of artistic distance, a prerequisite for 'objective vision'. Subjective authorial expression has been replaced by a subjectivity that can confuse intimate and professional roles, mix genres with extreme eclecticism, can be ugly and intrusive and approach bad taste.[20]

Works of 'pure' description, which doggedly resist ulterior meaning, such as Beat Streuli's apparent non-discrimination or Thomas Ruff's attenuated portraits, present the contradiction of a transparent, bare record and an opaqueness of consequent meaning, which give us simple appearances that ultimately obscure.[21] These methods of depiction abandon the intervention of 'photographic' expression or the search *for* expression in the subject and are both non-expressive and expressionless. Ruff plays out Baudrillard's impossible realm of reality in photographic practice, the realm of no representation and no meaning. His authenticity lies with the primacy of the image and his determination not to succumb to the illusion of being able to represent, which he implicitly holds as a weakness. He appropriates and combines two forms – the formal portrait and the passport photograph – and presents the person as a reductive abstraction rather than a reference (Baudrillard's second phase of reality), which is a 'thing' rather than a person. (See also contribution by Neil Matheson, below.) The physical presence of the subject in the photograph approaches a condition in which it refers only to itself. He arrives at a version of simplicity: his own brand of purity which avoids the dilemma of subjectivity and confrontation.

The possibility of 'pure' description, discussed in 'The Reality Effect', is an interesting one when translated in relation to photographs.[22] Here Barthes distinguishes descriptive detail that is 'irrelevant' to the narrative structure, 'attached to no functional sequence, nor to any signified characteristics, atmosphere or information'. He suggests that such description is interwoven with the 'imperatives of realism', so that 'referential constraints' are interwoven with 'aesthetic constraints'. He also suggests

Ulf Lundin, from the series *Pictures of a Family*, 1996. Copyright Ulf Lundin.

that it is the *genre* that represents the 'real', the *category* that acts on behalf of the 'real' and 'not its various contents, which is being signified; in other words, the very *absence* of the signified… becomes the true signifier of realism'. This asserts the significance of absence over the certainty of the detail's contribution; that we cannot 'see' the photographic content for the 'reality' we 'see' (understand) as being depicted by it.

Expectations of what is 'real' reside persistently in truth, verisimilitude and 'realism', where the implicit and particular nature of 'purpose' is obscurely embedded and established by the current norm of 'reality'. As the notion of 'realism' is not a law but a habit, and need not be constrained by verifiable 'truth', it is possible that meaning can be more directly symbolic, less plausible and more 'overtly discursive', with aspects of description not essential to the message but integrated with the illusion of realism. Baudrillard's term 'irreal' encompasses the instability of reality and certainty. His project, which seeks to upturn the basic premise of causality and reason, of the supremacy of the subject and 'objectivity', challenges what is 'obvious' and 'natural'. It focuses on the 'particular being or thing' rather than depending on universal determination and the reassurance of the subject. It promotes a fundamental shift in consciousness. Baudrillard sees banality as the inevitable consequence of our belief in and reliance on representation and verisimilitude, where the photograph, aware of its own deceit and self-conscious in its fabrication, absorbs the consequences of cause and effect and creates an 'implosion of meaning'.[23] His critique of our acceptance of the 'referent' as 'real' in its absence, where we are expected 'to glide in a kind of frictionless space from the perceptual to the conceptual', parallels description of the photographic contradiction that leaves us believing in what is not there.[24] In the context of the photograph, this argument comes to rest in his reference to Barthes' 'punctum': 'that figure of nothingness, absence and unreality which stands opposed to the "studium", the whole context of meaning and references. It is the nothingness at the heart of the image which lends it its magic and its power and which is most driven out by significations.'[25]

Baudrillard's theme of absence and nothingness echoes Barthes, whose writing about 'meaning' repeatedly assigns importance to the role of the insignificant. The specificity of context and the visually insignificant is vital to photographs if they are to retain an inexplicable, elusive quality, and not be clothed in symbolism or mythic representation.[26] And a translated image, already explained by the author, can miss the essential and raw import (or reality) of what is photographed. He suggests that the 'invented' image leaves the viewer no room for response or interpretation because the image is already loaded with obvious meaning.[27] Any expectation of some special quality in a photograph is closely allied to an expectation of the author translating experience, via commentary or metaphor, into some universal meaning. If, to achieve this quality of being 'universally true', photographs must signify more generally, must lose particularity, then – according to Barthes – they must lose their history, their context and ultimately their potential power as images.[28] His brief explanation of 'pure meaning' importantly distinguishes between the degree of meaning and effect, explaining the contradiction that an image must 'perform' and surpass its subject to be 'good'.[29] He states that, as every photograph refers to the specific, in order to generate general meaning and thereby 'signify' in a universal way, it has to assume a mask – a definitive, mythic image that will sustain, such as Richard Avedon's portrait of William Casby ('the essence of slavery is here laid bare', the 'mask is the meaning'). Society wants meaning, but translated ('less acute') as opposed to 'absolutely pure'. It mistrusts pure, raw meaning, without a mask, which is more dangerous. Barthes' reflection here points to the degree of balance between being explicit enough to be readable generally, and discreet enough not to disturb too much; enough 'to disturb', but not so discreet as to be ineffective. A photograph, then, is most *effective* 'not when it frightens or repels… but when it is pensive, when it thinks'.[30] How general or specific an image must be to be meaning*ful* or meaning*less* and how meaning and potency are constituted is clearly confusing. Barthes implies that universal narrative (meaning that is trans-historical and trans-cultural) might make it insignificant – that is to say that generality leads to insignificance and that significance must therefore require particularity. If nothing is left for the viewer to contribute, Barthes' indefinable quality cannot exist and the image is ultimately meaningless. Barthes' discussion is difficult, perhaps because he relies on the distinctions between political and aesthetic, between generality and particularity and, implicitly, between public and private, whereas contemporary uses of photography no longer retain these distinctions. (See chapter by Damian Sutton, below.) The position and clarity of purpose or effectiveness is central to the condition of 'meaning' and its status of quality. For an image to be powerful, it requires a position at the extreme edge of purpose or effectiveness, approaching insignificance. If we separate effectiveness from potency and assert that one does not derive from the other, we establish a place prior to the persistent assumption of cause and effect, regarding 'good' and powerful photographs.

Boris Mikhailov's brutal images are situated between pictures being too confrontational and being illegible.[31] Are these an example of what Barthes called literal, pure meaning: too raw to be effective? They present brutality in a theatrical way, a deliberately posed way that is obviously not a 'realistic' presentation in the sense of a likeness that is 'true', 'sincere' and 'revealing' in the humanist tradition. What is impressive about these alarming images is the way they cut through the search for a definitive statement that might express dignity and eventually senti-mentality. They disrupt sympathetic perception, they are so awful. Their exposure repels us. They distort and subvert that temptation to 'prettify', sanitise or exalt in a way that alienates us from his subjects, rather than creating the illusion of bringing them nearer as part of a shared humanity. This photographic illusion of nearness is what Baudrillard despises in the presentation of images that express, above all, the photo-grapher's opinion or vision. Mikhailov and Richard Billingham in different ways seem to have avoided mythic representation in presenting unrefined versions of being there. Margarita Tupitsyn says of Mikhailov's work that 'being part of it' makes the 'intrinsic meaning' unavoidable.[32] Involve-ment 'from below' rather than 'from above' explains and gives his work its precipitous position – on the edge of decency and documentary. The abandonment of analysis or comment on the Russian situation *is* the comment. Mikhailov himself talks about 'being' rather than seeking an event ('the more we can exclude [event] from representation, the closer we can approach the most important thing – being'), advocating 'being' or 'the real' as unremarkable and *non*-eventful.[33]

Perversely, photography cannot help but elevate the subject into an object of display, elevate the insignificant into the 'significant', and traditionally it has been the purposeful photographer's obligation to do

Boris Mikhailov, from the series *Case History*, 1999. Copyright Boris Mikhailov.

so, to transcend what is commonplace. Barthes and Baudrillard share a horror of over-construction and both encourage the possibility of a 'pure event…that can no longer be manipulated, interpreted or deciphered by any historical subjectivity'.[34] They are looking instead for something 'without culture',[35] something 'more radical'. Baudrillard warns that 'when the image is buried beneath commentary…walled up in aesthetic celebration, it is finished' – becomes 'aesthetic stupefaction'.[36] Ultimately, they both suggest that photographs with 'artistic' intention lose their potency, and both move towards a poetic, rather than eventful resolution, which defies logic. It is this defiance of logic, the elusive quality, the concept of raw apprehension approaching non-meaning, which is being simultaneously pursued and obscured, repeatedly, in contemporary practice – Barthes' 'absolutely pure', Baudrillard's 'figure of nothingness, absence and unreality'.

Whilst the condition and role of 'postmodernism' is currently being questioned, there appears to be confirmation, in photographic practice at least, of Lyotard's assertion that the project of modernity, as 'the realisation of universality',[37] has been relinquished. It is evident in an avoidance of translation and a preference for particularity and insignificance. The dominant Western aesthetic, habitually driven by the goal of finding a unifying principle or meaning, has promoted one version of 'good' art. The current (anti-)aesthetic has assumed the unremarkable and the awful as 'good', typically disregarding 'objective vision', along with modernist assumptions to complete, to define or mythologise. Images that dismantle photographic assumptions of control and objectivity, that disturb conventional subject/object relations, sit on the edge of a kind of non-aesthetic. Examples of photographic practice present expressions of an aesthetic *without* translation, interpretation or taste, and *without* direction. Avoiding interaction and expression, they are effectively a 'disappearance'. Frequently, there is almost an abdication of authorial responsibility, an undercurrent of denial, an aesthetic of 'without'.[38] But a raft of ironies follow an active avoidance of the aesthetics of 'good photography'. As a phenomenon, 'postmodern' photography borrows the appearance of genres, of photographic tradition, but is oblique, attenuated and contradictory. It embraces an idea of 'the real' – in the sense that it struggles to defy the denotative power of the photograph and move towards a conceptual form – not in the sense of documenting an idea as it did in the 1970s, but by using its obviousness to conceptualise. As Baudrillard suggests, indexical representation is repositioned as meaningless – echoing Barthes' distinction between meaninglessly effective and ineffectively meaningful. Liberated from an expectation of representation, denotation is paradoxically used in a way that is a form of abstraction. A kind of non-representation has developed through the play of avoidance. Baudrillard's 'irreal' negates the power of the controlling subject and asserts the object, 'which seduces'. His discussion advocates a 'naïve eye', an avoidance of photography that is 'aestheticised, calculated and composed'.[39] However, his own photographic practice reveals the difficulty in denying inherent taste, and an implicit restraint betrays a composed and Western aesthetic. Ultimately, attempts to avoid culture, to avoid formalism, to avoid the persistent compulsion to search beyond and transcend appearance have become a discussion of the possibility or the impossibility of a non-aesthetic. Most recent uses of photography can be seen to combine conceptual content with a more traditional photographic aesthetic that embraces the direct pleasure of what might be termed 'beauty'.[40]

Photographs that in different ways circumvent intentional search – looking sideways, outside the frame, via anonymity, banality and intimacy – arrive ultimately at the same place, in an affirmation of 'the real' displaced as 'irreal'. In avoiding the extraordinary and the transcendent, we achieve a provocative banal. Photographs 'apparently created in an artificial manner…reveal the natural'.[41] Coming full circle, in avoiding one kind of objectivity (or subjectivity) there is immersion in another. Rather than interpreting conditions of representation, such as avoidance, denial and disappearance, as problematic, it is suggested here that photographic practice, as an 'irreal' discourse, affirms a positive reaction. Beyond demonstrating a *reflection* of the contemporary condition, in visualising its own interventions, contemporary photography at least *parallels*, if not anticipates, written debate.

2 Gursky, Ruff, Demand: allegories of the real and the return of history

Neil Matheson

Of all media, it is surely photography that has the greatest problem with the issue of realism and, more specifically, with the related issue of truth. Usually considered as an essentially *indexical* medium – as a direct light imprint on the model of the fingerprint or death mask – photography is still widely assumed to have a hotline to history, a direct link with the real. When used as an art medium the question of the 'truth' of the photograph is not usually so much at issue; but, in works of art that do engage with current affairs or with questions of history, we are again confronted with the spectre of the real. This chapter takes as its focus the work of the German photographer Thomas Demand, work which, like that of Gerhard Richter or Luc Tuymans, challenges any easy distinction between the work of art and the interrogation of contemporary history. First, however, Demand's practice is sited in relation to that of the so-called 'Becher School' – the work of Bernd and Hilla Becher and their students at the Kunstakademie in Düsseldorf, particularly Andreas Gursky and Thomas Ruff. In so doing, an attempt is made to break with the aesthetic discourse within which this work is usually framed and to consider it instead in terms of its engagement with post-war European history. The work's relationship with historical reality is also considered, not in terms of indexical or 'literal' reality, but rather in terms of an *allegorical* interpretation of the history that is to be found there.

The Becher School and the Problem of the Body

One of the central problems to emerge is that of the body; there is quite clearly some deep malaise in the depiction of the body in much post-war

German photography. With the figurative tradition utterly discredited by the art of the inter-war period – whether in the celebration of the superman in the sculpture of Arno Breker, or in the disciplined, idealised bodies of Leni Riefenstahl's *Olympia* (1936) – the depiction of the human figure becomes deeply problematic for post-war German art. This problem with the body is apparent in the work of the Bechers, with their clinical series of blast furnaces, water towers and gasometers, where we encounter a true sense of trauma – an absolute shunning of the human and a taking refuge in the world of the inanimate object. There is an emphasis upon order, clarity, system, and an absolute refusal to express any subjective view. Hilla Becher insists: 'we bear no judgement...Our practice is objective. In this we are comparable to historians who forbid themselves all judgement of value.'[1] Taken up early on by American minimalists such as Carl André, the Bechers' oeuvre was quickly assimilated within an art discourse that focused on the sculptural quality of the motif, or that privileged seriality and grids, in an essentially formalist reading of the work. What is surely striking about this work, though, is the avoidance of the body. Hilla Becher has insisted: 'The presence of a single human being would lead the spectator's gaze towards something else.'[2] In a curious way the work becomes a kind of substitute for the body: Hilla Becher has said it 'can be compared to portraiture. You have to show the skin and the structure,'[3] and also that their work can be seen as a kind of 'comparative anatomy' of industrial remains.[4] This same dilemma is continued in the work of many of the Bechers' students, as in the case of Thomas Ruff, where we encounter this same unyielding blankness in the imagery. Anne Wauters has said that Ruff's images of public housing 'allowed him to focus on what he perceived as the sense of self-effacement and guilt pervading post-war Germany'.[5] His images again make use of a repetitive insistence upon inanimate objects, particularly buildings and architectural spaces, and the same avoidance of the inter-subjective relationship – what we might characterise as a kind of *visual autism*. Even when the body does appear, as in Ruff's portraits, the images seem impassive, mute and suggestive of a refusal to comment or respond. On one level this is expressed in the question of scale – the body is always either too big (Ruff) or too small (Gursky) – through either the macro or the micro viewpoint. Whereas with Ruff the face swells to fill the frame and is massively enlarged, such that we see every pore, with Gursky it is the opposite effect, as humans are reduced to swarming anthills, existing only as a mass. We find the same clinical objectivity of the Bechers in Gursky, where people are entirely subsumed by their social roles, whether industrial workers, share traders or executives. With Demand the logical conclusion is reached, as the body disappears entirely, figuring only as a ghostly absence haunting empty stage sets.

Gerhard Richter and the Return of History

Rather than read Demand's work through the Bechers, however, it might better be channelled via that of Gerhard Richter and in particular his *Oktober 18 1977* series (1988). This series focuses upon the aftermath of the arrest of members of the Baader–Meinhof group and their subsequent controversial deaths on 18 October 1977 – whether suicide or state-sponsored assassination – in Stammheim prison. Desa Philippi found Richter's series 'deeply troubling' insofar as it 'seems to simultaneously announce and cancel a possible relation between art and politics' – a judgement that might be extended to the political engagement of the photographic work under discussion here.[6] Richter represents a particular moment when German art came to struggle with its troubled past – not only in relation to Baader–Meinhof and the Red Army Faction, but, by contagion, with all that lies repressed in Germany after World War II. What is particularly significant here is that Richter based his series on news photos. For example, his *Atlas*, a selection of his source imagery, contains many images of the Third Reich, the Holocaust and post-war German history, and we find similar material in Ruff's *Zeitungsfotos*, a series that embraces political and military figures, portraits and current events. The demise of allegory in painting coincided in part with the decline of history painting, so that a return to history might also favour a revival of allegory. There appears to be a turn to a kind of photographic version of 'history painting' in the work under analysis here. It is frequently the case with Ruff, Gursky and Demand that the engagement with history is allusive, metaphoric, and that the theory of allegory in fact provides a more incisive tool for their analysis than any concern with the literally denoted or indexical content of the imagery.

Ruff's blank portraits of compatriots of his own generation are usually subsumed within a discussion of portraiture. For the French critic Régis Durand, Ruff's work critiques the popular notion of photographic transparency precisely by going along with that logic of the medium – by *exacerbating* it – so that the photographs become hyper-objective, hyper-detailed.[7] Durand observes of these images that 'they have the power (illusion) of an analogy of the real world, and at the same time are completely artificial'.[8] But Ruff's portraits might also be argued to hold political meanings, pointing as they do to bureaucracy, surveillance and the role of the state. While these images are often characterised as giant passport photos, some observers have noted that they are in fact closer to police mugshots.[9] The images also suggest quite specific references to the police wanted posters of the Baader–Meinhof gang, whose anti-state activities marked Ruff's own youth.[10] This reading is confirmed by Ruff's *Andere Porträts* series, in which he blends the faces of pairs of individuals produced, significantly, for the German pavilion at the Venice Biennale of 1995. For these images, again of fellow students but now in black and white, Ruff used a Minolta Montage Unit, as used by the German police in the 1970s to make identikit pictures – a by then archaic technology which thus serves to evoke a repressed period in German history.[11] And Ruff himself has insisted that 'my work has always been political…The portraits were done in the years leading up to 1984…We in Germany had the RAF in the '70s, with the hysteria and the control that went with it…'[12]

Ruff's *Zeitungsfotos* share a concern with mugshots and other imagery from the period of political unrest in the seventies. How, though, might such work be read in terms of 'allegory'?

History as Allegory

The word 'allegory' mixes *allos*, 'other', and *agoreuein*, 'to speak in the market place or common political arena'.[13] It means to speak of the esoteric or of the politically taboo, and to speak 'otherwise' – to say something other than what is literally said. Allegory is also parasitic, insofar as it feeds upon some other text or image, drawing its lifeblood from some other, culturally significant scene. But, as Paul de Man observes, the two never coincide, so that allegory also 'designates a distance in relation to its own origin'.[14] Craig Owens argues that allegory does not 'restore an original meaning' to an image but rather *adds another meaning*, and that, as such, it is a *supplement*, which is why allegory is condemned.[15] For Owens, what is proper to allegory is 'its capacity to rescue from historical oblivion that which threatens to disappear', and it appears, he says, 'whenever one text is doubled by another'.[16] Allegory is also *opaque* – it may figure as enigmatic or obscure, perhaps as images that are incomplete, mere fragments – and hence it both fascinates and frustrates our desire, as meaning is both offered and deferred. Owens therefore characterises allegory as 'the epitome of anti-narrative'.

Walter Benjamin, in his *Trauerspiel* study, contrasts allegory with symbolism: the symbol, he says, reveals itself in a 'mystical instant', whereas allegory has a 'worldly, historical breadth'.[17] Aligning allegory with history, Benjamin adds: 'everything about history that, from the very beginning, has been untimely, sorrowful, unsuccessful, is expressed in a face – or rather in a death's head.'[18]

And for Benjamin, the obscure and the *enigmatic* were part of allegory from the outset. 'Any person,' he writes, 'any object, any relationship can mean absolutely anything else.' The central motif of allegory, for Benjamin, is the *ruin*. 'In the ruin history has physically merged into the setting,' and assumes the form not of 'eternal life' but rather of 'irresistible decay'.[19] And Benjamin also adds: 'Allegories are, in the realm of thoughts, what ruins are in the realm of things.'

In terms of structure, as Owens observes, allegory is static, ritualistic, repetitive. It is disjunctive, disruptive of narrative: 'allegory,' says Owens, 'superinduces a vertical or paradigmatic reading of correspondences upon a horizontal or syntagmatic chain of events'.[20] The result is that, whereas history unfolds horizontally, syntagmatically, allegory cuts across this vertically, in a paradigmatic sequence of related images, each feeding upon the others. Nowhere is this more clear than in the work of Thomas Demand, where each image becomes a dense knot which references a specific, iconic image as well as pointing to a set of connected images. Demand's starting point, he says, is a: 'specific point in reality overgrown with photos and films, a cluster of fantasies', and from which 'chains of images' emerge which Demand says his work aims to investigate.[21]

Architecture and Utopia in Post-war Germany

Demand trained not as a photographer but as a sculptor, and his works are in fact carefully crafted simulacra, constructed only to be photographed. Based largely on news images, these photographs have a complex relationship with any reality they purport to represent and are several times removed from that primal reality. The objects themselves have a pristine, unused quality that Demand sees as liberating them from the confines of time and hence as denoting a utopian dimension in the work – so that allegory is already inherent in Demand's technique.[22] Bathed in an even light, these spaces seem to exist outside time. We might posit 'Zeichensaal/ Drafting Room' (1996) as a kind of ur-image within Demand's oeuvre. The photograph depicts a deserted architects' studio and is based on an image of a drafting room where the post-war reconstruction of Munich was planned. A light, airy space, where the future is still a blank page, its message is utopian, suggesting limitless possibilities for a brighter future, and as such acts as a foil against which are set images of the betrayal of that optimism – whether in banal post-war architecture or the corruption of politicians.

Anne Wauters has observed: 'In a country stuffed full of Third Reich buildings...the postwar reconstruction effort attempted to infuse architecture with what was left of Bauhaus ideals, a sort of faded utopianism that became part of the daily landscape...'[23]

This precisely characterises Demand's image 'Treppenhaus/Staircase' (1995), a deserted staircase which relates to the college, built in the 1950s, in which he himself was taught and which has echoes of Oskar Schlemmer's celebrated 'Bauhaustreppe/Bauhaus Staircase' (1932). It is significant that Schlemmer produced this painting from memory – that it is a *retrospective* view of the Bauhaus – and that it featured in a show that was closed down by the Nazis. The staircase here is animated by dynamic, youthful figures and clearly embodies the idealistic aspirations of the Bauhaus schools. We could also add a further, photographic, source in the photographs by Erich Consemüller of Gropius' Bauhaus staircases at Dessau. In this way Demand's image becomes an allegory of the cycles of utopian aspiration and their subsequent betrayal, first in the Weimar period and then again with post-war reconstruction.

With Demand's 'Parkgarage/Car Park' (1996) we are given the betrayal of that utopianism in the multi-storey car park, as the epitome of function-alist rationality[24] and as expressed in the brutalism of much concrete architecture of this type – for example, the Züblin multi-storey car park in Stuttgart (1962). W.G. Sebald, in his book *On the Natural History of Destruction*, writes of the post-war reconstruction of his own home town:

> A few years later a self-service shop opened on the site of the Herz-Schloss, an ugly, windowless single-storey building, and the once beautiful garden of the villa finally disappeared under the tarmac of a car park. That, reduced to its lowest common denominator, is the main theme of the history of post-war Germany.[25]

One could also contrast Demand's image of brutalist functionalism with far more elegant designs, as for example the Cäcilienstraße car park in Cologne, built in the fifties, which *does* embody that early post-war utopianism of the Bauhaus tradition.[26]

Thomas Demand, 'Parkgarage/ Car Park', 1996. Copyright DACS 2005.

Car park,
Stuttgart, from
Dietrich Klose,
*Multi-Storey
Car Parks and
Garages.*
Courtesy of
Elsevier and
Hatje Cantz
Verlag.

Bureaucracy, Memory and Modern History

Demand's 'Archiv/Archive' (1995) is at first sight a fairly innocuous signifier of record-keeping, the preservation of documents and of memory.
But in its obsessive concern with order and its lack of human presence,
the image becomes rather more disturbing. Durand notes its 'smooth,
gloomy aspect', which evokes 'the deathly quality of the contemporary
archive, that tomb of living memory'.[27] If we then add that Demand has
closely based his image upon a photograph documenting the archiving
of Leni Riefenstahl's film *Olympia*, the official record of the 1936 Berlin
Olympics, the work becomes an allegory of the inherent tendency towards
the bureaucratisation of modern life, while also recalling the reasons
why the figurative became so discredited in German art of the period.
The archive becomes a vault, suggestive of the death cult of Fascist
aesthetics. And insofar as the image is rooted in the documentation
of the era of the Third Reich it also points us to the terminal point of
the bureaucratic mind – to a Spartan room in the camp of Theresienstadt
in which long rows of prisoners' records were methodically stored, and
as recorded in an image in Dirk Reinartz' series *Deathly Still*. Time here
is on hold, with the office clock for ever frozen at six o'clock. Demand
has observed of his own work: 'What's involved here is that photographs are a metaphor of death. Because time stands still in them
and because they illustrate the passing of time so clearly.'[28] We should
recall too that, for Benjamin, allegory is centrally concerned with this
procedure of rescuing materiality from the unfolding of history as a
process of decay.

While the British media continue to feed on the corpse of Diana (an
issue treated in Demand's film-loop *Tunnel*, 1999), the German equivalent

is probably the mysterious death of the prominent politician Uwe Barschel. Barschel was head of the state of Schleswig-Holstein and a candidate for the right-wing Christian Democratic Union party in elections to be held in September 1987. Just before polling day the respected political journal *Der Spiegel* published highly damaging allegations about Barschel running a dirty tricks campaign against his Social Democratic Party opponents, thus launching one of the biggest political scandals in post-war German history. *Der Spiegel*, along with the rest of the German media, maintained the pressure on Barschel with further revelations. Soon after a press conference in which he gave his 'word of honour' that the accusations were false, Barschel flew to Geneva, where he was subsequently found dead in the bathroom of the hotel Beau Rivage in circumstances never fully explained. The case quickly became a lightning rod for conspiracy

Thomas Demand,
'Archiv / Archive', 1995.
Copyright DACS 2005.

Production still from Leni
Riefenstahl's *Olympia*, 1937.
Copyright Leni Riefenstahl.

theories, usually blaming either the former STASI, or Mossad, the Israeli secret service.[29]

In 1997 Demand produced 'Badezimmer (Beau Rivage)/Bathroom' based directly on the Barschel case. The bath has been run, the door is open, but the body is missing: we are left only with the crime scene itself. The image becomes an enigma, and, I would argue, an allegory on the theme of political corruption and murder. Instead of unfolding syntagmatically as a narrative on the Barschel case, Demand's image leaps vertically, allegorically, to a series of visual parallels. Firstly, the image obviously refers to the series of sensational photographs taken by a reporter who gained access to the hotel room immediately after the death, and subsequently published in *Stern*. Secondly, Demand's image makes an allegorical leap to David's *Death of Marat* (1793) – a key source for Richter's *October 18* series – whereby the image is drawn within the ambit of modern history painting, with Marat signifying the betrayal of revolutionary ideals. We could also include here an image of Artaud in the role of Marat in Abel Gance's *Napoleon* (1927), lying dead in his bath, a dagger in his chest – Artaud, in the late stages of cancer, was to take his own life in 1948. The corpse is, for Benjamin, the allegorical emblem par excellence. In the *Trauerspiel* he argues that people die 'not for the sake of immortality ... but for the sake of the corpse', 'because it is only as corpses that they can enter into the homeland of allegory'.[30] We might

Thomas Demand, 'Badezimmer (Beau Rivage)/ Bathroom', 1997. Copyright DACS 2005.

The death of Uwe Barschel, *Stern*, no. 44, 1987. Courtesy of *Stern*.

also draw a parallel with one of the earliest photographs ever made – Hippolyte Bayard's somewhat macabre 'Self-portrait as a Drowned Man' (1839) – a spoof suicide at the very origin of photography, complete with suicide note on the back which includes the extraordinary claim that the photograph is so realistic that one can smell the decaying flesh.[31] It is surely striking that right at the roots of the medium we should discover this allegory on the realism of the photograph, on mortality and human ambition, and on the fatal consequences of the new technologies.

History as Ruins: the firebombing of Dresden

In a final work by Demand, 'Exit' (2000), one is confronted with a simple metal staircase leading down into a basement. Functional and somewhat sinister, the steps perhaps suggest a descent into hell. In fact, Demand based the image on a wartime shelter in Dresden and the work was shown, symbolically, upon a bare brick wall in Dresden itself. The allegorical leap here is therefore to the Allied firebombing of Dresden and other German cities during the Second World War. Sebald speculates on the curious reticence of the Germans on this subject, which he says 'remained under a kind of taboo like a shameful family secret.'[32] Thus Demand's image points to a trauma still not laid to rest in the collective unconscious, as evidenced by the huge controversy in Germany over recent books by the revisionist historian Jörg Friedrich, arguing that air raids by the RAF should be classed as war crimes. In *Der Brand* ('The Fire', 2002), Friedrich claims that some 600,000 civilians died needlessly in those raids, many asphyxiated in cellars, leaving 'an entire generation trauma-tised'.[33] Friedrich's latest book, *Brandstätten* ('Fire Sites', 2003), consists of controversial images of the victims of Allied raids on Dresden and other cities. One image from that book seems to relate to an incident described by Sebald, when, in the Altmarkt in Dresden, '6,865 corpses were burned on pyres in February 1945 by an SS detachment which had gained its experience at Treblinka'.[34] Demand's staircase thus becomes an emblem in the allegorical sense, raising still uncomfortable, unspoken issues about the attribution of guilt over the war.

To conclude, then, these images function as allegories dealing with privileged moments within cultural memory. Benjamin viewed allegory as the antidote to myth, and, throughout this body of work, photography itself reflects allegorically upon its own constructedness, deploying allegory against the myths of photographic realism, immediacy and indexicality.[35] Photography's engagement with reality – and hence with history – thus emerges as both more complex than and as inseparable from a politics of memory.

3 Between the Hyperrepresentational and the Real: a sampling sensibility

Susanne Østby Sæther

Since the beginning of the 1990s there has been an international current of ambitious exhibitions showing works of art that employ material, or traces of material, originating from the media. Among the most influential are *Spellbound: Art and film* at the Hayward Gallery (1996), *Scream and Scream Again: Film in art* in Oxford, (1996), *Cinéma Cinéma: Contemporary art and the cinematic experience* in Eindhoven (1999) and *Passages de l'image* at Centre de Pompidou, Paris (1990). The scale of these exhibitions suggests that a prominent characteristic of much of today's audiovisual art proceeds from an interest in, and an application of, the technological means, material sources, 'language', iconography and motives of the mass media; in short, a re-articulation of elements of what we have come to refer to as 'media culture'. What challenges do such re-presentations pose for the state of the real?

The aim here is not to give an exhaustive answer to this question, but rather to interrogate one particular problem that follows from it. This problem concerns the existence of an apparent paradox in contemporary audiovisual culture: an excess of intertextual references and re-presentational strategies on the one hand, and a highly realist aesthetic on the other. Intensified by the ongoing digitalisation of reproduction media, this paradox is particularly pressing in photography-based articulations, grounded in photography's already complex relations to reality and the real.[1] It is not necessary here to repeat the familiar claim that the ongoing digitalisation of reproduction technologies has resulted in a rupture between the cultures of chemical photography and the digitally produced image (whether virtual or as an imprint of a pre-photographic existence), leaving us in a 'post-photographical era' that is characterised by a 'loss of the real'.[2] What is maintained is that the digitalisation of reproduction technologies further enables and enhances certain aesthetic practices and cultural forms already present in the 'old' regime of mechanical repro-duction media. One of these aesthetic practices consists in the prevalent re-presentation of fragments and/or traces of pre-existing media material.

A matter that surfaces with some urgency from this is the issue of repetition. While the process of repetition is inherent in reproduction media, the aesthetic practice sketched out above brings this process to the fore: the presence of pre-existing material draws attention to the return of a certain object, motive or form. Hence, the notion of repetition and return is at the core of the exploration of the paradoxical co-existence of excessively intertextual strategies with a highly realist aesthetic. It is suggested that one way to come to terms with this paradox is by intro-ducing the concept of sampling, as it is used in the field of musicology and electronic music. Hopefully, by this move it will be possible to map out some of the characteristics of what is called here the aesthetics of sampling, as it is played out in the tension between the prevailing documentary or 'realist' aesthetics and what W.J.T. Mitchell has termed 'hyperrepresentation'.[3]

This discussion will be extended through an analysis of *Dial H-I-S-T-O-R-Y* (Johan Grimonprez, 1997), an influential video work which consists mainly of imagery from pre-existing television material. As such, the work stands as an example of the paradox sketched out above. It demonstrates the preoccupation with the re-presentation of media material in contemporary art and audiovisual practices, but neverthe-less activates a highly 'realist' discourse through its documentary style and historical subject matter. After a brief introduction to the work, this chapter goes on to discuss the concept of sampling in relation to other, but related, conceptualisations of aesthetic re-presentational strategies dealing with repetition and return. This will be followed by a closer examination of *Dial H-I-S-T-O-R-Y* with respect to the tension between a hyperrepresentational and a more 'realist' aesthetic. The chapter will conclude by suggesting how the concept of sampling can provide one way to account for what can be shown to be a major paradox in con-temporary audiovisual culture.

Dial H-I-S-T-O-R-Y – an introduction to the work

Johan Grimonprez's video is a 68-minute compilation assembled from amateur recordings, television news, commercials, fiction films and self-produced material that chronicles the history of aeroplane hijacking. The soundtrack consists partly of diegetic sound from these recordings, partly of two male voice-overs reading what Grimonprez himself has characterised as 'a more critical personal commentary', as well as short fictional texts derived from Don DeLillo's novels *White Noise* and *Mao II*.[4] Added to this is the melodic and rhythmic disco-score *Do the Hustle* from 1976. Together these separate sound sources make up a smooth musical collage, edited by the American composer David Shea.[5] Hence, the imagery and the soundtrack consist of material that is both pre-existing and newly produced, both fictional and documentary.

In terms of the work's installation context, *Dial H-I-S-T-O-R-Y* is generally exhibited as a single-channel video installation consisting of the projection of a digital video onto a facing screen. However, the screening schedule, the size of the screen and the sound transmission have been subject to variation. At Galleri Riis in Oslo, Norway (1999), the work was exhibited at fixed hours in a specially designated and enclosed space, with the sound transmitted through loudspeakers adjusted to a predetermined volume. At Smack Mellon Gallery in Brooklyn, New York City (2004), the work was screened in a loop, in a large, multi-levelled exhibition space that also included several other video works. In this case the sound was channelled through earphones, and the audience could freely adjust the volume. Occasionally the work has been accompanied by *INFLIGHT*, a 126-page publication in the form of the airline magazines found on commercial flights.

Partly financed by Centre de Pompidou in Paris, and commissioned for Documenta X in 1997, the work was a success with critics and audiences alike. Since its premiere, the work has been acquired by several museums and galleries, among them the Museum of Contemporary Art in Oslo, Norway. In addition to traditional art venues, *Dial H-I-S-T-O-R-Y* has a recent history of being circulated in the commercial media system. It was, for example, aired on the American network television channel Trio-TV several times during 2004, and was released for commercial distribution by Other Cinema DVD in the same year, in collaboration with the artist.

Re-presentation and Sampling

The imagery employed in *Dial H-I-S-T-O-R-Y* presents itself as found footage: footage that already exists – such as amateur recordings, news reports and television commercials – and that Grimonprez recycles in the work. The term 'found footage' is related to the French term *objet trouvé*, which is often used as a (not very precise) synonym for a 'readymade'. As we know, the idea of the readymade was initiated by Marcel Duchamp by transporting a manufactured everyday object – a snow shovel, a urinal – into the art scene in a way that would challenge conventional art theory for several decades. But can the pre-existing material here be conceived as a readymade?

According to Thierry de Duve, 'the readymade is simultaneously the operation that reduces the work of art to its enunciative function and the "result" of this operation, a work of art reduced to the statement "this is art"'.[6] De Duve locates this operation within what he terms 'the enunciative paradigm', where the baptising of the object in question as art is the paradigmatic characteristic. Even if the found footage does meet the criterion of transposition from the context of everyday life, represented by television, to the context of the art institution, such an act of baptism does not seem to be the concern in *Dial H-I-S-T-O-R-Y*. Duchamp's objects were not of great significance in themselves, so that attention was directed towards the process of transposition rather than upon the meanings attached to the objects themselves. *Dial H-I-S-T-O-R-Y*, by contrast, brings politics, life and death, human grief and so on to the centre of attention, by using imagery that is already significant and meaningful in terms of these issues. Thus, it seems that the re-presentation in *Dial H-I-S-T-O-R-Y* shares the material aspect of the readymade – the recontextualised material is perceived as 'the same' as in its original context – but the re-presentation diverges from that in the readymade by not being primarily a nominalist act.

Historically, the readymade was succeeded by appropriation art, a form associated with the American 'Pictures Generation' of the late 1970s and early 1980s, and represented by artists such as Sherrie Levine and Robert Longo. However, there are some important distinctions between appropriation and the readymade. The American art critic Daniela Salvioni emphasises these distinctions when she states that in readymade art 'the found object itself is lifted from its native context in the public domain and transferred to the artist's own', while in appropriation art 'the image or object is repeated'.[7] In the terminology of Walter Benjamin's seminal essay 'The Work of Art in the Age of Mechanical Reproduction' (1936), one could say that, while the readymade confers cult value on an object that had none in the first place, appropriation art questions the cult value of the original work by means of mechanical reproduction.[8]

Appropriation implies that new associations are produced by placing elements from a work already known within a new framework. Hence, while the readymade presupposes a factual transfer of context – from the bathroom to the art gallery – the act of appropriation presupposes a more diffuse contextual transfer. The recontextualisation at work in appropriation art may consist of media translation, or the fragmentation of the 'original' work or its context. Rather than ask the question 'what is art?', appropriation implies a questioning of the relation between the new work and the 'original'. In other words, the material aspect is more present in the readymade than in appropriation art,[9] but at the same time appropriation is open to the possibility of fragmentation in a way that the readymade is not.

If we relate these concepts to *Dial H-I-S-T-O-R-Y*, we find that the work displays the fragmentation and the repetitive aspect of appropriation art. It is produced as a compilation of television clips, some of which are briefly contextualised (identified by place and date and introduced by subtitles), some of which are not. The rhythm and confrontational editing of the work adds to its generally fragmentary appearance. In spite of, or maybe because of, this fragmented appearance the imagery comes across as televisual, and in this way foregrounds the pre-existing dimensions of the footage. Hence, the work also shares the foregrounding of the material qualities of the pre-manufactured object with the readymade. As such, the work bridges the definition of appropriation art and the readymade, but leaving it neither one nor the other. It seems that *Dial H-I-S-T-O-R-Y* calls for alternative conceptualisations of the aesthetic strategies at work.

The concept of sampling might constitute a meaningful alternative to the related, but theoretically distinct, notions of the readymade and appropriation art. In his comprehensive book *Electronic and Experimental Music*, Thom Holmes defines (digital) sampling as 'a form of recording that uses software to further manipulate and modify recorded sounds'.[10] In the wider discourse of popular music, sampling is the term for 'stealing' or 'borrowing' a sound from a pre-recorded source: cassette, CD, vinyl or video.[11] The sampler can be defined as a technological instrument enabling this reproduction of stored or recorded sounds. The German pop music theorist Ulf Poschardt chronicles how the development of the sampler in the late 1970s was a result of the individualised appropriation by entrepreneurial DJs of various reproductive technologies – such as the use of the mixing desk and the record player – for purposes other than their primary intent. But the sampler was in itself a product of digital high technology. A consequence of this interplay between individual innovative technological appropriation and the industrial development and manufacturing of new production technologies, he argues, is that the eclecticism and historicism of the DJ must be understood as derived from production technology.[12] Sampling as an aesthetic practice and cultural form could therefore be conceived of as conditioned by, but at the same time influential on, developments in reproduction technology. Lev Manovich articulates a similar position, when he uses sampling as an example of 'operations embedded in software and hardware and found at work in contemporary culture at large'.[13]

On the basis of this brief discussion of different conceptions of artistic re-presentation, it can be argued that the concept of sampling (as defined here) highlights the material aspect of the re-presentational act shared with the readymade, but at the same time shares the possibility of fragmentation with appropriation art in a way that the readymade does not. Additionally, the concept of sampling signals the closeness of audiovisual expressions to the sonic arts, as well as the importance of the technological conditions required for engaging in such an aesthetic of re-presentation. In this, the concept of sampling implies an aesthetic sensibility and signification process which is dispersed across different media, each with their own specificities, but which still insists on the material dimension of the practice – the fact that it is constituted by the selection and re-contextualisation of pre-existing material produced for and by one particular medium. In addition, it is important to note that sampling is a term already in use by artists themselves, not only within the sonic arts but also by artists working within visual and literary practices. This migration of the concept from one art form to others indicates the sense of a shared aesthetic sensibility.

A Paradox in Visual Culture?

Dial H-I-S-T-O-R-Y brings together a wide array of media footage, arranging it in changing time intervals to form a confrontational montage. As such, the work mimics the tempo and rhythm of television zapping: fast, syncopated, abrupt. The temporal arrangement of television and newsreel footage in the manner of zapping seems to comment upon how extensive and influential our mass-mediated audiovisual discourse is for engineering our sense of history and reality, with television as the primary source. However, the soundtrack contrasts this confrontational montage with a musical score that, combined with a soothing male voice-over, sutures this fragmented imagery. Thus, on the image track, the work applies the signifying practices of television, while the easy listening soundtrack lends a smooth, polished quality to the work.

By virtue of this obvious televisuality and aestheticised smoothness, *Dial H-I-S-T-O-R-Y* can be characterised as *hyperrepresentational*, which W.J.T. Mitchell describes in the following way: 'Postmodern culture is often characterized as an era of "hyperrepresentation", in which abstract, formalist painting has been replaced by experiments like photorealism, and reality itself begins to be experienced as an endless network of representations.'[14]

This echoes Jean Baudrillard's writings on the 'hyperrealism of sim-ulation', which, in brief, implies that we no are longer able to distinguish between the real world and its representations.[15] In addition to the formal features of *Dial H-I-S-T-O-R-Y* there are also semantic elements that activate the notion of hyperrealism. Through the text passages inspired by Don DeLillo's novel *Mao II*, the voice-over establishes a relation between the terrorist and the novelist, questioning the status of the literary artist vis-à-vis the TV image: *Novelists and terrorists play a zero-sum game; what terrorists gain, novelists lose.* The implication is that the terrorist has taken the writer's role in society, because he is able to 'manipulate the media', as Grimonprez puts it in a 1998 interview, referring to how the terrorist is able to stage, and consequently get broadcast, spectacular and violent imagery.[16] Hence, *Dial H-I-S-T-O-R-Y* seems to reflect the view that image has replaced reality to such an extent that violence and terrorism are considered the only possible way to reclaim authenticity and reality. The juxtaposition of footage of different kinds and origins – of colour and black and white, accelerated and slow motion, circular motion and fast-paced editing, nappy commercials and plane crashes – demonstrates the conflation of personal memory and collective history, subjective and common experience, reality and its televised images, implying that it is pointless, if not impossible, to try and untangle these processes.

Implicit in the above is the critical consensus surrounding *Dial H-I-S-T-O-R-Y*: the reading of the work as merely media-critical, commenting upon the hyperrepresentationalism of a media-saturated society, questioning the truthfulness of images and 'the experiences of man in a post-modern society'.[17] At the same time, however, the work also evokes various 'realist' strategies. Firstly, *Dial H-I-S-T-O-R-Y* employs aesthetic conventions traditionally associated with fact-based, document-ary genres, such as unfocused images, jump cuts and the hand-held camera. Such an apparently amateur aesthetic is conventionalised as signifying authenticity and indexicality; the restless movements and unfocused lens of the camera are understood as a product of the chaotic circumstances in which the recording was made. Grimonprez's aesthet-icised montage does not change this potential for referentiality in the pre-existing media material. Rather, the work trades upon the interplay between the conventional and the referential in this particular amateur aesthetic. Secondly, the fact that the pre-existing material represents highly spectacular and violent content can also be taken to signify authenticity and in general a documentary mode. As John Durham Peters (among others) has argued, the body, with its capacity for pain and even death, is often used in the broadcast media as 'a criterion of truth and truthfulness'.[18] Consequently, *Dial H-I-S-T-O-R-Y* can be shown to insist on the reality of the violent, and often lethal, events represented, as well as the authenticity of their *televisual* representations. Thirdly, and most importantly, the work also insists on the reality and tangibility of audio-visual reproduction media and their material manifestations. This argument will be explored in more detail below. At this point it is enough simply to establish that these three rationales locate *Dial H-I-S-T-O-R-Y* in the current desire for reality and the real manifested in contemporary art and visual culture generally.

At first sight it seems that the co-existence of these two represent-ational tendencies apparent in *Dial H-I-S-T-O-R-Y* reflects a paradox within contemporary photography-based culture. On one side we have the hyperrepresentational strategies that might be interpreted as yet another manifestation of the self-reflexive art and media culture of the late 1970s and the 1980s, exemplified, for instance, by appropriation artists such as Martha Rosler and Sherrie Levine, and the self-referentiality of television series such as *Moonlighting*.[19] On the other we have the present desire for reality and the real in audiovisual culture, 'the return of the real' chronicled by Hal Foster and expressed in various representational styles and artistic methods.[20] These range from the 'new realism' demonstrated in the prevalence of the snapshot aesthetic in photography, the ethnographic methods of artists such as Lothar Baumgarten, Fred Wilson and Andrea Fraser,[21] the presence of a variety of documentary expressions at Documenta XI in 2003, to the influence of the Danish Dogme films and the vast amount of reality programming in commercial television.

This paradox could be traced back to two basic models of representation that, according to Hal Foster, dominate most accounts of post-war art grounded in photography. One states that 'images are attached to referents, to iconographic themes or real things in the world'; the other that 'all images can do is represent other images, that all forms of representation (including realism) are auto-referential codes'.[22] By relating the work to the simulacrum model of representation, and to Mitchell's description of 'hyperrepresentation', one could argue that *Dial H-I-S-T-O-R-Y* mainly represents 'other images', through its recycling of pre-existing material and its mimicking of the signifying conventions of television. By relating it to the referential model, however, one could state that *Dial H-I-S-T-O-R-Y* is, on the contrary, working to claim the authenticity and 'reality' of the catastrophic events chronicled.

Database Realism

Rather than characterising the relationship between the hyperrepresentational and the referential models of representation as one of conflict, it could be argued that these seemingly contradictory tendencies are in fact tightly interrelated, perhaps even conditioned by one another. This argument will be further supported by showing how *Dial H-I-S-T-O-R-Y* could be read as commenting upon specific information structures characterising the relations between media representations and the representational technologies and systems producing them, possibly establishing a connection between the two tendencies.

The relationship between representation and reproduction technologies is particularly explicit in one of the last sequences of *Dial H-I-S-T-O-R-Y*. Recalling the camcorder revolution, we are shown how honeymooners who taped a crashing hijacked Boeing 767 off the Comoros coast in 1996 were immediately invited to participate in Larry King's talk show on CNN. As a coda for the work as a whole, the footage of the happy couple recounting the excited shock of the event seems to comment upon how documentation of historical events, catastrophes and everyday life is increasingly turning into a media spectacle. In this way, *Dial H-I-S-T-O-R-Y* also reminds us, such documenting material is becoming much more accessible to artists and audiences alike. The increasing prevalence of so-called enabling technologies is crucial to this ease of access. Miniaturised video cameras, digital photographic equipment, cellphones and MP3 players with recording capabilities all encourage the proliferation of amateur recording, while digital storage technology aids audiences and artists in the retrieval, organisation, dissemination and sharing of the recorded information. From this abundance of recorded material new structures for organising this information are generated.

In *Dial H-I-S-T-O-R-Y*, history seems to be represented as an *archive*, both in the literal and metaphorical sense of the term, indicating that the archive might be a central information structure in the work. In a recent article, Hal Foster identifies what he terms an 'archival impulse' at work in contemporary art.[23] According to Foster, archival art 'seeks to make historical information, often lost or displaced, physically present', and is 'concerned less with absolute origins than with obscure traces'.[24] As such, archival art is engaged in processes of re-presenting historical information in its various material manifestations, activating this material's circulation histories, yet leaving the material open for further reworking – 'in art and in history alike'. Hence, archival art 'not only draws on informal archives, but produces them as well'.[25] Whether or not *Dial H-I-S-T-O-R-Y* could be considered a case of archival art is not really the point here. Rather, what is worth emphasising is that the work evokes an archival model for the presentation of information: *Dial H-I-S-T-O-R-Y* re-presents pre-existing media material as historical information, making it present in time as well as space. The telephone, as an interpersonal communication medium, is represented as a tool for moving within this archive of historical information: images of telephones and people speaking on the phone are repeated throughout the work – animated, documentary and fictional. As one of the voice-overs states, accompanying black-and-white, unidentified imagery of air-hostesses speaking on the phone, *the real terrorists make their phone calls after the damage is done, if at all*. Mediating between individual agency and collective history, the telephone is presented as an important terrorist tool, but also as a communication technology making it possible for media consumers to partake individually in the construction of what the artist has referred to as a 'push-button' history.[26] You can just dial HISTORY to access the desired information.

However, in spite of the importance attached to such 'analogue' technologies as the aeroplane and the telephone as metaphoric figures for the archive in the work, I will suggest that a more appropriate model for the organisation of the pre-existing material in *Dial H-I-S-T-O-R-Y* is the *database*, established by Lev Manovich as one of the key forms of new media.[27] Foster distinguishes archival art from 'the mega-archive of the Internet' primarily because of their different material manifestations.[28] Compared to what he very briefly describes as database art, archival art is 'far more tactile and face-to-face than any Web interface'.[29] Even if *Dial H-I-S-T-O-R-Y* does not actually make use of the Internet in any perceivable way, it still shares the two-dimensional screen with the Web interface Foster refers to – whether on a computer or in front of a video projector. Together with the compilation of pre-existing material from different sources, this fact may position the work closer to database art than the 'tactility' and three-dimensionality of the installations mostly referred to as 'archival' by Foster. But more important than the medium in question is the actual way the information is organised in and by this medium. According to Manovich, a database is 'a structured collective of data' that 'represents the world as a list of items', but that 'refuses to order the list'.[30] This implies that the database, at least in its immediate appearance,[31] stands in opposition to traditional linear narrative. *Dial H-I-S-T-O-R-Y*'s non-chronological organising of the hijacking footage – the mix of material from different sources, times and places – suggests a database matrix for the organisation of the pre-existing material. Digital reproduction media record fragments of reality, subsequently processed as digital data constituting a database structure, Manovich states.[32] Here he points to the relations, also commented upon in *Dial H-I-S-T-O-R-Y*, between the increased proliferation of enabling media technologies, the abundance of media material following from it and the new ways this material is organised, stored, manipulated and accessed. Accordingly, in *Dial H-I-S-T-O-R-Y* it seems that the pre-existing material evokes the 'old' model of the archive, through the work's foregrounding of the materiality

Johan Grimonprez, 'Three hijacked jets on desert airstrip, Amman, Jordan, 12 September 1970', 1997. Still from *Dial H-I-S-T-O-R-Y*. Copyright Johan Grimonprez. Photo Ronny Vissers.

and circulation history of the audiovisual fragments employed. Nonetheless, this material appears to be structured according to a database model, by virtue of the work's challenging of linear narrative and chronological history – or, in Manovich's words, its evident refusal to 'order the list'.

The increased proliferation of media technologies, together with the new information structures that have resulted from them, have considerable aesthetic consequences. With reference to the increased use of digital technologies in experimental music production, the musicologist Simon Waters notes that it has brought about a change in sensibility from what he characterises as 'an acousmatic culture (broadly concerned with sounds as "material", and based – in historical practice – on analogue technology)' to a 'sampling culture (concerned with context, and based on digital technology)'.[33] This can be understood as reflecting a general cultural shift from a (modernist) focus on the intrinsic properties of the text/work to a (postmodernist) interest in the remediation and re-articulation of already existing material. A necessary consequence of this interest in remediations and re-articulations is a preoccupation with processes of repetition and return, in motives, formal features and material. The discussion of the paradox outlined above will therefore be continued by foregrounding the figure of repetition and its manifestation in *Dial H-I-S-T-O-R-Y*, focusing especially on the repetitive aspects of the work as a 'realist' strategy.

The notion of repetition inherent in reproduction media has most often focused on the distance between the recorded material and the original event or object, as a legacy of Walter Benjamin's description of how the mechanically reproduced work of art loses its aura, its 'presence in time and space, its unique existence at the place where it happens to be'.[34] In his article on witnessing and the media, John Durham Peters understands the 'infinite repetition' of a television recording as a 'copy' of the original event, distancing it from the time and space of this initial event.[35] While Peters' account implies that every repetition is 'the same', regardless of its new use/context, it is also important to take into account not only the initial event prior to the recording but also the ever-changing context(s) of the recorded material. This is especially important when exploring media objects employing pre-existing material, as such an approach makes it possible to distinguish between the various copies generated from an event, as well as to identify the relationship between them caused by their new contexts. In other words, it is not only the initial events themselves (the hijackings in the case of *Dial H-I-S-T-O-R-Y*) that are re-presented through repetition, but the (first-generation) re-cording of the events as well. In *Dial H-I-S-T-O-R-Y* this process is linked to the re-presentation of the already existing archival material, exposing the layers of repetition at work, making the television recordings present as such: as material manifestations with specific circulation histories, now returned in a new context. In the new context of *Dial H-I-S-T-O-R-Y,* the employed archival imagery thus constitutes both the 'raw' material for the work as well as artefacts with a story of their own.

As a formal feature of a work relying on pre-existing photography-based material, the figure of repetition has also, as an exception rather than the rule, been presented as construing a privileged connection with the real. For example, Hal Foster has, against the critical consensus, shown how Andy Warhol's well-known *Death in America* images from the early 1960s can be read as cases of 'traumatic realism'.[36] Focusing on the repetitive nature of the image series and Freud's notion of trauma as 'deferred action', Foster establishes a rapport between repetition and trauma. What Foster conceptualises as traumatic realism in Warhol's work is thus constituted not so much through the dramatic nature of their motives, consisting of mass-mediated (often press) photographs of spectacular and violent accidents, as through the serialised repetition of these motives. A less psychoanalytically charged, and in this context more interesting, version of the relation between the figure of repetition and realist aesthetics is articulated in Mette Sandbye's reading of the German artist Hans-Peter Feldmann's photoworks from the late 1960s to the late 1970s. With reference to his booklet's containing uniformly sized black-and-white photographs (some of which are his own, others found or 'sampled') that repeat a motive of a mundane and trivial nature, she notes that the snapshots become a 'repeated assertion of the real, rather than an interpretive representation of it'.[37] The assertive, tautological aesthetic that results is characterised as 'archival realism'. Archival realism, then, is to be understood as social activity and intervention where the images 'point to the images as images, rather than windows to certain themes'.[38]

Johan Grimonprez, 'Raffaele Minichiello, first transatlantic hijack, Rome, November 1969', 1997. Still from *Dial H-I-S-T-O-R-Y.* Copyright Johan Grimonprez.

In spite of the obvious differences between these two works concerning media, motives and formal features (Feldmann's work implies a repetition in space and consists of trivial motives; *Dial H-I-S-T-O-R-Y* implies a repetition in time and employs highly spectacular motives), Sandbye's notion of 'archival realism' may help to account for the figure of repetition in *Dial H-I-S-T-O-R-Y*. However, it was earlier suggested that the database might be the proper matrix for characterising the organisation of the pre-existing material in *Dial H-I-S-T-O-R-Y*. Following from this, it is possible to conceive of the aesthetic strategies at work in *Dial H-I-S-T-O-R-Y* as a form of *database realism*. The work feeds upon the recognition of the employed television imagery as pre-existing, tangible and 'real' material, as images 'pointing to the images as images'. This imagery is mainly selected according to the theme of hijacking, as what Manovich calls 'a list of items', but without the list being ordered in an easily identifiable structure – as in a database.[39]

A Matter of Sampling Sensibility

In the earlier part of the discussion three important features were singled out characterising what we may now identify as an aesthetic of sampling, and which were put to work in the subsequent examination of *Dial H-I-S-T-O-R-Y*. Firstly, sampling is engaged in questions of *materiality*, in the face of the ephemeral nature of current screen culture on the one hand, and the increasing proliferation of digital technologies for storing, manipulating and accessing information on the other. In *Dial H-I-S-T-O-R-Y* this comes across as an acknowledgement of the materiality of the imagery employed, its status as pre-existing cultural artefacts. Secondly, an aesthetic of sampling implies a fragmentation of the original material, giving priority to a non-linear representation, possibly organised in a database structure. Thirdly, the concept of sampling focuses the technological investment involved in the reproduction and subsequent repetition of the pre-existing material. Even if the material employed might be identified as having originated from a known source, its return in the new context implies not only that its formal and semantic meanings might change – it might even, and most often does, return in a medium other than that by which it was originally recorded. Sampling, as a consequence, necessarily involves processes of repetition and return, in material manifestations as well as the media technologies repre-senting them.

Applying the logic of sampling to *Dial H-I-S-T-O-R-Y*, we are now able to argue that what was previously designated as a 'hyperrepresentational' aesthetic, in which images refer to other images rather than 'real things in the world', is in fact also what in the end makes it possible to establish the work as realist: *Dial H-I-S-T-O-R-Y* seems to be insisting on the material reality and social, political and cultural effects of the re-presented media material, and thereby 'representing other images'.[40] However, it is exactly through this process or re-presentation, the gesture of pointing 'to the images as images', as Sandbye puts it, that these same images are acknowledged as 'real things in the world'.[41]

4 Performing the Real

Lennaart van Oldenborgh

All the Discourses of the Real

One could distinguish, broadly, three major genres within reality TV: witness TV, docusoaps and reality gameshows (which also appeared roughly in that order). None of these could plausibly be included in the category of documentary (although the boundaries are far from distinct, especially in relation to docusoaps), but they do share with documentary a certain 'claim to the real', which distinguishes them from other kinds of programming. It also makes it possible to examine their massive appeal in the last decade by mobilising theories of documentary, which have often, and often agonisingly, addressed this very 'claim to the real'. So what exactly is the 'real' in reality TV, and can it help to explain its popularity?

Central to documentary theories, but usually elided, is a workable definition of what is understood by the real. Indeed a lot of the agonising seems to derive from either a confusion of what is to be understood by the real, or a recognition that subscribing to any deep philosophical definition immediately implies subscribing to one philosophical system over another. In lieu of a discussion of various philosophical discourses of the real, most writers on documentary practice appear to plump for an everyday definition of the real as perceptual, lived reality, without making this explicit.[1] Even though there is by now a general consensus that the representation of the real also necessarily means a mediation of the real (recognising the naïvety of some documentary makers' claim to present an 'unmediated' account[2]), only some writers address the potential problems of unmediated access to the real itself – that is, if the real is knowable at all – usually in terms of Jean Baudrillard's simulation.[3]

John Grierson's famous definition of documentary as 'the creative treatment of actuality' is comprehensively deconstructed by Brian Winston, who demonstrates that the documentary 'claim to the real' is based on the nineteenth-century description of the camera as a scientific instrument, therefore guaranteeing the indexical truth of the photograph, referring to an empirical reality.[4] This idea is connected to the legal use of photography as evidence, as a 'document' (the original use of the word was in a legal framework). Hence this indexical status still clings to recorded images, allowing André Bazin to claim their 'essential objectivity' because 'for the first time an image of the world is formed automatically, without the intervention of man'.[6] Meanwhile, according to Bill Nichols 'all films are documentaries' in the sense that all films document what is in front of the camera;[7] the real is here seen as the 'pro-filmic event', one could say a phenomenological definition of the real.[8]

Jon Dovey does cite Baudrillard's claim of a 'loss of the real', of the referent, in our comprehensively mediated culture, but counters it with sociological research,[9] salvaging the 'empirical real'. Michael Renov problematises the notion of the real much further, citing both Jacques Derrida ('what is neither true nor false is reality') and Jacques Lacan's description of the real as 'beyond discourse', to address the post-structuralist notion of the '"truth" of the text',[10] and attracting the impatience of Stella Bruzzi, who writes that sometimes 'it seems necessary to remind writers on documentary that reality does exist and that it can be represented without such a representation either invalidating or having to be synonymous with the reality that preceded it'.[11]

Although such an everyday definition of the real will do for most purposes, it appears to be insufficient to account for the kind of fascination that the various kinds of reality TV held, and continue to hold, for so many viewers. Quite aside from the *truth* of an image, 'realness' does have a great effect on its reception; it changes the way the image *performs on the viewer*. One could call this the special effect of the real.

To address this 'special effect', it might be useful to look at the distinction Lacan makes between the real and (symbolic) reality, in which the latter is understood to be the everyday, lived reality, as we perceive and understand it, and the former the formless, primordial real which underlies this, and which we encounter only in moments of crisis when the cohesion of the symbolic reality breaks down.[12] I will be looking for signs of such a structure of the real underlying my three main categories of reality TV.

Witness TV: trauma and compulsion

What we now call reality TV has been around for the last 20 years or so. First, the 'witness video' genre of 'coincidental' recordings of domestic mishaps, accidents, crime and natural disasters was facilitated by the widespread dissemination of cheap, portable consumer camcorders from the mid-1980s,[13] combined with the simultaneous widespread use of CCTV surveillance systems. In fact these technologies each spawned their own subgenres: from the 'accidental slapstick' of *You've Been Framed* (1990–present) and the accidents and disasters caught by amateur camcorders in *Caught on Camera* (1999), to the surveillance-footage-based real crime programmes such as *Really Caught in the Act* (2003–2004) and *Crimewatch UK* (1984–present). The latter is already a hybrid involving reconstructions and 'ambulance chasing', which have become the mainstay of what Dovey has called alternately 'emergency service TV' and 'flashing blue light TV', a subgenre that is particularly popular in the United States.[14] Typically, the authenticity of events is emphatically stressed by taglines such as 'Shocking, real footage you have to see to believe' (*Cops*), or 'No scripts! No actors! No reconstructions!' (*Caught on Camera*).[15]

Dovey locates the pleasure of reality TV in a combination of home-movie intimacy of address, an affirmation of popularly held prejudices by the indexical 'accuracy' of machine-generated images, and the voyeuristic pleasure of attraction and repulsion by the deviance and horror on show.[16] However, I would argue that Dovey misses one aspect of the fascination exerted by the genre I have described as witness TV: the 'real' provenance of the images holds a fascination for the viewer simply on account of the idea that it provides an indexical trace of a 'real' world in which extraordinary things (things that don't normally happen to us) really happen: a world which is experienced as somehow *more real than our own reality*. What is remarkable about a lot of this footage is that the thrill, the crucial tension, is usually provided by extremely dangerous, life-and-death situations.[17] Even though the protagonists tend to miraculously survive their ordeals – sometimes to provide a first-person accompanying account – it is clear that it is only a small step from here to the rather mythical genre of snuff videos. This is where the distinction between fact and fiction, which might otherwise be allowed to blur, suddenly needs to come into sharp focus for the viewer: did someone actually die here? Did we witness the passing of a life? Is this recorded image the last surviving, indexical trace of a human being?[18]

What is at work here is the promise of a glimpse of the real in the Lacanian sense, of that impossible realm which is beyond our symbolic and imaginary reality, and which we catch sight of only at moments of trauma and revelation.[19] Both Bill Nichols and Jon Dovey drop hints in this direction: Nichols when he speaks of 'a fascination with that which exceeds the grasp which prepares the way for fetishism',[20] and Dovey when he states:

> the video clip is more reality fetish than evidence, as it is replayed over and over, slowed down, grabbed, processed, de- and re-constructed for our entertainment and horror. The video clip here stands for a reality (of horror) that cannot be known but which must at the same time be contained.[21]

Although the reference to fetishistic disavowal, an acknowledgement of the crisis that simultaneously 'neutralises its symbolic efficacy',[22] appears to be relevant, the stronger association, in my opinion, is with the structure of trauma.[23] Since Sigmund Freud described the connection between trauma and the compulsion to repeat in 1920, based on his observations of soldiers returning from the front in World War I, the idea of repetition has been central to the psychoanalytic structure of trauma. In this analysis 'traumatic neurosis' was irreconcilable with the founding psychoanalytic idea of the 'pleasure principle', and Freud was forced to conceive of a primary 'death instinct', described as an urge in organic life to restore an earlier, inanimate state of things.[24]

In *The Return of the Real* Hal Foster has described repetition in art, especially in Warhol's work, as symptomatic of trauma, grounding his analysis on Lacan's reworking of Freud's ideas on the subject. Lacan defines trauma as 'a missed encounter with the real', which, as missed, cannot be represented, only repeated. According to Foster, 'repetition serves to *screen* the real understood as traumatic. But this very need also *points* to the real, and at this point the real *ruptures* the screen of repetition.'[25] The compulsion to repeat which is symptomatic of trauma can be seen as a crisis of the symbolic, as an attempt to absorb what it cannot absorb, what can only be bound, or screened, by repetition. If this crisis is not overcome (by signification, some narrative of truth), the very stability of the ego is threatened, and thought becomes impossible. Consequently, the following stands out: the real cannot be encountered as such, it can only be approached obliquely, and it appears as *unassimilable*.[26]

What seems clear to me is that the fascination of the violent reality TV clip lies exactly in its traumatic character, compelling us to replay it, slow it down, allowing us to search for this impossible moment when the order of things is disrupted as life becomes death, while at the same time this very horror needs to be contained in a frame of fetishistic disavowal. What is interesting is that there is always something in this process that is radically missed: the form inevitably comes up against the limits of the medium, and peering into the grain, trying to see between the successive frames, we, as viewers, keep missing something, and the more we repeat it the more we miss it, losing our grasp of some impossible real we glimpsed out of the corner of the eye.[27] It is in this sense that Dovey is indeed justified in invoking pornography as a paradigmatic form of reality TV;[28] isn't this after all the place where we are always looking for 'the real thing', but where this sublime Thing, the 'substance of enjoyment', the forbidden object, is somehow always 'radically lost'?[29]

At the time that the very fact of a reality TV clip's violence becomes the object of our fascination it appears as a guarantee of its 'realness'. So paradoxically, violence and death, the unassimilable, become our touchstone of the real. Slavoj Žižek writes that in World War I Ernst Jünger 'was already celebrating face-to-face combat as the authentic intersubjective encounter: authenticity resides in the act of violent transgression'.[30] Žižek goes on to claim that the 'ultimate and defining moment of the twentieth century was the direct experience of the Real as opposed to everyday reality – the Real in its extreme violence as the price to be paid for peeling off the deceptive layers of reality'.[31] What is striking here of course is the representation of reality as an onion, or as a series of masks, suggesting that underneath these layers of deception some 'hard kernel of the real' is to be detected. This is, I would argue, precisely the structure of the real that informs viewers' fascination with docusoaps and other character-driven representations of the real, according to which some 'hard kernel' of identity, of a *real self*, can be found underneath the deceptive layers of people's self-presentation.

Docusoaps: the flicker of authenticity

The second major form of reality TV to hit television screens in the UK in the mid-1990s was the docusoap, a form apparently based on the 'fly-on-the-wall' observational documentary but with a host of elements that characterise it as a hybrid form. Ongoing documentary series such as *Sylvania Waters* (1992) and *The House* (1995) prefigured the format that really came into its own with such programmes as *Driving School* (1997), *Vets in Practice* (1996–2000) and *The Cruise* (1998).[32] In common with most observational documentaries, docusoaps tend to focus on a few central characters, but they also rely heavily on parallel editing to mimic the structure of the soap opera, weaving together several strands of narrative in brief scenes, with as many mini-cliffhangers as possible. In addition, brief bursts of explanatory, and frequently 'ironic', voice-over, and lots of quick, on-the-spot interviews with the central characters take the form even further away from the Direct Cinema conception of the 'pure' observational documentary.[33]

Since the docusoap relies so heavily on the central characters the issues of casting and performance become major preoccupations for the producers involved in this genre. This has traditionally been an issue for observational documentary as well, which is why one of its favoured subjects has been the portrayal of people who were somehow in the business of public performance anyway. Similarly, many docusoaps (such as *The Cruise*) have leisure or show business as their subject, providing them with the larger-than-life characters that are so crucial to their success.[34] What is needed from the performers in this genre is not just that they are 'relaxed in front of the camera', in other words that they can give a convincing performance of themselves, but also that they are able to deliver, in 'confessional-style' interviews, the kind of brief, telegenic articulations of their feelings that fit the format. Without question the successful docusoap 'stars' develop a strong sense of what kind of performance is expected from them, and a real skill in striking the right balance between playing up to the camera and presenting a convincing, intimate portrait of themselves.[35]

The dominance of the docusoap in the British TV schedules in the late 1990s coincided with a rash of 'scandals' in the British printed press about 'fakery' in documentary, starting with revelations in the *Guardian*, in 1998, about fabricated sequences in the award-winning Carlton documentary *The Connection*, which looked at the drug trade between Colombia and the UK. Several other documentaries were swept up in the moral panic that ensued (a headline in the *Daily Mail* shrieked: 'Can We Believe Anything We See On TV?' in February 1999), as well as the confessional talk show *Vanessa* (some 'fake' guests had been hired through an agency) and, predictably, a handful of docusoaps. What most of these cases focused on were interventions *by the filmmakers* to shape or influence what was happening in front of the camera, and the extent to which such interventions, and reconstructions in documentary in general, can be considered legitimate. Reconstructions have been standard practice in most of the history of documentary filmmaking, certainly in the early days of Robert Flaherty and John Grierson, so effectively it was the strict rules of observational 'purity' of American Direct Cinema (see note 11) which, rather inexplicably, were invoked by the regulators and the press during the 'fakery' scandals.[36] It is also interesting that, although some of the controversies involved the manipulative 'casting' of factual formats (notably in *Vanessa*), the inherent slippage of the real in the practice of characters 'performing themselves', common to docusoaps, was never part of the panic. Perhaps there is an implicit acknowledgement that, common to some sociological theories, people present themselves in daily life in a form of public performance in any case.[37]

Jane Roscoe makes the point that in docusoaps the acknowledgement by the subject of the camera implies an acknowledgement of the centrality of performance in the genre, and that this centrality implies a 'knowing' type of looking for the audience, which is put in the position of evaluating how well the participants play their role. Crucially, she locates the pleasure of the audience in their perception of 'flickers of authenticity – moments *when the performance breaks down* […] moments when we think we see the real person', and it is precisely in these moments that the audience locates the 'real'.[38] The idea that it is these moments that make docusoap compelling reflects the 'passion for the real' expressed in audience's compulsive viewing of witness TV formats, and suggests a similar underlying perceptual structure.

The importance of the idea that behind the performance we can still glimpse the 'real person' explains why one of the 'fakery' scandals *did* concern the question of performance. It involved the subjects of a presumably serious documentary, *Daddy's Girl* (1998), about, according to its billing, the 'often intense relationship between fathers and daughters', who misled the filmmakers into believing they were father and daughter, when in fact they were lovers. For three months, the crew followed Victoria Greetham and her fictional father 'Marcus' (whose real name was Stuart) through the ups and downs of their relationship, focusing for a large part on the disapproval by father 'Marcus' of Victoria's irresponsible boyfriend 'Stuart' (a role performed by Dan, a friend of the real Stuart). The transmission of the film was cancelled at the last minute after the real father of Victoria spotted a trailer for the film and called Channel 4 to inform them they had been deceived. The whole fiasco then became the subject of *Who's Been Framed?*, a documentary by Riete Oord for Channel 4 in 1999.

When Riete Oord confronts Marcus and Victoria with their deception in the latter film, they display a perfect understanding of the postmodern loss of the real: 'nothing on television is real,' says Victoria, before claiming that 'it was good telly […] they got exactly what they wanted […] it would have been pretty boring if it had just been me and my real dad'. Their knack for anticipating what the producer was looking for was made even more explicit by Stuart, who said: 'they never told us what to do, but it were [sic] obvious…we just sensed it'. In what was to be the climax of *Daddy's Girl*, Stuart drags his friend Dan out of a taxi and starts roughing him up, a scene that, according to Stuart, 'we didn't plan at all…I just knew we had to do something, give them something, and I just…there's a word for that…improvisation, yes, we were just improvising.' It might have made them perfect docusoap stars if they hadn't given their performance on a false premise, thereby breaking the documentary format's 'contract with the viewer'.[39] What this effectively meant was that any perceived, pleasurable 'flickers of the real' would have also been false, leaving the viewer feeling betrayed. In addition, given that they were media outsiders, *amateurs*, the 'contract with the viewer' was not theirs to break.

However, the fact that their performance was so successful under-mines the status of *all* 'flickers of the real', not least in *Who's Been Framed?* itself. After all, throughout this double-take on a documentary Victoria and Stuart give an excellent performance as well, clearly familiar enough with the codes of various kinds of factual television to slip effortlessly into the appropriately confessional style (and in the terms of Jean Baudrillard both simulations would be equally 'real'). So their *account* of *Daddy's Girl* is, in a sense, just as much open to question as their initial performance in it: in both cases they were playing up to the filmmakers' expectations, eager to give them 'exactly what they wanted', creating a performance that fundamentally responded to the interpellation of the filmmakers. This is where a post-structuralist account of identity or sub-jectivity comes into play, problematising the idea of a 'hard kernel' of the self, and shedding a different light on the idea of performance.

Judith Butler bases her argument about performance on the Lacanian idea that the subject's accession to language, and thus to symbolic reality (allowing reality to be *thought*), involves the submission to a name, by which we are situated in discourse, and which guarantees the temporal cohesion of the ego. This 'interpellation' simultaneously means submission to the Law of the Father, the symbolic authority that provides the name (or, to use the Lacanian phrase, 'in the name of which one speaks'),[40] the first rule of which is the rule of sexual differentiation.[41] Indeed it is the slippage in this process, the degree to which we can 'bend' the rules of the symbolic, through performance, to open up spaces for multiple or ambiguous genders, that is at the heart of Butler's project.[42] However, what is interesting is the possibility that 'self-performances' in reality television might be part of a process of 'self-enunciation', of *speaking oneself into being*, in an act of performative speech.

Reality Gameshows: the spectacle of identification

The *legitimate* way for amateurs to 'break into' the media and create their own mediated performances is through the still continuing wave of what are called 'reality gameshows',[43] the most well-known of which are *Survivor* and *Big Brother*.[44] There is a spectrum of transitional formats between the docusoap and the reality gameshow, from the set-up situation which is otherwise treated like a docusoap, exemplified by *Wife Swap* and *1900 House*, via the 'classic' live/semi-live form of *Big Brother*, with its focus on interrelational dynamics and a high level of audience participation, to the straightforward talent contests such as *Popstars* (2001–present) and *Pop Idol* (2001–present).

According to Roscoe, the audience's pleasure in reality gameshows is also to be found in the evaluation of the performances of the contestants,

heightened on the one hand by the fact that we can judge their performances towards the others while we also have a (hidden camera) view on
'how they really are', and on the other hand, in the case of shows such
as *Big Brother* and *Pop Idol*, by the fact that we can exercise our voting
power to punish the contestants we do not like.[45] In addition, in the case
of *Big Brother*, we can scan the webcams and the live transmission on E4
to catch ever more convincing 'flickers of authenticity', the most eagerly
anticipated of which of course was the possibility of witnessing *real sex*
among the contestants.[46] Again, in our 'passion for the real', we desire
the sublime, pornographic moment, even if we fully realise that, given
that the contestants will be well aware that we are watching, it could be
classed as a sexual performance.

Indeed, the claim to the real of these shows is often called into question,
on the grounds that 'the situation is contrived and the protagonists
handpicked',[47] and that the contestants frequently declare that they are
motivated by a desire to launch a media career. And yet it is precisely in
this last aspect that I believe there is *another* aspect of the real that can be
glimpsed in the *Big Brother* format. After all, what we witness is the
transformation, to a greater or lesser degree, of amateurs into celebrities.
I would argue that this is not just a matter of professional status, but that
to a significant degree they *really become celebrities*. The television apparatus
as a whole can be seen as a mirror in which the participants are reflected
back to themselves. While in the house, the contestant is cocooned,
fully isolated from the outside world,[48] but when he (let us assume he is
male) emerges from the house, and is confronted with his own image
disseminated through the media, this results in what we could describe,
after Lacan, as the 'jubilant assumption of his specular image'.[49] The
identification that takes place can be seen as an identification in the full
psychoanalytical sense, namely 'the transformation that takes place in
the subject when he assumes an image'.[50]

However, in the case of *Big Brother* this identification is specular *as
well as discursive*; the TV apparatus does not simply reflect back an image,
but an image embedded in a specific discursive practice, namely the
'language' of television, which interpellates the contestant as a media
subject. What comes into play is a process that parallels the submission
of the subject to the Law of the Father. Again one could dispute the
degree to which the contestant is wholly subjected to the authority of
the media apparatus, and the degree to which the subject enunciates
him/herself by his/her own performance.[51] Here, then, is that glimpse
of the real we witness when the contestant first recognises the reality of
his celebrity: isn't this a moment when his symbolic reality momentarily
falls apart, a point of crisis which forces him to re-situate himself in
discourse?[52] Of course the precise moment of this crisis is impossible to
determine, but we could justifiably say that the moment the contestant

emerges from the house, accompanied by the shrieks and howls of the collected fans, is, at the very least, the moment that *stands in* for this temporary loss of the symbolic.[53]

In conclusion, a Lacanian understanding of the Real goes a long way to help us understand why reality TV has proved to be so compelling to contemporary audiences. First, our passion for the real of violence, 'stripping away the deceptive layers of reality' (a kind of 'purgatory real') underlies the pornographic fascination with witness TV formats. Then, the 'flickers of authenticity' we discern in docusoap similarly suggest to us moments of crisis, when the deceptive layers of performance are stripped away. Finally, in reality gameshows we look for the same 'flickers of authenticity', especially during live broadcasts, trying to catch the contestants off guard, but we are also witness to an inherent crisis of reality for the contestants to the extent that they *identify* with their newly mediated image.

Is the 'Special Effect of the Real' Really Our Passion for the Sublime?

By way of an epilogue it might be useful to revisit Žižek's 'passion for the Real', and his argument that, paradoxically, *because* we long for a 'return' to the violent authenticity of the real, it culminates in its apparent opposite, in a *theatrical spectacle*,[54] a spectacle that plays out this return as a fantasy. Indeed Hollywood has created a whole genre of this apocalyptic fantasy: *Independence Day* (1996), *Planet of the Apes* (1968/2001) and *The Matrix* (1999) (to name but a few) are all spectacles in which we are not only confronted with images of sublime violence, but also with a post-apocalyptic reality marked by widespread destruction. This was, of course, exactly the fantasy that was played out, *performed*, by the terrorists crashing the planes into the World Trade Center on 11 September 2001.[55] This brings us to another violent fantasy played out as a reality event on television in the autumn of 2003: the 'Live Russian Roulette' by Derren Brown on Channel 4. Many commentators suggested that the only way they could believe in the reality of the experiment was for Derren Brown to blow his own brains out, again positing the lethalness of the experiment as the guarantee for its realness.[56] However, the question Žižek asks in connection with the terrorist attacks on 11 September – *Where have we already seen the same thing over and over again?* – is the same we might ask of Derren Brown. The fact that we have been collectively fantasising a return to the violence of the real is precisely what makes us experience them as unreal: after all, wasn't one of the most common responses by witnesses of the attacks on 11 September that it felt just like being in a movie? To Žižek, the danger is not that we should mistake fiction for reality, which was the spectre raised by the moral panic around documentary hoaxes in the British press, but its opposite: that we should not 'mistake reality for fiction'.[57] After all, what would have happened if Derren Brown had blown his brains out? Surely we would not have believed in the reality of it. We would have assumed C4 would not have allowed a situation that had a serious risk of going wrong, and that we would see Derren Brown a couple of weeks later for his next blockbuster stunt. Surely we would have mistaken reality for a fiction, at least initially.[58] As it happened, of course, Derren Brown's revolver contained a blank, but that does not deny the realness of our fantasy, the reality of our desire. As Victoria Greetham said, 'nothing on television is real', but then again it might be more real than we think.

II / REALISM IN PRACTICE

Introduction

Art, by its very nature, is understood as speaking through the language of representation. This second section contains for the most part contributions by artists who also write about their practice and the research behind it. Greater weight may appear to be given, consequently, to the artists' analyses of their work than the visual realisation of their ideas. The combination of text and image, though, is intended to give particular insight into the motivations these and other artists have to address 'the Real' as a subject. The contributions also draw attention to the different media, strategies and reference points that contemporary artists adopt to bring their ideas and interpretations to resolution. By their proximity, the contributions reveal a shared concern with certain binary relationships – of self and other, interior and exterior, microcosm and macrocosm, material and immaterial, intellectual and experiential, the imagined and the haptic. As a result, a preoccupation with the body as the site of understanding is revealed as a recurrent theme. Rather than focusing entirely on subjectivity and emotive expression, however, the artists are here concerned with the individual's relationship to 'the Real' as experienced through time, space and context, and through knowledge systems in particular.

The plate section is preceded by Andrew Lee's photographic essay 'Centres', which resonates with James Coupe's contribution, 'Art, Representation and Responsibility: towards a system aesthetic'. In his essay he discusses intelligent art and systems theory in direct relation to his own practice. Employing technologies commonly available, he discusses the generation of a 'conscious artwork' that integrates itself into the world of which it is a part. The artist detaches himself as far as possible from imposing his subjectivity upon the work by allowing the system's logic to create meaning.

Complete human detachment from an artwork is neither possible nor desirable and, within Coupe's artwork, human interactivity is essential to the evolution of the work: the viewer's 'own body confronting and integrating with a system'. A 'mobile' text is generated by the exhibition visitor and distributed via a computer network. It momentarily appears to float free from both sources of 'consciousness', somewhere in the ether, during the process of transmission. However, not only is a 'limit' reached but a boundary crossed when the messaging system begins to create a relationship with the corporate body that runs a mobile phone network. Implicitly Coupe's work raises questions about what or who now has control over us, within or outside the gallery. In a secular society, what form of consciousness monitors our actions? Not, it might seem, the consciousness of a benevolent omnipresence but that of potentially malevolent and, arguably, equally unknowable corporate forces. In facilitating an artwork that is created through the interaction between a network and its own audience, Coupe challenges notions not only of authorship but also of authority.

The contrast between Coupe's and Kate Robinson's texts makes explicit the change in Western thinking identified in Slavoj Žižek's contribution to this compilation. That is, a shift towards explanations of the postmodern world, objectively defined by a combination of global capitalism, scientific rationalism and psychoanalytic theory, from an earlier understanding of reality based on faith, truth and meaning.

In 'Real Streams' Robinson asks us to reconsider the significance of a mystical understanding and experiential knowledge of the phenomenal, and the numenal, world.[1] Through her study of the spiritual and philosophical writings of Hildegard of Bingen and Guilio Camillo, in contrast with her use of computer-generated images and Virtual Reality Modelling Language (VRML), we are asked to rethink what our intuitive understanding of the world might contain: to use it not instead of but in addition to our rational knowledge, as a way of approaching or interpreting the void that appears to be Reality.

Kate Robinson is writing about the significance of understanding through the body and through the experiential, rather than the mind and the intellect alone; of ideas being transmitted via streams of energy rather than as information. She traces how knowledge of reality and of the self is understood through attempting to relate to the macrocosm; through awareness of a presence outside and apart from one's own body but experienced or understood through or within it. These are difficult ideas for a rational, secular world to accommodate; attempting to speak about an ineffable Reality. Yet, in a variety of guises, it has been the subject of art for hundreds of years. Perhaps it is the very fact of its ineffability that drives artists to continually attempt to express what it is to be in the world. Perhaps art is one of the few spaces where these ideas can be most directly expressed. Art provides a space of representation where we accept that we can never express the totality of Reality but understand that what we can experience through the act of looking simultaneously within and outside ourselves is as close as we can get to being fully conscious or present.

In this context, Alan Dunning and Paul Woodrow's work with haptics on the *Einstein's Brain Project* can be read as a means of objectifying what the self feels and experiences. The artists have fabricated 'a body-double', which is 'viewed and experienced outside the actual body'. Using virtual reality technology the Project discusses the (possible or impossible) separation of the mind from the body.

In 'The Shape of the Real', Dunning and Woodrow discuss installations that 'direct the output of the human body to virtual environments'. The environments are constantly being altered through feedback from a participant's body. By the artists' use of haptics an invitation is made to the audience to become a part of the making of an artwork and, at the same time, to focus more clearly on perceived reality and physical consciousness. In the process, interestingly, the limits of the physical body are dissolved as sensation moves between the surface and the interior, and between the virtual and the real. In the Lacanian sense, the gap between self and other, or image and source, is potentially, in that moment of looking at the artwork, closed.

In contrast to the hermetic physical body explored in Dunning and Woodrow's work, the relationship of the self to the world is examined through the visceral body, literally, in the work of Jennifer Willet and Shawn Bailey. Through their work we come to see and understand the physical self as emanating from the microcosmic cells. We know that the body is a delicate thing but, given advances in scientific knowledge, so too is the balance to be struck between the natural and the selected.

In their project, 'BIOTEKNICA', Willet and Bailey employ scientific means and human tissue samples in the laboratory to explore living artworks and to draw attention to what they perceive as the lack of debate surrounding bio-ethical issues. They describe their project as a 'timely meditation on the ultimate fragility of the "natural" body'. Looking themselves at 'bio-manipulations and bio-invasions of the physical and social body', they ask us to consider both the beautiful and the grotesque. Artists and viewers together, we look at re-presentations of biotech-nology and its role in the 'future definition of humanity'. Occupying an ambivalent position, Willet and Bailey ask us, and the scientists whom they work alongside, to think about how we behave: morally, politically and ethically.

In the process of creating and presenting their works, all the artists included in this publication are calling themselves and their audiences to consciousness. Through a complex mix of intuitive, intellectual and formal devices, they ask us to question how we experience the world and make meaning from it. They ask themselves and us, as viewers, questions about what it is to be in and of the world. Their artworks ask that we are conscious of the world of which we are a part; that we think about the context or reality that we are creating for ourselves.

5 Art, Representation and Responsibility: towards a systems aesthetic

James Coupe

The outcomes from *I, Project*, a one-year funded research project (funded by the Arts and Humanities Research Board) to build a self-representing artwork, address a series of questions discussed here. Does an artwork need to be representational? What happens when an artwork is emulation rather than simulation? What are the implications for authorship and audience within such work? Where does responsibility for the activities of an autonomous, unpredictable art system lie? What role does computer technology play in exploring art that is ontologically autonomous?

The motivation for asking many of these questions emerged from an installation made in 2001, entitled *Digital Warfare Network* (*Project Phase Two*).[1] The theorist Nicolas Bourriaud recently described art as a 'state of encounter', a kind of bonding agent that keeps together moments of subjectivity associated with singular experiences.[2] In *Digital Warfare Network*, I created a system that could connect together all the people who had visited it in the gallery by behaving as a conduit for the sending and receiving of mobile phone text messages.

When a visitor approached the installation inside the gallery, a computer screen would display a message inviting them to send it a mobile phone text message. If they complied, the installation would immediately send a text message to the visitor, telling them that they had become part of the *Digital Warfare Network*. All the information that the system could get from the visitor's message was automatically stored inside the system's database: message, phone number, date, time, etc. Every ten minutes the system would select a message and a phone number from its database and send it. The effect was that, in the course of the time that the installation was exhibited, over 2,000 people intermittently received messages from each other.

Initially people looked to blame me, the artist, and would contact the gallery to complain that I was sending them text messages:

> *When did you decide 2 stoop down low 2 use 'art' (DWN) 2 get the girl?*
> *What do I look like? U easy flatterer…* [3]

After a while, however, the visitors who had become connected to the system became aware that other visitors were generating the messages, and that it was the installation itself that was distributing them. In other words, they realised that there was a system in place, of which they were a part and which extended far beyond the physical object within the gallery. The autonomy of this system, as something that had been initiated by the artist but which was now evolving in response to the visitors' input, became an important focus for how people responded to the messages they received. Rather than directing their messages towards other people, they began to direct them towards the 'system' itself:

> *FIGHT THE SYSTEM*

> *IM SURE THAT THERE IS A LOT OF PEOPLE IN HERE TRYING TO COMMUNICATE BUT THE MACHINE IS INTERFEARING BY BREKING CONTINUITY*

> *YES, PLEASE MAKE IT STOP.*

I wanted to absent myself as much as possible from the artwork: to become a client, as opposed to an administrator. I also wanted the visitors to acknowledge this and become aware that they were dealing with a system, rather than an individual. In order to achieve this, it was important that the installation was parasitical – it contained a Vodafone SIM card – rather than operating within its own independent space. So in effect the artwork was in the same place as the Vodafone network, yet it was not. As Bourriaud says, 'an artwork is a dot on a line.'[4] This can be illustrated by an incident that occurred during the exhibition. A Vodafone salesman attempted to sell cheaper text messages to the installation's SIM card and inadvertently inserted Vodafone into the *Digital Warfare Network*:

> *Call 09067 367721 To reduce your high mobile call charges. Calls cost 1p/m.*

> *BB po box 235 TQ12 6ZR.*

> *F:Richard Starkey S:NUISANCE CALLS M:PLS DO NOT SEND ANY MORE NUISANCE SMS TO 07990 525681 . Vodafone Cust svs.*

The Vodafone incident was a good example of how the system's autonomy afforded it a clear agenda. As a parasite, it was able to critique the politics of its host system. Due to the installation being essentially unstoppable as a system, issues of responsibility, intentionality and authorship arguably lay with the artwork. Such a scenario forced the relationship between artwork, artist and audience to shift: the artwork developed behavioural patterns and goals that were not necessarily in the artist's original conception, leaving the audience exposed. We can further understand this displacement by drawing analogies with systems analysis, specifically its concern with the idea of emergent properties that are generated by the system itself. Once a system develops such properties it becomes more than the sum of its parts, due to the fact that it incorporates functions that do not exist in any of its individual components. It thereby becomes difficult to comprehend the system by analysing the activities of its constituent parts, requiring instead that we look at the system in terms of its overall goals and behaviour. Thus, if an artwork is able to transcend its own mechanics, and engender an evolutionary advantage with which to engage other systems or audiences in meaningful, two-way discourse, then we are faced with a fait accompli in which the artwork's ontological reflexivity effectively usurps its instinct for representation.

Digital Warfare Network (Project Phase Two) raises questions that have a well-established art historical precedent. Far from being technologically driven, its concerns are intimately linked with core avant-garde themes such as alienation, utilitarianism and disruption. In the period 1968–1975, theorist Jack Burnham wrote widely on a perceived shift from art objects to art systems, describing a 'systems aesthetic'[5] where work focused less on things and more on the way that things were done, and where process began to supersede results. Burnham's methodology for understanding this kind of work can be broken down into three key premises, all of which were integral to the way in which *I, Project* was approached.

First, Burnham states that a systems aesthetic operates within an open, rather than a closed, environment. In other words, systems art responds, changes and adapts to its own context, rather than ignores it:

> [systems oriented art] will deal less with artifacts contrived from their formal value, and increasingly with men enmeshed with and within purposeful responsive systems. Such a change should gradually diminish the distinction between biological and non-biological systems, i.e. man and the system as similarly functioning but organisationally separate entities. The outcome will neither be the fragile cybernetic organisms now built nor the cumbersome electronic environments just coming into being. Rather, the system itself will be made intelligent and sensitive to the human invading its territorial and sensorial domain.[6]

Essentially, the work does not simply change its form or state (what it looks like) but also updates its ontological relationship with the context in which it is situated; that is, the way in which the system behaves and acts evolves from an exchange with its environment that provokes an alteration of its holistic purpose.

Secondly, Burnham stipulates that systems art places equal aesthetic value upon visible and invisible information, saying: 'formalist art embodies the idea of a deterministic relationship between a composition's visible elements. But...systems exist as on-going independent entities away from the viewer.'[7]

So here Burnham is making a key distinction between the idea of an empirically available 'total' visual presentation, as manifested in object-based art, and the distribution of absent and present elements that we encounter with systems-based work. We can see the realisation of Burnham's scenario within the *Digital Warfare Network*'s use of telematics: the system's appropriation of Vodafone's network allowed it to activate a kind of virtual private-public space of which no participant had a complete knowledge. The system was not being physically mapped; there was no diagram explaining who was connected and where they were. The conversations occurring within the system were providing moments of subjective connection that were geographically grounded via short messages, and which demonstrated the scale of the system without ever showing its entirety. In other words, the project was not defining itself simply through its material components, but also through the visitors' understanding of the *system* as an independent, autonomous and persistent entity that operated beyond any particular device.

The third element of Burnham's theory states that a systems aesthetic is not concerned with simulation. It is not interested in building representations; its relationship with the world is parasitical rather than parallel. Rather than building a system from scratch, an artist will tend to take an existing system (environment, network, musical instrument, law of physics) and manipulate it. This is what Burnham termed in 1975 'real-time political art'.[8] From this perspective, *Digital Warfare Network (Project Phase Two)* should not be seen as a representation of the sense of displacement that remote technology provides, but rather as a real experience of it, built upon the backbone of an actual network. Hans Haacke has described this process eloquently:

> A 'sculpture' that physically reacts to its environment is no longer to be regarded as an object. The range of outside factors affecting it, as well as its own radius of action, reach beyond the space it materially occupies. It thus merges with the environment in a relationship that is better understood as a 'system' of interdependent processes. These processes evolve without the viewer's empathy. He becomes a witness. A system is not imagined, it is real.[9]

Through appropriating the very systems that it aimed to critique, the project could occupy rather than re-present this space of phenomenological engagement, on a synchronous discursive level.

The research carried out within *I, Project* closely investigated these three principles of Burnham's, specifically in relation to large-scale distributed art systems. Within such systems, there is an inherent tension between the fact that they are too spread out for any single individual to get a real sense of their whole and the expectation that art should be made accessible to human beings through anthropocentric representation. The use of 'real-time' systems, in Burnham's sense of the term, hints at a kind of posthuman art, where the focal point is no longer the human body but, rather, a broader field of conditions, structures, environments and relationships. In his early writings, Burnham had spoken of a 'systems consciousness' superseding the art object.[10] Later, however, he believed that artists would eventually develop a means of producing artwork that was 'alive', and that would perhaps ultimately replace the human organism.

> The stabilized dynamic system will become not only a symbol of life but literally life in the artist's hands and the dominant medium of further aesthetic ventures … As the Cybernetic Art of this generation grows more intelligent and sensitive, the Greek obsession with 'living' sculpture will take on an undreamed reality.[11]

So Burnham was interested in projects that were intelligent on anthropocentric terms, not on their own terms – indeed he rejected potentially useful terms such as truth to materials as 'ambiguous'.[12] Burnham, despite advocating the real-time aesthetic outlined above, was unable to disregard his instinct for representation on a human scale. If he had followed the logic of his own theory, he would have had to accept the possibility that an artwork could develop its own field of relations, and its own boundaries, through a constant process of reinvention and reconstruction via existing systems. This denial rooted his theories within Modernism and effectively depoliticised his influence. This aspect of Burnham's theory was ultimately its downfall, leading to a dramatic retraction in the 1980 essay 'The Panacea that Failed', in which he confesses to having 'anthropomorphised the goals of technology'.[13] Burnham had effectively fallen into a representational trap, wanting to use technology to author systems that could imitate biological life and become real, rather than looking to explore the intrinsic properties of emerging technological systems as a means to critique social information structures.

The nature of this representational trap is particularly interesting in terms of its cross-disciplinary relevance. Art is not alone in facing this problem: it is a general symptom of our engagement with technology in computer science, engineering, medicine, oceanography and so on. We generally struggle when challenged to see ourselves as anything other than the central player within a technological construct. The vast networked information systems that we engage with on a daily basis today, however, are beginning to construct particular ontologies and autonomies that make them more than the sum of their parts. The process of making sense of the world as a single individual is extremely complicated, and is no longer a case of interacting with organic interlocutors such as human beings or 'nature'. Often and increasingly we find ourselves as partial performers within sophisticated, autonomous, database-driven systems controlling things such as money, food, conversations, warmth, travel and entertainment. The consequence of this is that such systems are constructing representational syntaxes for themselves, and we create disciplines such as 'human–computer interaction' in order to work out how to enable us to best understand them, rather than the other way round.

I, Project's research team sought to address the above questions and issues through concentrating upon the relationship between art and Artificial Intelligence (AI).[14] This seemed an appropriate choice due to the fact that for both disciplines, representation is a central concept. Artificial Intelligence, the science of making machines do the kind of things that humans can do, focuses upon the creation of computer programs designed to construct, adapt and link representations in the production of intelligent responses. The representational trap that Burnham's systems art fell into again features prominently: the responses are generally 'intelligent' in human terms, and aim to override the 'natural' impulses of a machine in order for it to convince the viewer or user that it is something it is not.

This 'classic' interpretation of AI often finds itself accused of lacking intentionality, due to the fact that its systems do not have the capacity to relate their internal processes and representations to the external world. John Searle, for example, criticised purely computational AI systems in his famous 'Chinese Room' argument, and reasoned that in order for a computer to be intelligent in the world, it would need some way of physically experiencing the world.[15] In other words, Searle was accusing the proponents of classic AI of dualism, for their belief that disembodied computer programs could be intelligent.

Within the last two decades, AI researchers have responded by developing systems premised upon notions of situated and embodied intelligence. This 'bottom-up' approach concentrates upon the ways in which autonomous systems can perceive and act within their immediate environments. Using this method, software and hardware agents are programmed to actually 'experience' and interact with their environment rather than simply manipulate its symbols. In other words, artefacts are no longer expected to learn human language but their own language, one that is about 'the world as it appears to them' and that helps them to communicate with other agents (no longer humans) in order to better cope with that world. So here Searle's objections are dealt with by building robots that are computer programs operating simultaneously in the physical world as well as in their own perceptual world (or *Merkwelt*). The robots are programmed to construct their own world-view on the basis of their immediate environments, and respond to them so as to avoid obstacles, follow objects and so on. Once again, however, such an approach is limited by the fact that the robots' behaviour is understood and interpreted as a success or a failure according to human criteria. As long as the robots can be seen to imitate real-world organisms, such as insects, they will not have their own intrinsic 'life tasks'.[16]

It seems clear, then, that the issue of situated and embodied representational syntax brings AI into shared territory with art: art is also reliant upon properties such as context, environment and language. Within both art and AI, dichotomies emerge between internal and external processes – between an appearance and a 'thing in itself'. And interestingly, the territory that this dichotomy occupies is precisely where each field's central question lies: 'is it art?' and 'is it intelligent?' Furthermore, it seems likely that each field is able to answer the other's question: abstract art indicates that an artwork can create its own universe rather than need to imitate a real-world organism; AI shows us that a system can exhibit intelligent behaviour without needing to share a human world-view. Speculating about the possibility of a system that could not just begin to answer, but also *be* an answer to both of those questions, we can consider an artwork that can construct an understanding of itself with which to develop autonomously its own set of presentational goals.

The fulfilment of this possibility is a long-term project, but I believe that *I, Project* succeeded in defining an appropriate methodology for approaching its problems. In a final discussion I will refer to another art project, carried out collaboratively by *I, Project*'s research team, which progresses some of the themes encountered in *Digital Warfare Network (Project Phase Two)*. Entitled *9PIN++*, the work was initially conceived in response to a commission from SCAN (Southern Collaborative Art Network) to 'map' the nine galleries that their organisation supported. The project involved an unprecedented level of access to the internal workings of the various galleries, media labs and committees that SCAN supported. This gave us the opportunity to embed *9PIN++* deeply within the institutional fabric of the galleries through a number of strategies. Initially, the research team opened a series of dialogues to discover each gallery's presentational boundaries and negotiate how and where the project could co-exist with their social and organisational spaces. We then installed a complex array of computers, sensors and actuators within each gallery, all networked together into one large system that could monitor movement, sound, video, light levels, air quality, temperature and humidity. In doing this, we were looking to provide the system with as much access as possible to the network of people, spaces, events and meetings that constituted each of the institutions that it was occupying.

The choice of sensors and actuators was also very carefully determined: our aim was to create a large range of potential feedback loops with which the system could express itself. For instance, the system could both monitor the gallery's air quality and adjust its air-conditioning; it could sense the gallery's light level and control its lighting; it could detect sound levels as well as make noise, and so on. Decisions over what to do with the data that the system collected from its sensors was made by a series of AI algorithms hosted on a central server, and built according to a model of computational creativity. Each gallery within the system became a node manipulated by 'curious' software design agents. The agents used specialised neural networks called 'novelty detectors' to explore autonomously each node's design spaces and evolve an independent level of interest in them, effectively seeking out the defining characteristics that made each node unique.

The server would process the sensor data using the AI algorithms and then send back a sequence of instructions to each gallery. The instructions took the form of sensor-actuator routines that provided new data to satisfy the agents' curiosity. So, for example, an agent that had become interested in the relationship between sound and light within its node would send routines that would continually adjust the light levels in the gallery and then listen for unusual changes in sound data via its microphones. Through this input-output loop, the system would attempt to reconcile a system-level desire to remain balanced and stable with the curious agents' drive to discover difference. The dynamic between these two competing goals provided the system with scope for unpredictable, emergent behaviour, where each node could become interested in itself, or aspects of itself which had emerged computationally rather than via explicit instructions from the artist. By monitoring the ways in which particular actions were received, each agent could construct a unique presentation of its current 'state' through exploring the impact of its various interventions within its own *Merkwelt*.

In conclusion, we can see that 9PIN++ also fits into the system aesthetic outlined by *I, Project*. It is an open system that deploys feedback techniques to update itself in response to its local environment. It is composed of sequences of visible and invisible properties due to its geographical dispersion, its use of software agents in symbiosis with real-world hardware, and the manner in which each system is literally embedded within the gallery. Perhaps most significantly, 9PIN++ is not a simulation: it works to construct its own representational syntax that, being appropriately situated within its own world-view, allows it to better understand itself and its context.

Its process involves a renegotiation of authorship, as the responsibility for decision-making transfers from artist to artwork. The artwork occupies a set of information spaces that are unavailable to human perception; the agents' interventions within the gallery are evidence of an internal logic and set of goals but they are not centred on the audience; rather they incorporate them as system properties. The question then arises: how do we experience this kind of work, where the inner workings are out of our reach? This is at once a communicative challenge for an artist and a philosophical question for an AI scientist.[17] The answer is the same for both fields: what we see is not the thing itself, but it must function to convey enough of the 99.9% of the system that is beyond our grasp. So, just as we do not need to understand everything about another human being, or a banking system, or spam email, in order to concede to it some kind of autonomy, work that coheres with a system aesthetic needs to be able to provide a partial experience that alludes to a dynamic series of life tasks. We are asked to encounter these tasks through a symbolic language that the system constructs for itself from within its own world-view. Operating as a kind of first-hand semantics, patterns of activity and behaviour emerge that ask the audience to develop a shared level of discourse with the system, in the same way that we are asked to develop shared discursive operating spaces with many 'industry standard' autonomous systems. Within the field of digital art, there are numerous recent examples of data visualisations, which take statistical data from systems such as stock exchanges, postal addresses, Internet usage and so on, and abstract it into colours, shapes and patterns.[18] *9PIN++* is clearly distinct from this in that it is not seeking to re-represent anything or to fit its data into easily graspable anthropocentric conventions such as computer graphics, melodies or user interfaces. The potential of such an approach to art is vast, and will no doubt result in an expanded understanding of where, how and when art can find itself.

6 Real Streams

Kate Robinson

The concept of the 'mystic' or 'visionary' has changed through the ages. The 'mystical' has always been on the borderline between emotion and rationality, the fabulous and the concrete, while the 'visionary' image is an important vehicle for expressing complex philosophical or theological ideas. The visionary images of the Benedictine nun Hildegard of Bingen are here explored with reference to a twelfth-century Scottish theologian, Richard of St Victor (died 1173). Her subjective experiences provide the starting point from which to understand the world and, implicitly, reality. By tracing the persistence of certain visual motifs from Hildegard's *Scivias* through the ideas of a sixteenth-century Italian natural philosopher, Guilio Camillo, a contemporary interpretation of Camillo's imagery emerges. The discussion concludes with the twentieth-century German philosopher Edith Stein's view of reality, as expressed in her final work, *The Science of the Cross*.[1]

It was Richard of St Victor who coined the phrase 'the science of the heart'.[2] He was describing what he meant by the term 'mystical'. Richard left Scotland to live and work at the monastery of St Victor, in Paris, where he became the Superior and Prior. He wrote extensively on matters of secular learning and law, though in fact he regarded secular education as worthless as an end in itself if divorced from a spiritual dimension. Richard's most renowned legacy is to be found in his mystical writings, such as *The Twelve Patriarchs* and *The Mystical Ark*.[3]

'Mystic' comes from the Greek *mystikos*; a *mystagogos* was one who was initiated. Originally it referred specifically to knowledge of the Greek mystery cults. Louis Dupré and James Wiseman have charted the changes in emphasis of the word over the centuries. They say that the 'objective quality of the original concept' persisted into the sixth century.[4] It was only by the late Middle Ages that the idea of mysticism had changed to admit a 'private, inner experience'. However, even then 'the emphasis on contemplation which to us appears such a distinct characteristic of the mystical could not have served as a specific difference, for the active life of good works counted as equally "mystical"'.[5]

The physical human body and all its mundane functions, as much as the stars and the earth and sky, were generally seen as part of an organic whole, a functioning mechanism that reflected the mystical workings of God. According to Dupré and Wiseman, it was only towards the end of the Middle Ages that the term moved towards 'the highly individual, subjective meaning we tend to regard as its very essence'.[6] They conclude by saying that all mystical texts right up to the present time – and here they cite, for example, Krishnamurti and Thomas Merton – place greater emphasis on the importance of what they call, in Latin, *sapere*, 'the experiential "tasting" of truth', rather than *cognoscere*, which implies a 'purely intellectual knowledge'.[7]

The *Concise Oxford English Dictionary*, 1956 edition, describes the mystic as one who 'seeks by contemplation and self-surrender to obtain union with or absorption into the Deity'. It goes on to say that the term is often used to describe someone 'who believes in spiritual apprehension of truths beyond the understanding', hence the term 'mysticism'. This, it says, is often used in a derogatory sense. Mysticism, in the negative sense of the word, is close to 'mystify', defined as to '[h]oax, play on credulity of; bewilder; wrap up in mystery'. We are in borderline country here, in no-man's land. To 'wrap up in mystery', to cocoon, swaddle, and conceal is the opposite of the original sense of *mystikos*. The earlier versions are instead far more to do with a peeling away of confusion to reveal a deeper truth, a truth not necessarily based on rational analysis but on existential understanding, on what the philosopher Eugene Gendlin has called 'felt sense', or *sapere*.[8]

Perhaps it is not surprising that this borderline country between truth and untruth, reality and fantasy, is the domain of 'the science of the heart'. On the one hand, a blood pump, an oxygen carrier, a double-chambered administration system; on the other, the region we have come to associate with our *emotions*: love and hatred, sorrow and humour, the things that make us human. The American actor and playwright Wallace Shawn once said that if he were to write a chronicle of the things that he *did* in his life, it would fill a few pages. But if he were to write a chronicle of the things that he *felt* in his life, it would be a vast work running to hundreds of volumes.

Let us return to Richard of St Victor. Despite, or perhaps because of, his interest in the mystical, he believed that we 'should seek always to comprehend by reason what we hold by faith'.[9] In step with the intellectual climate of the day, he believed that his analysis of the way the world worked, which included the mystical experience and mystical knowledge, needed to be systematised and analysed through reason.

A contemporary of Richard was Hildegard of Bingen (1098–1179), a female mystic who lived in the German Rhineland. Interest in Hildegard has grown, and today she is undoubtedly better known than Richard of St. Victor.[10] However, that was probably the case even in the twelfth century. Hildegard was famous throughout Europe as the Seer, the Prophetess of the Rhine. Brought up in the male environment of a Benedictine monastery, abandoned there by her parents at the age of eight (and by all accounts having a pretty miserable time), Hildegard eventually owned up to having 'visions' sent from God when she was in her late thirties. She had experienced the visions from when she was a small child, but had kept them secret 'for fear of the scepticism of others, the shrugging of shoulders, and the manifold gossip of mankind'.[11]

However, spurred on by encouragement from the eminent intellectual heavyweight of the day, Bernard of Clairvaux, and subsequently by papal approval, Hildegard dictated descriptions of her visions to her faithful scribe and secretary, the monk Volmar. The first of her books, *Scivias* (1141–1151), or 'Know the Way', took ten years to write. Subsequently, among others, came *Physica* (c.1151–1158) and the *Book of Divine Works* (1163–c.1174). She was prolific in her correspondence, writing around four hundred letters to popes, emperors, secular rulers, monks and nuns all over Europe. She also wrote a series of song cycles for voice and instrumental accompaniment, such as *The Play of the Virtues* (c.1150) and *The Symphony of the Harmony of Celestial Revelations* (c.1151–1158).

In her letters Hildegard betrays a fierce and fiery but also gentle character. She always professed to be an illiterate and uneducated woman. She also maintained that her understanding of medical and cosmological matters, as well as the way of life that the nuns in her community followed, were directly inspired by visions. Similarly, Hildegard's music was also 'visionary'. John Stevens has made a thorough examination of the music, contrasting it with medieval liturgical forms. While the basic structure of the music is of its time, the 'words and the melodies…give the impression of outpourings, unrestrained spontaneous utterances'. They are, according to Stevens, 'musical crystallizations of moments of vision'.[12]

Hildegard's music could be said to have a fractal structure, in that each element of the music reiterates, or reflects, the larger pattern. A fractal is a fragment in which a pattern of meaning points to the larger whole, or perhaps more accurately the whole is embedded within the part – 'the closer you come, the more detail you see'.[13] While '[i]nfinity is implicit and invisible in the computations of calculus…[it is] explicit and graphically manifest in fractals'.[14] As Stevens discusses, Hildegard used the form of musical liturgy as a 'frame, a mould into which she could pour her creativity'.[15] While, from a distance, the music appears to be of its time, the closer the listener attends, the more original and untamed it becomes.

The structure of a snowflake is fractal, and so are the contours of coastlines, mountains, clouds and galaxy clusters. Fractal geometry is a key element in computer graphics. I think that a fractal motif occurs in many of the illuminations that accompany Hildegard's text. The image of 'The Fall', in her *Scivias*, for example, illustrates how the whole is united through the repeated pattern.

At the corners are images to represent air, fire, earth and water. The border is made of a repeated motif of the winds blowing in opposite directions. This is to suggest the sense of dynamism and movement in the scene. Elsewhere Hildegard talks about the idea of the winds pushing and pulling, creating dynamism. The upper part is devoted to planets and stars in a blue heaven. Air and fire, or the sun, act downwards from the heavens; water and earth are below, at the terrestrial level. A large black serpent, rising like smoke, from an earthy cauldron of flames at the very base of the picture, pierces the sky. Meanwhile Adam, levitating horizontally above flowering trees – the Garden of Eden – cups his hand to his ear as he listens to the roaring flames of the inferno below. He is mid-way between heaven and earth. The flames themselves, to which he is listening, are in diagonal opposition to the benevolent flames of the sun in the top right-hand corner of the picture. From Adam's rib sprouts a cloud of stars. This is Hildegard's un-bodied image of Eve, the Mother of All Living. The stars of Eve, shooting out of Adam, reflect the stars of

Hildegard of Bingen, 'The Fall' (detail from *Scivias*), 1141–1151. Photo: Rheinisches Bildarchiv.

the sky. They also make a pun on the idea of *Stella maris*, a name of Mary, star of the sea, the sea of heaven. Reiterating the piercing of the sky, the serpent pierces the cloud of stars with a triple-pronged tongue. This image is sexual as well as referring to speech: the active serpent speaks while the passive Adam listens. But there is also a subtle symbiosis in the relationship between Adam and the serpent. The serpent's smoky emanations pierce into the lower level of the sky; in the meantime, Adam's head pierces the side of the serpent, his hand stretching out along the level of its neck. Turning the whole image on its head, it looks as though Adam is simultaneously being crushed by the weight of the serpent while also actually holding him up. The picture is very finely balanced.

Hildegard herself said: 'The visions which I saw I did not perceive in dreams nor when asleep nor in a delirium nor with the eyes or ears of the body. I received them when I was awake and looking around with a clear mind, with the inner eyes and ears, in open places according to the will of God.'[16]

The neurologist Dr Oliver Sacks has suggested that Hildegard's visions were the result of migraine attacks. This theory picks up on ideas first mooted in 1917 by the historian of science Charles Singer. For Sacks, Hildegard's 'splendid and beautiful' stars become 'a shower of phosphenes [tiny sparks common in the early stages of migraine] in transit across the visual field, their passage succeeded by a negative scotoma [shadow]'.[17]

He suggests that her images of the City of God represent a pixellated disturbance of the visual field common to migraine sufferers, and describes her 'Head of God' as depicting a 'typically migrainous fortification figure...radiating from a central point, which...is brilliantly luminous and coloured'.[18] This also appears in 'The Tower of Preparation'.

That Hildegard may or may not have suffered from migraine, and whether or not we can believe her when she says that she was an uneducated woman, her writings belie knowledge of some of the important texts of the day.[19] The two communities she founded (each of around twenty nuns following the Benedictine rule) were at Rupertsberg and at Eibingen, near Mainz, and were very close to the great libraries and centres of scholarship at Worms, Metz and Trier.

The egg-shaped image from *Scivias*, entitled 'The Universe', follows the contemporary Aristotelian understanding of the make-up of the earth and planets, though in a particularly beautiful way.[20] The earth at the centre is made up of the four elements, earth, air, fire and water – each one represented in the same way as in 'The Fall', just like a kind of elemental key. Surrounding the earth are the fixed stars and planets – shown as fiery shapes, the smaller ones in white, the larger in yellow gold. Both the full and crescent Moon is clearly visible amidst the stars; directly above the Moon are two fiery shapes in orange and white representing Mercury and Venus. Above this, the Sun is shown as a large orange and gold fiery shape surmounted by three further planet forms that represent Mars, Jupiter and Saturn. One of the unusual aspects of this mandala-like picture is the absence of an obvious image of God. Only the flames piercing the very frame of the picture point to a numinous dimension.

In 'The God of Illumination', also from *Scivias*, the wings of the Creator God pierce the frame. The image is in three parts: at the top is a golden image of the Divine; in the centre is a mountain with people; at the bottom, on an abstract background of stars, are two conceptual figures. In the bottom left is an apocalyptic figure that we know from the text is called 'Fear of the Lord'. This tall figure, giving a key to the picture as a whole, is covered in a pattern of eyes. It is an image of illumination, of vision. The great Illuminator is on the top of the mountain, which itself is covered with a pattern of apertures in which are revealed the faces of people watching the spectacle that unfolds before their eyes, like so many little television sets. A river of gold runs down from the figure on the mountain to cover the head, eyes, ears and mouth, and all of the figure at the bottom right of the picture. This is an image of a little girl, called 'Poverty of Spirit'. The implication is that the senses should be filled up with an image of the Divine.

The idea of the golden stream connecting the three levels of the world, the divine, the earthly and the inner experience, or spiritual essence

Hildegard of Bingen, 'The Universe in the Shape of an Egg' (detail from *Scivias*), 1141–1151. Photo: Rheinisches Bildarchiv.

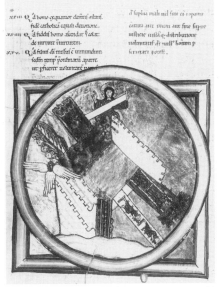

Hildegard of Bingen, 'The Tower of Preparation' (detail from *Scivias*), 1141–1151. Photo: Rheinisches Bildarchiv.

of mankind, appears to have persisted as an image for at least another four hundred years. One such image, and one that bears resemblance to Hildegard's 'Poverty of Spirit', occurs in the work of the Italian philosopher Giulio Camillo (c.1480–1544), who lived in Venice in the early sixteenth century. He worked closely with the painter Titian and devoted his life to creating his 'Idea for the Theatre', the layout of which he dictated to an agent three months before he died in 1544.[21] The Theatre itself was a highly complex model of the universe composed of over two hundred textual descriptions of images. The layout of Camillo's Theatre has been discussed in detail elsewhere.[22] The references inherent in the images themselves come from a wide range of source material: a bricolage of mythological pagan, Christian and classical motifs. It is thought that Camillo was attempting a kind of calculus based on the visual image and language. One of the images that he repeatedly uses is that of a 'Young Girl with her Hair Raised to the Heavens', which is meant to symbolise 'a vigorous thing either strong or trustworthy'.[23] He explains that the image is based on Plato's idea of man being a tree upside down 'since the tree has its roots below and man has his above'.[24] He goes on, citing Origen and Jerome, to explain that the hair should be understood metaphorically as representing a part of the soul. In the same way, the 'beard, eyes, and other parts corresponding to the body' should be interpreted, in biblical terms, as correspondent to an aspect of what

Hildegard of Bingen, 'The God of Illumination', also known as 'The Light Streaming to the Blessedness of Poverty of Spirit' (detail from *Scivias*), 1141–51. Photo: Rheinisches Bildarchiv.

he calls the 'interior man'. In this way, just as 'the tree draws to itself through its roots the nutritive moisture from the earth, so the beard and hair of our interior man should draw dew, that is, the living moisture from the influxes of the celestial channels, from whence comes all its strength'.[25]

Camillo, like Hildegard, envisages a vital equivalence between the body and the cosmos. For Camillo, this is activated through 'celestial channels', streams of cosmic, or divine, energy that flow into the earth from the heavens.[26] These heavenly streams move through the very capillaries of the skin, of every single hair of man. Camillo distinguishes between the 'supercelestial streams which do not wet' and the 'waters of this world, which do wet'. The 'supercelestial streams' are from 'the waters above the Heavens'.[27] Elsewhere he discusses the 'moist heat' of heaven, saying that it is 'liquid, fluid, agile, slippery and pleasing and sweet to the touch of nature'.[28] The waters above the firmament are a macrocosmic version of the earthly element of water, which is manifested in streams, rivers and oceans.

For Camillo, the spiritual or mystical aspect of creation is inseparable from the physical. Correspondent with the heavenly waters above the firmament, the celestial streams inseminate earthly matter not only with life but also with the 'spirit of life'. The 'streams', 'channels', and what he elsewhere calls the 'dew' of heaven constitute the vehicle by which this seminal heavenly influence is imparted.[29]

Camillo's extraordinarily visual descriptions provided rich source material for the author's contemporary version of his *L'Idea del Theatro*, made in 2001.[30] Interpretations of the world described by him were created using computer technology, including Virtual Reality Modelling Language.[31] A small selection is reproduced here. 'Atoms', for example, which in the Theatre would be placed on the level of 'The Sandals of Mercury' under the influence of Venus, represents diminishment and dissolving. 'Narcissus' (illustrated), at the level of the 'Cave', and also under the influence of Venus, represents the beauty of things in this world. 'Gordian's Knot', also at the level of the 'Cave', under the influence of Mercury, represents continuity. There are nearly three hundred images of this type allocated throughout the Theatre, their interpretation dependent on their place and content.[32] Placed inside a virtual model, all these images were set to float in a theoretical universe. The viewer, who enters the space of this virtual 'world', is able to manoeuvre through a stream of images.

For Camillo, as for Hildegard – and as the author hopes was represented in the VRML model mentioned above – the method by which the participant can optimally navigate the streams of imagery is from the perspective of the centre. The idea of the centre is physical and metaphysical. Both Camillo and Hildegard attempt a synthesis of science and art: for Hildegard, this is cosmological, musical and visual; for Camillo, it is cosmological and theatrical. They also share a reliance on the subject's response to phenomena, in the participation of the senses – in seeing, listening, feeling. For both it is through bodily participation – in the singing and the hearing, the imagination and the seeing, the energy and its flow – that their synthesis is realised.

This text concludes by looking at the writings of a twentieth-century philosopher. Edith Stein's interpretations of a historical mystic look at the physical world – like Camillo and Hildegard – through a metaphysical lens. She also shares with her predecessors a view of the world that imbues the body itself with spiritual significance. As we shall see, reflected in both Stein's life and art, this involved a passage through darkness.

Edith Stein (1891–1942) was a German intellectual who became a nun of the Order of the Discalced Carmelites. Unlike Hildegard of Bingen, Stein was a highly educated woman. Receiving her doctorate from the University of Freiburg under the guidance of Edmund Husserl, she was an associate of the philosophers Hedwig Conrad Martius and Martin Heidegger. While Stein was drawn initially to the discipline of phenomenology, in her final work she focused on a late Renaissance mystic, interpreting visionary and ecstatic poetry.

Stein was Jewish and, despite her conversion, was in danger in Germany at this time. Along with her sister Rosa, who had also taken the veil, Stein moved to the convent of Echt, in the Netherlands. But even here she was not safe. In her last months, before the Nazis abducted her and Rosa, Stein wrote an exegesis on the writings of St John of the Cross (1542–1591). She called this work *The Science of the Cross*. On 2 August 1942 Stein had probably been working on the manuscript, the final pages written in fainter and fainter ink, as she was forcibly removed from the convent. The book and much of her other writing was saved, however, hidden in an attic for the remainder of the war and published posthumously.

Stein defines a 'theology…derived from inner experience' as being a science of the cross.[33] A living theology, St John's doctrine, she says, 'can be likened to the wide-spread branches of a tree that has sunk its root in the greatest depth of a soul and which has been nourished by the heart's blood'.[34]

In *The Science of the Cross* Stein discusses the nature of the visionary experience – which she treats with caution, even though she values it.[35] Her science is based on a time when the soul 'is put into total darkness and emptiness'; only then will she, the soul, be granted the 'ray of darkness'.[36] God 'pours streams of love over her'.[37] She tells of 'the profound abyss of the caves of sense' – the caves of intellect, will and memory.[38]

One of the many images that Stein interprets is from St John's poem 'The Bridal Song'. In this image, like Hildegard and Camillo before her, Stein's focus is on hair. With the light that Edith Stein shone on 'that hair, that sole one',[39] an ancient mystical tradition is revivified. It is a single hair that is a bond of love:

We fashion crowns…and you
Weave love throughout their span
Which with one hair of mine is bound.[40]

7 Centres

Andrew Lee

This photo essay is taken from *Centres*, a series of photographs of telephone call centres across Scotland.

1. 'Thomas Cook Direct, Falkirk, 2001'.
2. 'Travel Choice Direct, Kilmarnock, 2003'.
3. 'First Direct, Hamilton, 2002'.
4. 'T-Mobile, Greenock, 2003'.
5. 'Esure, Glasgow, 2003'.
6. 'Kwik-Fit Insurance Services, Uddingston, 2002'.
7. 'CR Smith, Dunfermline, 2003'.
8. 'Scottish Environment Protection Agency, Perth, 2002'.

All images copyright Andrew Lee.

Plate section

When did you decide 2 stoop down low 2 use "art" (DWN) 2 get the girl? what do I look like? u easy flatterer...

REMOVED 24/06/2001   14:41:12

above James Coupe, 'Digital Warfare Network (Project Phase Two)', installation, 2001. Copyright the artist.

left James Coupe, 'Digital Warfare Network (Project Phase Two)', screenshot view, 2001. Copyright the artist.

above left Kate Robinson, 'Young Girl with Her Hair Raised to the Heavens', from the *Theatre of Memory*, 2001.

above right Kate Robinson, 'Narcissus', from the *Theatre of Memory*, 2001.

below Kate Robinson, Image from VRML of the *Theatre of Memory*, in collaboration with Carl Smith, 2001.

All images copyright the artist.

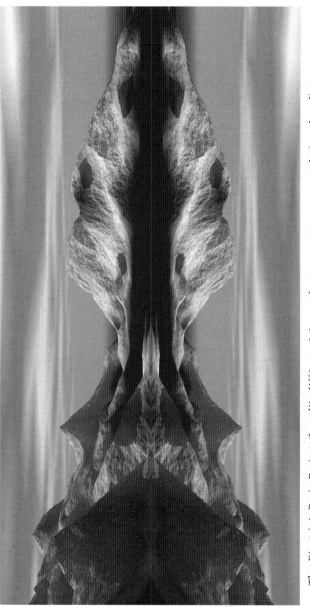

The *Einstein's Brain Project*, 'Lac d'indifférence', image from computer-generated virtual-reality environment, 1998. Copyright the artists.

Time 00:03:02:09

The *Einstein's Brain Project*, 'The Shape of Thought', computer-generated 3D model, 2004–2005. Copyright the artists.

The *Einstein's Brain Project*, 'Pandaemonium', interactive mixed-reality environment, 2001. Copyright the artists.

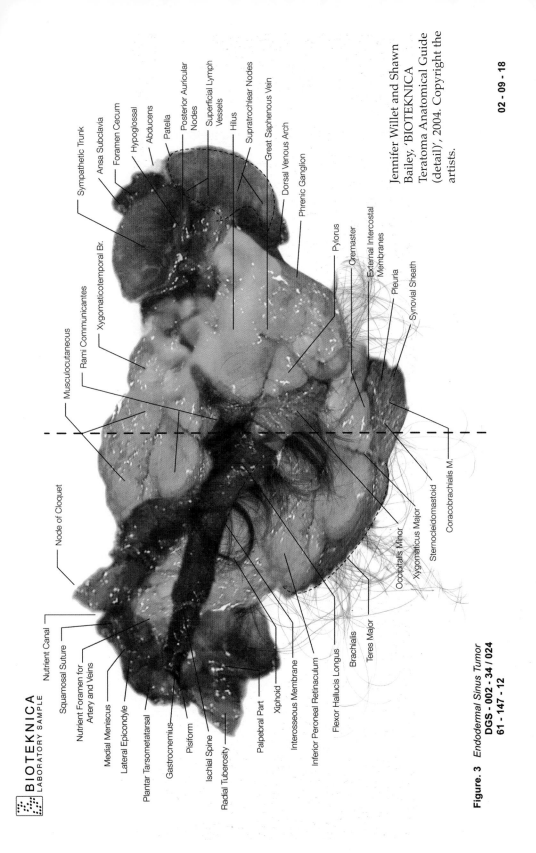

Jennifer Willet and Shawn Bailey, 'BIOTEKNICA Teratoma Anatomical Guide (detail)', 2004. Copyright the artists.

02 - 09 - 18

Figure. 3 *Endodermal Sinus Tumor*
DGS - 002 - 34 / 024
61 - 147 - 12

Nutrient Canal
Squamosal Suture
Nutrient Foramen for Artery and Veins
Medial Meniscus
Lateral Epicondyle
Plantar Tarsometatarsal
Gastrocnemius
Pisiform
Ischial Spine
Radial Tuberosity
Palpebral Part
Xiphoid
Interosseous Membrane
Inferior Peroneal Retinaculum
Flexor Hallucis Longus
Brachialis
Teres Major

Node of Cloquet
Musculocutaneous
Rami Communicantes
Xygomaticotemporal Br.

Sympathetic Trunk
Ansa Subclavia
Foramen Cecum
Hypoglossal
Abducens
Patella
Posterior Auricular Nodes
Superficial Lymph Vessels
Hilus
Supratrochlear Nodes
Great Saphenous Vein
Dorsal Venous Arch
Phrenic Ganglion

Pylorus
Cremaster
External Intercostal Membranes
Pleura
Synovial Sheath

Occipitalis Minor
Xygomaticus Major
Sternocleidomastoid
Coracobrachialis M.

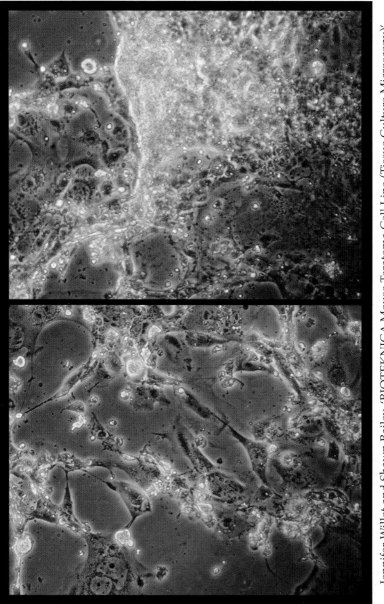

Jennifer Willet and Shawn Bailey, 'BIOTEKNICA Mouse Teratoma Cell Line (Tissue Culture Microscopy)', 2004. Copyright the artists.

8 The Shape of the Real: the work of the *Einstein's Brain Project*[1]

Alan Dunning and Paul Woodrow

Prevailing cognitive models describe the brain as following the forking paths of judgement that experience has established, shifting from one appropriate path to another in response to ever-changing sensory feedback.

Such wandering reminds us of the discrepant returns of memory found in the work of Alain Robbe-Grillet, and of Umberto Eco's inferential walks through a labyrinthine text. Again and again these works recognise a world reflected many times over, in which the means of negotiating the mirrored labyrinth must be constantly made anew. This is reminiscent of Elias Canetti's note for a novel: a man who always strays and has to find a new way home every night; or of Damasio's famous 'Boswell', a man with a memory that never reached back more than 30 seconds; or of Oliver Sacks' patient who constantly had to reinvent himself in the face of a perpetually fleeting memory.

> This self is an:
> …evanescent reference state, so continuously and consistently recon-structed that the owner never knows that it is being remade unless something goes wrong with the remaking…Present continuously becomes past, and by the time we take stock of it we are in another present, consumed with planning for the future, which we do on the stepping stones of the past. The present is never here.[2]

Our very organism, then, rather than some absolute experiential reality, is used as the frame of reference for the constructions we make of the world around us and for the construction of the ever-present sense of subjectivity. The body is turned inside out and placed beside and around itself like a Klein bottle, the latter being a closed, non-orientable surface that has no inside or outside. The distinctions between interior and exterior, between body and world, are broken down even as they are erected in the organism's moment-to-moment reconstruction of itself. This corporal literacy is a poetics of reversal – a jellyfish that physically inverts itself as a natural consequence of the flows it produces and navigates.

In 1998 Randall Rohrer, David Ebert and John Sibert described several techniques for text visualisation to aid in understanding document content and document relationships. Their paper 'The Shape of Shakespeare: visualizing text using implicit surfaces' provided a graphic represent-ation in three-dimensional space of essentially non-spatial information.[3]

Since 1996 a collaborative group of artists and scientists working under the name of the *Einstein's Brain Project* (hereafter the Project) has been engaged in a similar visualisation problem: that of visualising the bio-logical output of the human body. In doing so the Project has generated forms and shapes directly out of the human acts of living, acting and thinking. Is this the shape of the real?

One of the aims of the group is the visualisation of the biological state of the body through the fabrication of environments, simulations and installations. The Project has developed numerous installations, using analogue-to-digital interfaces, to direct the output of the human body to virtual environments that are constantly being altered through feedback from a participant's biological body. The core of the Project is a discursive space that engages with ideas about the constructed body in the world and its digital, cybernetic and posthuman forms.

Over the years the Project has worked to formulate and fabricate a body-double, which can be viewed and experienced outside the actual body. The form of this body is an aura or auratic presence generated by an actual and specific participant in a designated space. The auratic presence – a notional holographic double – exists outside the viewer's body and is a consequence of the biological functions of the participant's body (heartbeat, brainwaves, body heat, skin resistance, eye movements, blood pressure and so on). However, the auratic form does not necessarily reproduce or imitate the outward physical appearance of the viewer. In the lengthy series of works called 'Madhouses', the body is represented by dynamic abstract forms moving in virtual space. In ongoing works such as 'Errant Eye', the effects of biological data are represented by the distortions in the visual field. In more recent work the body's activity is represented by the following: three-dimensional blobs that slowly take shape over time from the effect of electroencephalogram (EEG) signals; robots swarming and flocking across a floor; a phosphorescent wall that briefly holds the traces of lights and lasers responding in real time to biological data; and pulses sent through a ferromagnetic fluid.

Core members are Alan Dunning, Chair of Alberta College of Art and Design's Media Arts and Digital Technologies Programme, and Professor

Paul Woodrow and Dr Morley Hollenberg from the University of Calgary, who have been working as an interdisciplinary collaborative team for the past ten years. This collaboration has regularly included other scientists, technologists, theorists and engineers brought to the Project to meet particular scientific, technical and theoretical requirements and to enlarge the vision of the Project. The Project has developed a large number of works that deal with issues of perception, representation of the human body and the construction of reality through immersive, shared, virtual reality environments and artworks.

The Project's early work (1996–1997) represented the notion of the body/brain as descriptive representations, physical spaces and metaphoric spaces, together evocative of a neurologically sensed world open to a variety of interpretations and perceptions in the struggle to establish the body in the world. The Project created realistic navigable virtual landscapes from models and images of human body parts. Working with the University of Calgary neurologist Dr Arthur Clark, microscopic sections of the brain were used as the basis for constructing a series of virtual reality landscapes. The landscapes were rendered and organised so as to present familiar, yet unnameable, highly naturalistic geological formations and geographic locations. Embedded in these scenes were semiotic references to literary, mythological, poetic and social content indicating that an appreciation of this artificial world through effect and appearance is congruent with a representation of the natural world inscribed over and over by mediating cultural bodies.

Following the representation of the body/brain as a realistic space, the Project's focus became the internal mechanisms of the brain itself, employing the notion of the brain's structure and neurological pathways as an interface. In a series of installations, 'The Fall, the Furnace and the Flesh' (1998–2000) and 'The Crucible' (2000–2001), the Project used nineteenth-century phrenological accounts of brain structure to construct an anatomical model of the human head. The head contains pressure-sensitive pads, light and sound sensors corresponding to the 37 organs of mental and moral faculties identified by the phrenologists Franz Joseph Gall and Johannes Caspar Spurzhiem, to enable a participant to engage with the installations. The recapitulation of the nineteenth-century model within the context of contemporary neurological science and digital representation was presented as a critique of outmoded representations of the brain. Based on ideas of interpreting the world contained within phrenology (as the participant literally feels the bumps on a head), the work explores cultural and social stereotyping. It also addresses issues arising out of the mass usage and adoption of scientific knowledge, as well as chemical, cultural, social and political constructions of reality.

The *Errant Eye* is an ongoing work begun in 1998. It deals with ideas about perception, consciousness and the construction of reality. It does so through an elaborate, immersive, VR environment that explores those functions of the brain associated with deficiencies in memory, sensation, perception and expression and makes them manifest. By linking brain activity with visual changes in the perception of a world, the Project provides a space where these manifestations of the inner workings of the brain problematise the relationship between a world apparent and a world perceived. It also continues the Project's interests in the converging disciplines of science, technology, art and philosophy in the study of consciousness.

The environment is entered by donning a stereoscopic head-mounted display, modified to accommodate electrodes and audio, and driven by workstations to provide different inputs to each eye for the construction of a familiar immersive world. Micro-voltages from the participant's scalp are sensed by the electrodes and used to track neuro-cognitive activity. The signals are analysed and routed to a computer where they modulate the form and content of the perceived virtual environment.

As the real-time EEG output is monitored and fed into the virtual worlds the signals continuously update the values of fields within the scenegraph, and initiate rapid changes in the world: colour, size, position, orientation, video texture and so on. Using a dataglove and context-dependent gesture recognition, the participant manipulates objects and effects changes in response to a world that is constantly in flux and requires constant renegotiation.

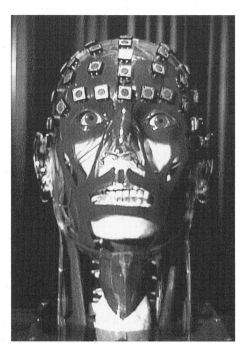

The *Einstein's Brain Project*, 'The Fall, The Furnace, The Flesh. Part II: The Furnace', interactive installation, 1998. Copyright the *Einstein's Brain Project*.

Various fields of enquiry, including epistemology and clinical neuro-science, have led to an understanding of the brain as less a passive receiver of information about the world and more a processor of data from the world in the synthesis of our perceptions. This project provides the par-ticipant with a graphic representation of this relationship, using brainwave patterns that have been well characterised for clinical neurology to generate images and environments of a particular type and form, which are navigated and interacted with by means of a dataglove. These in turn generate changes in the EEG output of a participant, which are fed back into the system and processed by artificial intelligence agents that produce variations in the form and content of the virtual environment, in real time.

The first of a series of works using the interface ALIBI (Anatomically Lifelike Interactive Biological Interface) were created in 2000. ALIBI is a life-size cast of a male human body filled with sensors that allow participants to interact with computer systems by touching, speaking to or breathing on the body. The body is covered with thermochromic paint that changes colour when touched. Used in conjunction with a brainwave recording device built into a heads-up display (HUD), the body interface monitors the biological and physical output of a participant's own body, including EEG data, skin temperature, electrical resistance, speech, gesture and motion.

The first of these works was 'Madhouse'. The interface ALIBI was placed in the centre of the room and participants stroked, or breathed upon, particular locations on the body to produce corresponding images (sometimes related to the body's function and at other times related to metaphor and simile) in a virtual world. The images were seen in a HUD worn by the participant and simultaneously viewed by the audience by means of projection onto a screen in the gallery.

When viewed by other observers, the participant resembles a patho-logist examining a corpse. The images seen in the HUD are degraded and in black and white. Distorted views of people, buildings, objects in motion and lights appear as semiotic ghosts: faded memories of the city or low-resolution recordings as if dredged up from some deep and long-forgotten time well. Attached to the HUD are electrodes that monitor the participant's brainwaves. These brainwaves are fed, in real time, into a three-dimensional virtual reality environment, and manifested as visual and aural equivalents that are projected onto the second screen and amplified in the space. This virtual reality simulation is in constant flux: a living phenomenon that evolves in infinite space and time and responds in real time to a participant's mental activity. What a participant sees is a real-time manifestation of his or her brain and biological activity. When the participant is at ease, the environments and sounds are fluid, slow-paced and smooth; as he or she responds to the images, the environments and audio become jagged, fast-paced and increasingly raucous. When a participant is again able to reach a tranquil state the work returns to a languid condition. As the participant touches the body, sounds are synthesised in real time and fill the gallery space. Moving hands across the surface of the body and placing them in different areas and in different relationships to each other produces and modifies the pitch, volume and timbre of the sounds.

Consistent in the Project's work is the use of maps of emotion and trace evidence. This involves the notion of the body and its environment as a recording medium, as well as the Situationist strategy of the *dérive*.

Madame Scudéry's 'Carte du Tendre' is a map of emotion.[4] Every rock, every hilltop and every natural feature is embedded with meaning. This is a world invested with signs and symbols and psycho-geographical contours that impact on the body and its agency. Filled with omens and portents, this kind of geography constructs the body in the world as it predicts a future predicated on the trace evidence of the past.

'Trace evidence' is a term that applies to all types of physical evidence that may be circumstantial in a trial. Forensic examination of substances found at a crime scene can often establish the presence of the suspect. An invisible unwitnessed body can be reanimated through the use of the techniques of the natural sciences to examine physical evidence. Forensic science reconstructs invisible bodies and unwitnessed events.[5] It is these events and bodies that are reanimated in the *dérive* as it constructs the body in the world.

In 1972 BBC Television broadcast the Nigel Kneale play *The Stone Tape*. In it a team of scientists examine a ghostly event in an old building. A programmer builds an application to analyse the nature of observed reality, and they discover the possibility of the stones themselves being a kind of recording medium for traumatic images and events that transmits its message directly to the brain.

The Stone Tape theory is a popular possibility for parapsychologists to explain ghostly events. For the Project, Kneale's play is an example of our ongoing sense that there is an invisible world that surrounds us.

At the heart of the Stone Tape theory is the notion that the experience of ghostly phenomena does not rely on the perception of a visible, external ghost. Rather, everything is perceived in the mind:

> It holds an image – and when people go in there they pick it up. What you hear or what you see is inside your own brain! […] Don't you get it yet? It must work like…a recording. Fixed in the floor and the walls, right in the substance of them. A trace…of what happened in there. And we pick it up. We act as detectors – decoders – amplifiers.[6]

Taken together, the ideas of trace evidence, the Stone Tape theory and maps of emotion suggest endless numbers of realities mapped on top of worlds. Using the coincidences of science, culture, technology and art, the Project examines the fundamentally contingent nature of consciousness and the making of meaning. The work of the Project has grown out of an interest in bodies in motion, worlds in flux and the endlessly recombinant texts and forms of our worlds. It has also emerged out of an interest in the seen and unseen, the half-perceived and misperceived things at the limits of our perception, and in the reanimation of the lost bodies and past events that constitute this invisible world. The world is not entirely what it appears to be, and the surface of the visible world needs only to be lightly scratched to reveal the invisible worlds above and below.

In 1957 Guy Debord published *The Naked City*. Consisting of randomly collaged fragments taken from a map of Paris linked together by directional arrows, the work summarised the Situationists' strategy for the exploration of urban space.[7] The map presents a structurally unintelligible view of Paris, the fragments having no clear relation to each other except that of being linked by the arrows. From a text on the reverse of the map we are told that the arrows describe 'the spontaneous turns of direction taken by a subject moving through these surroundings in disregard of the useful connections that ordinarily govern his conduct'.[8]

These spontaneous turns exemplify the type of action known to the Situationists as a *dérive*. The *dérive* (drift or drifting), and its accompanying sense of *dépaysement* (being disoriented or deceived), transformed the meaning of the city and its concrete social construction of space by changing the way in which it was inhabited. The original map of Paris is revealed as a seamless representation in which diversity and distinction are concealed. Debord's *The Naked City*, by contrast, is a city infinitely faceted, marked by division and difference.

The *dérive* mirrors Damasio's continual, moment-by-moment, construction of the self:

> the images in the consciousness narrative flow like shadows along with images of the object for which they are providing an unwitting unsolicited comment. To come back to the metaphor of the movie-in-the-brain they are within the movie. There is no external spectator… the core you is born as the story is told within the story itself.[9]

Given the complex relationship between the construction of the self and the construction of space, the body in virtual worlds has moved towards a hybrid state. Composed of biological organism and machine, it is not always precisely clear 'who makes and who is made'.[10]

In Debord's own words,

> the spatial field of the *dérive* may be precisely delimited or vague depending on whether the activity is aimed at studying a terrain or at an emotional disorientation. It must not be forgotten that these two

aspects of the *dérive* overlap in many ways so that it is impossible to isolate one of them in a pure state.[11]

In producing this series of works, the Project identifies five bodies. These are: the Conscious Body, the Absent Body, the Active Body, the Mnemonic Body and the Amplified Body.

The Conscious Body – the body-minded brain – is a notion of the body linked to consciousness, the awareness of both the external and internal functioning that can be felt, sensed and expressed through non-verbal feelings: all those conditions which create the apparent continuity in the brain. This is Edelman's and Damasio's notion of the 'movie-in-the-brain' – the sense of self in the act of knowing.

> For example, Gerald Edelman's proposal, perhaps the most comprehensive attempt to deal with the matter of consciousness published to date, uses an appealing biological framework to address the conditions under which the movie-in-the-brain can be generated. In recent work he carries the effort farther and specifies psychological conditions necessary for the creation of integrated scenes in the conscious mind. Other thoughtful attempts to deal with aspects of the movie-in-the-brain problem include Bernard Baars's global network hypothesis and Daniel Dennet's multiple draft model.[12]

The Absent Body is a virtual body that must be consciously and repeatedly reanimated to maintain its purchase in the culture and fabric of a virtual world. Bodies are, to varying degrees, absent in daily life – forgotten, veiled or masked, or even no longer in existence. However, in virtual environments the surrogate body – a 'replicant body' with all the difficulties of establishing one-to-one correspondence with a real world – becomes the only means for agency in cyberspace.[13]

The Active Body is a body considered as a point from which emanate events and forces that ripple through and alter the immediate and distant environment.

The Mnemonic Body is a repository for memory and events. The body becomes the object rather than the subject of important information if it is considered a recording medium – as a meat tape.

The Amplified Body is the body projected into the world. As the processes of the body are made visible and audible, the body is transformed to take on altered and enhanced personalities and shapes and is able to move in new, experimental, although often problematic ways.[14]

The novel movement of these bodies is what the Project terms 'hypermorphic' and 'transorganic'. Hypermorphism is the tendency of world components to change from one form to another so rapidly and continuously that, although they never fix on a form, they appear stable. 'Transorganic' is the term given to the nature of forms oscillating hypermorphically between the extremes of organic and non-organic.

In the Project's worlds, these themes of the hypermorphic and trans-organic are driven by the twin engines of parallaxis and hybridisation. Cameras oscillate rapidly between polar geometries in response to incoming biodata. Cubes, cones and spheres are used to construct a world in flux as objects blur into hybrid forms, never entirely a cube, cone or sphere. In the parallaxic remix, viewpoints move rapidly between spatial coordinates in response to incoming biodata. Like the experience of a traveller in a forest fixing on a constantly disappearing and reappearing navigation marker flickering through the trees, occluded objects are revealed and re-contextualised as the participant sees through the layered lattices of the world.

These hyperbodies can exist only in categorical, deeply nested, multi-plicitous environments. Spectator and spectacle are entwined, entangled in co-existent space. Perception enfolds us in matter and synthesises the perceived object and us. The modes of representation and 'being-in-the-world' are intimately intertwined in practice, for example in the way their relationship can be superimposed on the relation between subject and object: if the body is conceived of as an object, representations of the body are the site of subjectivity; if the body is conceived of as a subject, representations are objectifications of the body.[15]

If the body moves hypermorphically and transorganically between these two conceptions we move towards a version of the cyborg, 'a hybrid creature, composed of organism and machine'.[16] We enter a world in which it is no longer certain what the limits of our bodies are. Caught, like the deep-sea diver, in the rapture of the deep, we are aware only of the painful and unbearable separation from ourselves, surrounded as we are by amputated limbs and severed psyches. In our desire to reunite and recuperate our unnaturally divided bodies we are reconfigured as 'body-world'.

These worlds may correspond more or less with the world that we assume to be real. However, the frequent disruption of the stable world, of the assumed literal reality, by the introduction of other narrative structures or levels, such as *trompe l'oeil*, freeze-frame, reverse motion, spatial discontinuity and twisted hierarchies, leaves no distinction between literal reality and metaphoric reality.

In the construction of a dynamic self, the mind attempts to engage the worlds that lie behind appearances. These worlds are in perpetual motion and unstable transformation, without attributable frames of reference, without material bodies or finite borders, in constant flux, linking past to future and memory to prediction. It is as if we are inside ourselves, like a three-dimensional eye, which constructs itself as it moves through internal, haptic space.

In a world of objects, the subject is characterised and limited by boun-daries and frames, perceived as unvarying and outside natural morphic transformations. Now it is possible to view ourselves as dynamic entities continually engaged in perpetual iconoclastic, biological and social renovation and construction. We are able to recognise the transformations operating on our bodies and can acknowledge the hypermorphic and transorganic nature of our image of ourselves. In *The Saturated Self*, Kenneth Gergen describes these selves existing in 'a state of continuous construction and reconstruction. It is a world where anything goes that can be negotiated. Each reality of self gives way to reflexive questioning, irony and ultimately the playful probing of yet another reality. The center fails to hold.'[17]

Using the strategies of the Situationist Guy Debord's *dérive* and the retrievable histories and knowledge embedded in our material world, the installations produce spaces for understanding through close observation of the psycho-geographic world. Looked at this way, the *Einstein's Brain Project* concerns itself with the idea of the world as an enormous library where everything is out of order. Travel books sit next to philosophical treatises and first-aid manuals. The inexhaustible inventory of the streets contains endlessly varied and recombining bits of information, resulting in the most unlikely juxtapositions and unexpected events and discoveries. The world is layered with histories and distant geographies, invisible but waiting to be discovered like a new north-west passage in the backstreets of Paris.

In the end, perhaps, the work developed by the *Einstein's Brain Project* does not so much show the shape of the real but, instead, provides a space for the consideration of what such an idea might imply. This space is an environment in which subject and object are intertwined and in which reality emerges for what it is: layered and endlessly recombinant. In building an environment entirely generated by the biological output of the human body, the invisible processes of the body are turned inside out – its activity amplified and made visible. Look here and we might at least find the pattern of the symbolic, the imaginary and the artificial – the shadow of the shape of the real.

9 BIOTEKNICA: organic tissue prototypes

Jennifer Willet and Shawn Bailey

Do artists cross the line when they breed plants or animals, or use the tools of biotechnology? Scientists routinely cross the line. So do farmers, business people, military men, and doctors. Only artists and certain religious people hesitate. Of course one of the great human dilemmas is that we do not know the extent of our powers. We invent outrageously and casually as we breathe, but we have no idea where our inventions will take us. Extinction? Slavery? 1000 years in Disneyland? Even if the Holocaust had never happened, we would have good reason to worry about where knowledge of genetics and DNA will take us. We will need all the awareness we can muster to engage evolution. To the extent that art favors awareness, the more artists who cross the line the better.

George Gessert[1]

With recent advances in the biotechnological field, notions of reproduction, transformation and self/other distinctions have come to the forefront of public debate. We see ourselves facing an alarming threshold where humanity, as we understand it today, will be irrevocably changed by the technological trajectories we choose for ourselves. Biotechnology, and specifically projected cloning technologies, are seen as a Pandora's box. Paradoxically, these offer great humanitarian potential, particularly in the health care sector, yet simultaneously ensure a societal leap into a vast and possibly devastating unknown. In *The Biotech Century*, Jeremy Rifkin states : 'The biotechnology revolution *will* affect each of us more directly, forcefully, and intimately than any other technology revolution in history.'[2]

With such focus placed on predictions and forecasts – the hype and hysteria – surrounding biotechnology, we often overlook the very clear and present bio-manipulations and bio-invasions of the physical and social body occurring each and every day. Arguably, there is no impending biotechnological threshold, or, if there is, it has already been crossed. Quietly, and without pomp or circumstance, we have slipped into the biotech future.

On 5 July 1996 the now famous Dolly, a cloned Finn-Dorset ewe, was born to a research team directed by Dr Ian Wilmut in conjunction with Roslin Institute, PPL Therapeutics, and licensed by the BioMed division of Geron Corporation. This miraculous birth was celebrated in the now famous article published in *Nature* announcing her arrival in 1997.[3] Dolly captured the world's attention, inspiring public awareness and debate around evolving cloning technologies. Six years later, and long after the media spotlight was all but extinguished, Dolly was euthanised by her creators due to advanced lung disease encouraged by premature ageing. In December 2002 Dr Bridgette Boisselier, leader of Clonaid, the human cloning research group sponsored by the Quebec-based Raelian religious cult, announced the birth of the first viable human clone – a baby named Eve. Weeks later, with no quantifiable proof, no DNA evidence or independent verification, Eve was quickly dismissed from popular consciousness and relegated to the category of scientific hoax.

Though news of both Dolly and Clonaid's Eve was widely published at the time in the popular media, and therefore presumably discussed extensively in classrooms and at dinner tables around the world, neither is particularly reflective of the current state and awesome proliferation of contemporary biotechnological research. Thousands of research projects involving a range of different possible trajectories, biological materials, tools and methodologies are carried out today by universities, corporations and research organisations worldwide. However, only an infinitesimal number of these activities will be packaged and distributed for public consumption. Even fewer will be investigated and publicly debated by third-party interests. We can imagine a number of reasons for this. Perhaps it is the distraction offered up by the 'War on Terror', or a premeditated corporate thrust to protect vast investments from public scrutiny. Possibly it is the impenetrable authority and obscurity of scientific language.

For whatever reason, public dissemination, consultation and discussion surrounding contemporary biotechnological research is, at best, decidedly limited and, at worst, non-existent. For example, an announcement was made in 2003 by researchers from the Institute for Biological Energy Alternatives (IBEA), led by Dr J. Craig Venter and supported by the American Department of Energy, that the first entirely artificial life form had been created. It was a duplicate of the genome of a bacteriophage virus called phi X containing 5386 base pairs.[4] Though less televisable than Dolly, this research is significant and requires scrutiny and debate. For, if the required magnitude of processing power is available, this technology can generate artificial human genomic structures which, embedded into a shell ovum, will result in a viable human being (or a synth). This process is far beyond that of cloning, a phenomenon that is known to occur spontaneously in nature. It is actually a process that could lead to the artificial generation of unique human specimens. But what rights will an artificially generated organism have? What obligation will exist on the part of this individual to the corporate and industrial-technological base that is responsible for its existence? Who will be a synth's God?

With little rigorous media coverage, complex discussion about bio-technological research in the public sphere is unimaginable. In a culture of overspecialisation, the individual or lay person holds little claim to or interest in the unregulated pursuit of scientific-knowledge-cum-corporate-commodity or in the ethical and scientific ramifications of each new finding. As Richard Lewontin argues in his insightful lecture series *Biology as Ideology: The Doctrine of DNA*: 'We think that science is an institution, a set of methods, a set of people, a great body of knowledge that we call scientific, is somehow apart from the forces that rule our everyday lives and govern the structure of our society.'[5]

In response to this dictum, an apparent public malaise, and the dangers we see associated with the capitalist thrust of contemporary biotech-nological research, we have developed an interdisciplinary art project entitled BIOTEKNICA. BIOTEKNICA is a fictitious corporation, a parody of existing corporations and research groups, manufactured to engage critically with evolving notions of reproduction and self/other distinctions in relation to biotechnology. BIOTEKNICA has developed a virtual labo-ratory, where designer human organisms are generated based on consumer demand.[6] However, the organisms produced by BIOTEKNICA do not adhere to the structures and functionality normally manifest in a viable human subject. Similar to mutations depicted in *The Fly* (1986), *Rosemary's Baby* (1968) and *Alien Resurrection* (1997), our specimens are irrational and grotesque. They are modelled on the teratoma, an unusual cancerous growth containing multiple tissues, such as hair, skin, teeth, vascular systems and often an independent nervous system. Monstrous as this may seem, scientists today see the teratoma as a natural instance of spontaneous cloning and are conducting research into the growths with the goal of developing future therapeutic and cloning technologies. BIOTEKNICA both embraces and critiques these technologies, con-sidering the contradictions and deep underlying complexities of contemporary biotechnology and its role in the future definition of humanity. BIOTEKNICA is a timely meditation on the ultimate fragility of the 'natural' body.

The teratoma (known also as a dermatoid cyst, or an endodermal sinus tumour) is a relatively common abnormal growth, and quite often cancerous. It typically originates in foetal tissues, the sperm 'sac' or ovaries, though it can be located anywhere in the body. It is a germ cell tumour, meaning that, like an embryonic stem cell, it has the capacity to differentiate into a variety of tissues naturally found in the host organism. However, unlike a healthy embryo, it does not require fertilisation to instigate growth and differentiation. It possesses irrational or dysfunctional structural properties, and the malignant teratoma, like all forms of cancer, consists of immortal cells. Although the manifest structure of the teratoma is distinctly different from that of the host organism, it is genetically identical and is therefore understood essentially as an unsuccessful clone. This process of unfertilised cell differentiation is called parthenogenesis, and it is best described on the corporate website for Advanced Cell Technology:

> Parthenogenesis is the development of an organism from an unfertilized egg, a process that occurs infrequently in nature. In humans, parthenogenesis can result in an ovarian teratoma – a mass of tissue containing multiple cell types – and other abnormal entities, but cannot lead to a live birth.[7]

Scientists are looking to the teratoma to provide a possible model for the programmed growth of new tissues from harvested adult cells. It is believed that it might provide the key to understanding reverse cell differentiation. Scientists hope to replicate this process in the laboratory, and eventually learn to control the type of differentiation that occurs, with the future intention of cultivating genetically identical replacement parts for transplantation into the host organism or patient.[8] The irony is, of course, that the teratoma continues to be a dangerous form of cancer. It is considered one of the most frightening and repugnant tumours known to humankind, and its prognosis is still difficult to manage. Additionally, in a Frankensteinian turn, researchers are finding that in certain instances of the injection of healthy stem cells into animal subjects for therapeutic purposes, these cells are instead developing into teratoma tumours at the site of implantation.[9] In a reciprocal fashion, the teratoma appears to be not only a viable source for future successful stem cell and cloning technologies, but also the disastrous result of such technological research gone awry. It is with this double-edged meaning – that of the monster and the seed of scientific discovery – that we deploy the teratoma in BIOTEKNICA.

BIOTEKNICA has developed a number of installations and virtual environments in which the user, through a series of commands and choices, can produce and reproduce biologically engineered specimens. Our first prototypes were developed during a residency at The Banff Centre for the Arts, where we digitally generated a dozen specimen images utilising photographic source material from the human body, commercially purchased meat products and found animal carcasses. In a later incarnation of the BIOTEKNICA Virtual Laboratory we used these images as a model to establish the visual parameters for the BIOTEKNICA: Genetic Mix Module v.1, a digital interface where the user can design their own teratoma.[10] These works have been exhibited and presented at a number of venues and conferences across Canada and internationally, as well as online at www.bioteknica.org. Additionally, and arguably more importantly, BIOTEKNICA serves as a critical interpretive device that simultaneously collects and reproduces accurate information surrounding biotechnology, whilst at the same time making well-informed critical and artistic comment on the societal, scientific and political ramifications of these technologies. BIOTEKNICA implicates its user/viewer in the act of biotechnology, asking its participants to engage directly in a paradigm modelled on the reality of contemporary science. The user takes on the role of the scientist and constructs artificially engineered organisms, and, in a larger sense, constructs knowledge and discourse surrounding contemporary biotechnology.

Until 2003 BIOTEKNICA was manifest as a purely multimedia production. However, to reintegrate BIOTEKNICA with the site of the body – into a corporeal relationship with its viewers – we chose to pursue two viable forms of 'wet' artistic production to further enhance the slippage between fiction and reality in the propagation of our project. First, we devised a series of 'meat sculptures' as organic representations of the BIOTEKNICA Product Line. These sculptures were presented in tandem with other elements from the BIOTEKNICA Corporate Presence, as well as specimens in a series of public performances entitled BIOTEKNICA Public Autopsy. Secondly, during the summer of 2004 we worked for four months as Research Fellows in residence at SymbioticA: the Art and Science Collaborative Research Laboratory in the School of Anatomy and Human Biology at the University of Western Australia. There we developed strategies towards growing organic prototypes from animal and human cell cultures. We worked with tissue culture protocols in the production of artwork, as was pioneered by Oron Catts and Ionat Zurr, of the internationally recognised Tissue Culture and Art Project (TC&A), and SymbioticA founders. With their assistance and expertise, we practised utilising existing tissue culture technologies to develop a series of organic prototypes – soft sculptures or 'semi-living'[11] artworks – that tip the scales between representation and reality, contributing further to the complex questions that arise from the development of BIOTEKNICA. This marked our first foray into the field of 'wet' or biological art practice.

BioArt is an evolving field of contemporary art practice, where media can range from genetically modified plants to synthetic gene strings, to cultured organic cell structures, and beyond. Essentially, it is a form of art production where the medium consists of biological systems. Some of the most successful and provocative contemporary BioArtists include Eduardo Kac (Art Institute of Chicago), Joe Davis (Massachusetts Institute of Technology) and the Tissue Culture and Art Project (University of Western Australia). Kac states: 'transgenic Art is a new form based on the expression of synthetic genes in host organisms, or the expression of an existing gene in a different organisms...'[12]

Kac is most famous for representing a 'glow in the dark' bunny named Alba. He has since gone on to produce entire gardens filled with luminescent creatures, genetically engineered to glow a subtle greenish tint under special fluorescent lighting. This glow is achieved by a single gene from a jellyfish being inserted into the animals' genotype, altering the function of their surface tissues; a normalised marker system established in the laboratory is represented in the gallery as art. On the other hand, Joe Davis is best known as the first user of DNA sequencing technologies to encode linguistic passages from the Bible. He transcribed a Morse code substitution algorithm into a digital message, rapid-proto-typed it from a gene-sequencing device and inserted the strand of genetic information into living bacteria. The bacteria are allowed to grow, making Davis, as he states, 'the most prolific author in history'.[13] More fascinating yet is his exploration of further iterations in the make-up of the genotype, where spontaneous mutations enter errors into the translation of the code in subsequent generations.

By contrast, TC&A (Oron Catts, Ionat Zurr and Guy Ben-Ary) launched, in 2001, a work entitled *Worry Dolls*, where animal tissues were cultivated and sculpted into semi-living artworks. *Worry Dolls* is a complex installation comprising a biologically self-contained laboratory environment housing a series of tissue culture sculptures growing on-site in the gallery. These works are rooted in the tradition of Guatemalan worry dolls, which would be placed under the pillow of an individual with great worries. TC&A invites its viewers to place their worries in the hearts of the bio-engineered dolls to stave off pain. A biohazard sign hangs at the gallery entrance in order to warn viewers that their bodies and the external environment itself are hazards to the fragile art objects, which lack an immune system. A single touch by an unprotected hand results in the contamination and death of the carefully cultivated work.

In the instance of BioArt production, the boundaries between art and scientific investigation are deeply challenged. It is critical that artists and theorists contribute to the future trajectory of these technologies, but BioArt also poses a difficult dilemma. How does one engage in BioArt production in a critical and ethical manner? How are works of BioArt interpreted in the public sphere: as demonised or terrorist practices? Are they merely innovative bio-toys that reinforce – in fact advertise – the wonders of the biotech future? Is the artist in some way a public relations apologist for the whole industry? Is it socially and politically acceptable for artists and other non-specialists to participate in wet biological practices?

On 11 May 2004 Steve Kurtz, professor, artist and member of Critical Art Ensemble, woke up to find that his wife, Hope Kurtz, had suffered a cardiac arrest and had died in her sleep. He called 911. When the paramedics arrived, they observed laboratory equipment, samples of bacteria growing in Petri dishes, and books on biological warfare and bio-terrorism in his home. Kurtz, as a member of Critical Art Ensemble, had been engaged in BioArt production as a critical methodology for many years. Cranked up on the pervasive media rhetoric of the 'War on Terror', the police suspected that Kurtz's art supplies might be bio-terrorist weapons and contacted the FBI. The FBI abducted Kurtz without charge, sealed off his entire block, brought in a HAZMAT team dressed in biological hazard suits and confiscated his computers, manuscripts, art supplies – even his wife's body.

Subsequently Kurtz, along with nine of his colleagues, was subpoenaed to testify before a grand jury. The FBI was seeking charges of terrorist activity under Section 175 of the US Biological Weapons Anti-Terrorism Act of 1989, and the expanded USA Patriot Act. This law prohibits the possession of 'any biological agent, toxin, or delivery system' without the justification of 'prophylactic, protective, bona fide research, or other peaceful purpose'.[14] This law was applied to Kurtz' possession of equipment for DNA analysis and cultures of three common and harmless bacterial species (*Escherichia coli*, *Bacillus globigii*, and *Serratia marcescens*). Of course, the real danger posed by Kurtz and Critical Art Ensemble goes far beyond their possession of simple biological cultures. The true threat of Kurtz' practice is not to the health and safety of the American people but to the intellectual and ideological stronghold of the corporate and government monopoly over biotechnological practices. Critical Art Ensemble is threatening to established power structures only in that they have developed a scheme to drain President Bush's new homeland of its most prized commodity, the unregulated development and exploitation of new capital markets. What is at risk but the profits of such corporate Goliaths as Monsanto and Advanced Cell Technologies? Through *Tactical Media*, Critical Art Ensemble utilises various strategies, mainly electronic and scientific forms of communication, to engage the public in dialogue on new technologies.[15]

Several months later a four-count indictment, substantially downgraded from early investigations into biological terrorism handed down by the federal grand jury in Buffalo, saw Kurtz charged with wire fraud and mail fraud to the amount of $256.[16] Also indicted was Dr Robert Ferrell, Chairman of the University of Pittsburgh's Human Genetics

Department, for illegally providing Kurtz with biological materials. The laws under which the indictments were obtained are normally used against those defrauding others of money or property, as with telemarketing schemes.

With the Steve Kurtz case unfolding in the American media circus, and a heightened sense of scrutiny (even paranoia), we commenced our residency at SymbioticA. The message was clear: a critical artistic engagement with legitimated scientific practices is potentially dangerous. We followed the news reports carefully, from both intellectual and empathetic perspectives, and with great trepidation began training in basic tissue culture protocols.[17]

We began familiarising ourselves by cultivating the 3T3 mouse fibroblast cell line. Cell lines are specific cell sets developed purely for scientific research purposes. They are immortal. Their telomeres have been chemically treated with an enzyme so that the cells do not age; they do not experience cell death.[18] They are able to divide infinitely, in a similar manner to the uninhibited growth exhibited by cancerous cells. 3T3 is a mouse fibroblast cell line established in the early 1960s from an embryonic Swiss mouse.[19] Fibroblast tissue (scar tissue) is made up of extremely robust cells and is best for learning introductory tissue culture protocols on because of its virtual indestructibility, though it is still subject to contamination through human error. Miniscule samples of the cell line are cryogenically preserved, and distributed at cost to the research community. The goal, in this instance of tissue cultivation, is to quickly defrost and stimulate the cells in a friendly environment. This procedure provokes prolonged cellular division and the eventual cultivation of enough cells to fully seed a three-dimensional scaffold or manifest a perceptible tissue surface. The cells are maintained, or 'fed', with a nutrient solution consisting of Dulbecco's Modified Eagle's Medium (DMEM), Gluta Max (an amino acid), penicillin and foetal bovine serum. They are stored in an incubation environment with a modified atmosphere at 37° C. The 3T3 mouse has achieved a sort of immortality, as now, forty years after its death, scientists and students all over the world are conducting research with generations upon generations of this cell line. It is fascinating to reflect on how many kilograms of fibroblast tissue have been cultivated in tissue-engineering facilities since the time of this mouse embryo's original sacrifice.

When growing tissue cultures, the cultivated cells naturally attach themselves to each other and the bottom of the dish. Once the cells are confluent (or filling the entire surface of the dish) we redistribute the cells into multiple flasks to stimulate further growth. To redistribute these cells, they must first be shocked into releasing their natural bonds. Trypsin is used for this purpose. However, if the cells are overexposed to trypsin, not only are the bonds broken but the cellular membranes as well, effectively killing the cells. The procedure, called 'passaging', like many laboratory protocols is an artificial process developed to aid with cellular research. However, if not applied properly it has devastating consequences for the very cells it is intended to maintain.

After prolonged trials and a few instances of human error, we began cultivation of the P19 mouse teratoma cell line. The P19 cells distinguish themselves from the 3T3 line, amongst others, in terms of their irrationality and propensity for three-dimensional clumping, as well as differentiation. The P19s proved to be even more hearty than the fibroblast cells we originally trained with, confirming the veracity of cancerous cell proliferation. Interestingly enough, staff scientists with whom we shared the labs routinely commented on our choice of cells as an ugly one, suggesting that we might prefer to work with cells of a more 'predictable' or 'aesthetic' nature. We, on the other hand, are thrilled with the visual and intellectual contribution the P19 cells contribute to the BIOTEKNICA mandate.

Before completing our residency at SymbioticA we commenced experimentation with the cultivation of cells on a three-dimensional substrate. Using the Rotary Cell Culture System developed by Synthecon Inc. on behalf of NASA, the three-dimensional scaffolds are placed in a sterile cylindrical environment, filled with the prepared medium solution and a batch of freshly trypsonised 3T3 cells. The cylinder, continually rotating in an incubated environment, prevents the cells from attaching themselves to the bottom of the dish. Instead they fall continuously through the floating substrate – attaching, dividing and growing. With varying results in this complex protocol, the BIOTEKNICA Organic Tissue Prototypes Residency came to an end. The last day was spent in the laboratory terminating our cultures.

In conclusion, BIOTEKNICA is intentionally both aesthetic and horrific in its manifestation. It is a beautiful immersive environment rooted in scientific optimism, clean design and technological wizardry. It is also a freak show – a site where disease is allowed to grow and proliferate – all within the capitalist model of exploitation at any cost in exchange for financial gains. BIOTEKNICA generates more questions than answers, for both the audience and ourselves the producers. This is the functional crux of our project: to engage further in the questions and complexities that arise in the field of contemporary biotechnology. We see ourselves pursuing this line of research until we have achieved a series of six successful prototypes. We see great opportunity, conflict and complexity with this type of production – this instance of overlap between art and science. Returning to the case of Steve Kurtz, we can see now how this confirms Gessert's above statement that, '[t]o the extent that art favors awareness, the more artists who cross the line the better'.[20]

BIOTEKNICA purposefully plays on the greatest aspirations while confirming the worst fears of its users. It reveals the contradictions and deep complexities that one must consider when forming opinions about biotechnology. It insists that non-specialists escape the safe shelter of ignorance and participate in a very real and present debate surrounding contemporary biotechnological research.

III / HOW REAL IS THE REAL?

Introduction

This last section finally 'confronts' technology and its relationship to the real. For the most part this means 'new media', but there is a sense in all of these contributions that the real cannot escape technology itself. Whilst much of this book so far has explored the possibilities of new media in aesthetic practice and its subsequent criticism (indeed, technology itself pervades the book as a substratum of our experience of the real), this section directly addresses the often portrayed dialectical relationship that technology has with the real, mirroring as it does the psychoanalytic dialectic of the Real and reality. Indeed, it might have been logical, therefore, to place this section at the beginning of the book, since much of the discussion tacitly refers to new media as a new environment of creative and interpretive possibilities. Yet there are very good reasons to place this section here, as a final review of many of the underlying issues of the real and technology, but also as a setting-off point for a new ontological understanding of the reality of technology. As much as each contribution to this section reviews a substantial historical debate in individual as well as interrelated fields, each also tries to see through the simple binary dialectic of old and new (old/new methods, old/new ontologies, old/new subjectivities, old/new politics) that has characterised the adoption of new media technologies in aesthetic practice. Each beginning from a position in which the arrival of new technology is seen only through a 'loss' of the old, the texts in turn reveal how underlying ontological relationships between technology and the real not only follow ancient debates, but also continue to be a mainspring of creative and interpretive practice, as well as of contemporary political thought.

The new/old media dialectic has been a substantial element of aesthetic debates since at least the early 1990s, a period which saw creative and discursive signposts of the intervention of new media into our daily lives. Virtual reality, perhaps the most spectacular of these, emerged during this period as a technology intimately associated with new ways of experiencing our world, as well as new ways of envisioning other worlds. As VR captured the public imagination, new philosophies of aesthetics, based on its perceived potential for what the new media guru Jaron Lanier called 'post-symbolic communication', began to circulate in the new technological public sphere of the Internet. Virtual reality would reconnect us with experience by dissolving operation of language. Yet with the very sign of experience thus elided, the difference between the new, simulated reality and the world out there was similarly seen to be dissolving and, by the end of the 1990s, films such as *The Matrix* illustrated the vertiginous panic caused by our realisation of this effect. Yet, as suggested by Jenna Ng in this section, the proliferation of literature on *The Matrix* merely served to place it (and notions of the virtual/real dialectic) into a longer history of philosophical scepticism. If there is a lesson from VR, it is that once the elation and panic surrounding a new technology have each subsided, deeper questions of our experience of the real are uncovered.

As an artistic tool, VR remained in use only with a few practitioners, whereas in design and architecture it continues to displace older methods of visualisation, experimentation and 'pre-realisation'. Michael Smyth's chapter in this section considers this displacement from the point of view of what is lost in the design process. Smyth engages in a necessary refocusing of design processes away from the visual primacy of the graphical user interface and the VR simulation, suggesting reintroduction to the other senses, in particular through touch and the physical manipulation of space.

The loss of the object in creative practice is also addressed by Elizabeth Menon and Damian Sutton, who each consider the impact of new media on older ontologies. For Menon, only a return to an established rubric of art history can provide a viable context for a particular artwork when it appears on a computer screen. Whilst many important critiques of the art history canon have issued from the ranks of feminism and postmodernism, Menon suggests that a useful epistemological model is first required to begin to identify the work of art in new media, when the technology has a tendency to delimit the boundaries of the object and the gallery. Such a rubric would necessarily incorporate the political, cultural and subjective viewpoints from which the new art historical canon is created. For Sutton, the loss of the photographic object liberates photography discourse from the mire created by the art historical primacy of the unique photographic object. The deferment of photography technology from the analogue to digital is not seen as a break in this context, since it serves only to reveal photography as a creation of images defined by a relationship between old and new technologies. The screen of digital photography is pulled back to reveal – a screen, this time a social screen of immanent images.

Both Sutton and Ng make use of the debate (since the mid-1990s) surrounding the loss of a connection with reality that analogue photography has since been seen to embody. Despite 160 years of photographic manipulation, the relationship between the photograph and the object photographed remains fundamental to our conception of the medium, supported by a critical commentary from scholars such as André Bazin, and even strengthened by the apparent superficiality of the digital image. Yet, as Ng notes, virtual cinematography never leaves photography entirely behind, suggesting that the physical connection with reality is not lost in digital image capture, but that the digital image's connection with reality is established through its difference from the analogue.

It is photography's intervention in our experience of the real that gives it such dominance in this section, as well as throughout the whole of *The State of the Real*. Photography is a visible intervention of technology and the discourses of science in the relation of Real to reality, and this is why Slavoj Žižek's contribution makes such a useful coda. Žižek's review of the discourses of the real, covering the Real of Freud and Lacan, the real Event of Alain Badiou and Gilles Deleuze, as well as the appearance and subjectivity of science, provides an interrogative commentary on the aesthetic debates with which this book engages. What, for example, are the hyperbolic claims made for virtual cinematography if not Žižek's 'excess of obscene life'? The ethical debate that surrounds the blind faith in new media technologies of visualisation surely echoes Žižek's ethical 'crisis' of science and the condonement/containment of technical processes.

Ultimately, Žižek's contribution is important in its parsing of the appearance of the real. Just as much of this book's discussion moves beyond a binary analysis of real/virtual or referential/superficial, so Žižek destabilises this kind of dialectic – one that creates other binarisms (capitalism/democracy, Real/reality, science/religion) that give rise to the objects (the photograph, the model, the artwork) under threat from new technology. The real is therefore in the relationship between new and old, between technologies. The onset of a new technological paradigm, and its attendant euphoria and anxiety, are evoked in Žižek's irrational fear of torrential rain, the exhilaration and calamity of which is as real as the feelings of love, the surface of cartoons and the appearance of true and false.

10 Designing for Embodied Interaction: experiencing artefacts with and through the body

Michael Smyth

Introduction

The maxim states that 'seeing is believing', but that 'it is touch that determines reality'. Instinctively we reach out to touch those objects that attract or perplex. Touch conveys an intimacy both at a physical and emotional level. In the pursuit of the digital world, the sense of engagement that touch offers has largely been sacrificed. Instead the graphical user interface (GUI), with its windows, icons, menus and pointers has been created, the ubiquitous portal into the digital world, with its levels of indirection acting as a constant challenge to human–computer interaction (HCI) practitioners and users alike. Interaction with technology has lost its grounding in physicality.

The vision of an environment populated by interactive and interacting artefacts, as articulated by ubiquitous computing, offers the opportunity to reclaim the interface and return it to the physical world.[1] Form and function will be reunited, leading to the design of artefacts that both engage and provoke interaction. In the words of Bill Buxton, there will be a move away from the safety of the 'Henry Ford' school of design, resulting in a world populated by bespoke technologies.[2] To date the approach adopted by the majority of practitioners has resulted in the current generation of anonymous beige boxes. Breaking 'the box' raises the question of where these technological artefacts will go. Most probably, the migration from the desktop will be either into the environment or onto our skins. Technology will be more personal, and form will impact on how users relate to and interact with these devices. This is more than product semantics; form and function are inextricably linked to the affordances conveyed by these new artefacts. Touch is a pleasurable sensation: the sweep of a curve, the precision of an angle, the tactile quality of a material. What is less well understood is how such haptic qualities play a role in the creation of a sense of engagement and a linkage with the body that underpins much of our learning.

The phenomenologist Merleau-Ponty's account of 'being-in-the-world' emphasises the importance of the body. He places the body at the centre of our relation to the world and argues that it is only through having bodies that we can truly experience space. In the context of perception, Merleau-Ponty formulated what Hubert and Patricia Dreyfus have described as a sense of sight, as an embodied vision that is an incarnate part of the flesh of the world: 'our body is both an object among objects and that which sees and touches them'.[3] The body is interpreted as having a central role in how we engage with and learn about the environments we inhabit. Not surprisingly, a number of ideas underpinning phenomenology have been appropriated by the design community when discussing the acquisition of design skills. This in turn has led some researchers to comment that design-based skills are both bodily and cognitive.[4] In the context of how we interact with and through technology, such an emphasis on the role of the physical body raises various research issues. These can be seen in the work of a number of researchers, most notably at the Royal College of Art (RCA) and the Tangible Media Group at the Massachusetts Institute of Technology (MIT).[5] The Interaction Design Group at the RCA explores the role of technology in people's lives and imaginations,whilst the Tangible Media Group at MIT are investigating the relationship between the physical and virtual worlds and the subsequent implications for interaction.

Increasingly, the importance of the body in understanding and learning is being acknowledged within other disciplines. This can be seen from the tradition of experientialism, for example in the work of Lakoff and Johnson.[6] They argue that a fundamental part of cognition is the development and usage of base metaphors that are built up through the experience of the physical object. In the context of architecture, the feeling of buildings and our sense of dwelling within them are more fundamental to our architectural experience than the visual sensation that the building provides. If such a proposition is accepted then it is vital that tools that are aimed at supporting the design process seek to integrate and capitalise on all the body's senses. In particular, the haptic and orientation senses appear to contribute most to our understanding of three-dimensionality, what Bloomer and Moore refer to as 'the sine qua non of architectural experience'.[7]

Design for the Body

The emphasis on the visual sense in Western culture, coupled with the level of indirection introduced by the use of computer-aided design (CAD) technology during the design process, has resulted in 'designs which housed the intellect and the eye, but that have left the body and the senses, as well as our memories and dreams, homeless'.[8] Buildings are encountered, they are not merely observed. Their importance lies in their ability to articulate and give significance, which can only truly be achieved through physical encounter. This position is supported by Franck when she comments, with specific reference to the role of technology within the design process, that 'it seems likely that the opportunities afforded by the computer will increase the propensity that already exists in architecture for the form to be disconnected from everyday use and for vision to be the only sense attended to'.[9] This imbalance of our sensory system has prompted the suggestion that the increased experience of alienation, detachment and solitude in the world today may be related to a certain pathology of the senses, which has in turn led to isolation, detachment and exteriority.[10]

Such a demarcation, it is contended, will impact not only on the nature of the buildings with which we interact but also with the nature of the

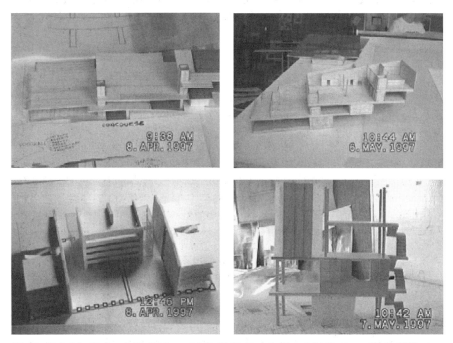

Physical Models #1 (top left), #2 (top right), #3 (bottom left) and #4 (bottom right), 2005. Copyright Michael Smyth.

design process through which they are created. As buildings lose their plasticity and their connection with the language and wisdom of the body, they become isolated in the cool and distant realm of vision. Increasingly, architecture is losing its tactility and measures designed for the body. Indeed the detachment of the construction process has prompted the view that architecture is rapidly turning into 'stage sets for the eye'.[11] The sense of 'aura', the authority of presence, which Walter Benjamin regarded as a necessary quality of an authentic piece of art, has been lost. Benjamin viewed aura as central to authenticity of art and explained it by analogy with the experience of nature. The experience of a mountain range is superseded by the experience of reproduced images that, however perfect, are missing the point of presence that in turn gives that object its aura.[12] In the context of the design process the role of the body has been diminished for architects who use CAD systems. Elaborate drawings, rendered objects and VR walk-throughs can be created with the movements of one hand. No longer is there the need for physical manipulation of material or tools, and the sense of engagement that this provides.

The Reintroduction of Touch as a Means of Interaction

Currently touch is a sense that is seldom explicitly supported by computer-based design tools, whereas a physical model enables designers to walk around it, handle it, touch its surfaces and immerse themselves in the representation.

A series of case studies of the use of tools by architects during the early phase of the design process revealed the importance of touch during design interaction.[13] The sense of engagement provided by tools, in particular the haptic qualities associated with physical models, was recognised by designers as being central to their understanding. For example, such physical models enable the consideration of the design problem in the context of the whole building, rather than the more limited views provided by hand drawings and CAD. A further quality attributed to physical models was that they enable the designer to manipulate, through touch, a three-dimensional representation of the building space. The sense of engagement provided by such models was viewed as something qualitatively different from that provided by drawings, whether produced by hand or by CAD. The characterisation of designers as 'thinking with their hands',[14] while creating or manipulating physical models supports the findings of Roy, and echoes the sentiment of Schön when the latter describes the act of drawing in terms of the designer 'conversing with an image'.[15] The haptic qualities of the physical model provides the necessary degree of intimacy in order to visualise, explore and understand the space. What is being proposed is that the body plays a part in how we make sense of, and interact with, the physical spaces that we design and inhabit and that constitute our environment. Indeed at a broader level the body plays a central role in how we experience all aspects of reality.

This raises the question of how technology might provide designers with such essential attributes? The level of indirection that technology introduces between users and their workaday world has been an important factor in its failure significantly to contribute to the early phase of design.[16] Designers demand tools that provide direct engagement. Current mainstream technologies fail to meet this basic requirement. Possible leverage on this problem might be found in research into tangible user interfaces. This work seeks to augment the real physical world by coupling digital information to everyday physical objects and environments, in order to explore how interaction with technology can migrate from the screen to the physical environment.[17] Translating this approach into a design context prompts the following question: why should the act of building a physical model or drawing a plan sketch not also act as a method of inputting that information into a knowledge-based system? This approach has been applied to the field of urban planning and design with the development of Urp.[18] Urp consists of a physical workbench which, through the use of back-projection techniques, allows planners to examine shadows, reflections and wind flow effects on proposed buildings. Interaction is through physical models of the buildings and control devices that are placed on the surface of the workbench. Physical manipulation of these artefacts then determines what is displayed on the workbench. A similar question was asked by John Frazer during his study of physical design models as input devices, in particular his work on the Walter Segal Model.[19] Segal developed a timber-framed building technique aimed at encouraging people to design and build their own homes. The technique used a two-foot grid which allowed the economic cutting of panels. Segal was anxious that his builders should also be designers and he encouraged them to visualise their plans. In keeping with this philosophy, Frazer built an electronic version of the panel model in which various panel combinations represented different elements of the building. The result was a system whereby people without any knowledge of architecture or computers could design a house by building a simple physical model.

In pursuit of such engagement, some model-makers have explored the use of film and slide projection as a means of enhancing communication. Examples of this approach can be seen in the early work of Daniel Libeskind, who fabricated models using texts and images torn from books and magazines. This approach enabled the designer to denote specific elements of the proposed building through the use of materials. An example of this technique can be seen in his *City Edge Project*. In this case the entire model is laminated with words and images taken from a variety of sources, including the Bible and telephone directories. Libeskind's later models have sought to utilise a variety of materials, not only as a means of expressing the radical geometric shapes characteristic of his work but also as a means of considering the use of materials in the final design – for example, the zinc-plated models of his design for the Jewish Museum in Berlin. Libeskind's work acts as an illustration of the intimate relationship between the physical model and the eventual design.

Increasingly complex technologies have been incorporated into physical models in the pursuit of communication. The architect John Neale has included timers and sensors, back-projected video and still images, models and part-models of varying scales and examples of building materials in a bid to convey a richer understanding of the proposed building. Indeed such an approach to model-making can begin to blur the distinction between the model and the design process that it is intended to support.

In a previous study of interior architects and their use of physical models during the design process, a finding that emerged was that the material chosen from which to construct a model could have a significant impact on the eventual design solution.[20] Tom Porter and John Neale support this position when they argue that the model-making fabric can influence the quality of the architecture it replicates. They cite examples of critics who have historically blamed the proliferation of severe Brutalist and bush-hammered concrete architecture of the 1950s and 1960s on the widespread use of balsa wood for modelling. Indeed others argue that 'those weaned on a Modernist tradition and who rely

Joe Colombo, Tube Chair, 1969. Photograph courtesy of Delft University of Technology, Virtual Design Museum.

on the pristine abstraction of white cardboard models, have helped spread the "International Style" anonymity of a raw concrete built environment stripped of ornamentation'.[21]

The level of sophistication of some physical models raises the question of the nature of their relationship with the building that they seek to represent – indeed, whether the production of the model becomes an end in itself. In the vast majority of cases, when physical models are constructed it is to articulate particular aspects of a final building. The end is certainly not the model. In certain circumstances this relationship can become blurred. This is particularly evident when the model becomes a full-size mock-up of an aspect of the proposed building. Porter and Neale provide two examples of the use of full-scale mock-ups, firstly with the work of Jacques Germain Soufflot, and in the current era by Nicholas Grimshaw & Partners.[22] Between 1755 and 1792, while building the Ste-Geneviève church in Paris, Soufflot created a virtual replica of the as yet unbuilt structure. Using painted canvas over a three-dimensional timber frame, he sought to simulate the appearance of the proposed church. The purpose behind such an approach was so that the citizens of Paris, in particular Louis XV, while laying the foundation stone, could appreciate the spatial effect of the building.

Nicholas Grimshaw & Partners found it necessary to fabricate a full-scale section of the roof for the Waterloo International Terminal in London. Primarily this was created for the testing of its accessibility for maintenance, an attribute which clearly could not be judged from a CAD-based model of the roof section.

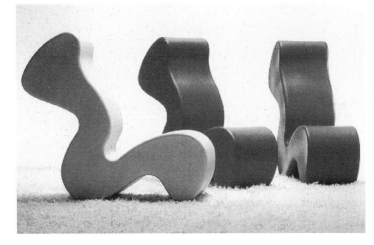

Verner Panton, Phantom Chair, 1998. Photograph courtesy of Delft University of Technology, Virtual Design Museum.

Transient Architecture

Why do architects build full-scale models? Is it their power to inspire at an emotional level, to literally position the observer within the idea of the architect and to enable interaction on a multitude of sensory levels? It is increasingly rare for architects to create full-scale models of the type described in the previous section, due mainly to financial restrictions imposed on most modern designs. Furthermore, with the increased use of VR walk-throughs, there is the perception that such physical models are superfluous. In architecture, perhaps the closest area which embodies the sentiment of full-scale models is portable or ephemeral architecture.[23] This encompasses buildings that are temporary in nature and are designed to be deployed in an existing environment. Examples of such architecture might include exhibition spaces, temporary accommodation, musical stage sets and installation artworks.

The remainder of this section will focus on those structures that seek to integrate art and architecture as a means to explore the idea of embodiment and its consequent impact on the richness of experience. Generally these structures are inflatable, multicellular structures which utilise space, colour, texture and sound as a means of communicating with individuals who traverse the structure. This is exemplified by the work of Alan Parkinson (Architects of Air) and Maurice Agis, in particular his 'Spaceplace' (1966–1967), 'Colourspace' (1980) and 'Dreamspace' (1996) structures. When discussing his work, Agis describes the crucial element as the movement of people through the unfolding space.[24] It is that feeling of connectivity with the self and with others in the space, and indeed with the space itself, that Agis attempts to facilitate with his structures. To enhance the experience further, Agis has collaborated with the contemporary composer Stephen Montague in the creation of 'Bright

Daniel Libeskind, model of the Jewish Museum, Berlin, 1989–1990. Photograph courtesy of Studio Daniel Libeskind.

Interiors', a soundtrack of 16 loops that endlessly repeat and interact, as the light and colour interact in the space. What is critical to both Agis' and Parkinson's work is the sense of scale, the fact that the structure is experienced from within and the sensory richness that such physical embodiment provides. All the senses are engaged and the result is a rich and intimate experience in which the individual is touched at a number of levels.

Reconnecting the Body to the Artefact

An issue that has permeated the discussion so far is that of engagement, and in particular how this is experienced through the body. All the artefacts, whether scaled or full-size, provide both a level of engagement and a degree of embodiment. The ability to touch and manipulate an object, to sense its weight and texture, are attributes that are possible only when interaction is conducted in the physical world. Such richness is further enhanced when the user is placed in the physical space of the artefact. Full-scale environments enable the experience of the concept they depict in the fullest sense. All our senses are engaged, resulting in a level of richness of experience the like of which most designers can only aspire to. It is contended that touch, and its associated intimacy with the body, provides a means through which interaction might be enriched. Touch has the ability to connect both the body to the artefact and the artefact to the body.

In order to illustrate how interaction can be designed to incorporate touch, a number of examples will be described in the remainder of this section. The first is Denis Santachiara's 'Stroke Lamp' of 1986, which was originally described by Anthony Dunne in the context of the new relationships between people and machines made possible through the use of new reactive materials.[25] In this example the lamp was activated by stroking its surface; the greater the intensity of stroke, the more brightly the light shone. A single touch extinguished the light. While maybe not the most practical way of controlling a light, what the Stroke Lamp illustrated was the possibility of a sensual and playful interaction with an everyday object. The second artefact that utilises touch was a prototype camera, produced by Ross Lovegrove for Olympus and entitled 'The Eye'. The camera was constructed out of a soft latex rubber, producing an extremely tactile object. This sense was further enhanced during use, as the camera was operated by squeezing its body rather than pressing a button. Lovegrove states that The Eye camera was 'originally designed to be touched and to acquire meaning from the way it related to your hand, the way you squeeze it and the way you stroke it. Sensuality therefore becomes a medium for aesthetic experience (aisthesis)'.[26] This refers to the important reflexive quality of touch, in that it formed a connection both to and from an object with the individual. The next example, which is also a domestic light, is entitled 'The Bubble Light' and was produced by Mathmos (2000). The light was an 8cm diameter sphere, also constructed from latex rubber and, in a similar fashion to the camera, operated by squeezing. The light has been designed to fit the palm of the hand, is highly portable and is powered by rechargeable batteries.

Several prototype devices have sought to investigate how touch might be incorporated into interaction so that an emotional aspect of communication can be conveyed between individuals. LumiTouch was one of a pair of interactive photograph frames which were designed to be exchanged between individuals in an existing relationship.[27] When one frame was touched this was signalled by the other by means of coloured lights. In a similar vein, the 'White Stone', reported on by Tollmar et al., sought to 'make sublime communication and a sense of presence between two people'.[28] The stone was the size of a pager and could detect when it was being held in the hand, initiating a response in the other stone, for example a beep. The final prototype was the Kiss Communicator, which was designed to communicate between people separated by physical distance.[29] The device explored ways of using technology to communicate in a subtle, sensual way, the aim being to let a partner know that you are thinking of them through touching or breathing on the device. The device then glowed, as a means of encouraging further communication and as a means of indicating a connection with the partner device.

Each of these artefacts was designed to be touched and to be operated through touch. It is instinctive to touch an object that attracts or perplexes. Touch is a display of tenderness and, it is contended, technologies which seek to avail of touch should also exhibit such tenderness in terms of design, implementation and deployment. Such tenderness should be manifest in how the technology handles both its communication and

Maurice Agis and Paloma Brotons, 'Dreamspace', 1996. Copyright Maurice Agis and Paloma Brotons.

expression. That is to say, such expression need not be overt; sometimes it must be subtle, private and accessible only to those with whom a history already exists. We can tell a lot not from what is said, but how it is said; not just from a touch but the way we are touched. The term 'tender technology' refers to those technologies that allow the communication of such context, which is usually lost in conventional devices.[30] It has been suggested that the study of implicit expression, coupled with the value placed on emotional connections, is indicative of new roles for technologies within our personal lives.[31] Touch is a means of conveying such expression and intimacy.

Conclusion

As technology moves from the desktop into the environment and onto our bodies, it is contended that touch will play an increasingly important part in connecting us with and through these artefacts. The role of materials, with their implications for authenticity, will further cement the reunification of form and function in the context of such devices. We are witnessing (and, critically, are part of) the early stages of the migration of technology from the purely virtual and intangible to the real and the physical. Such movements will provide new challenges for interaction designers, and the body will again return to the centre of their attention.

11 Virtual Realities, Techno-aesthetics and Metafictions of Digital Culture

Elizabeth K. Menon

Discussion of digital art within a constantly changing contemporary context presents special problems for art historians. Interactive video, web art, immersive multimedia environments and video installations have become the focus for discussion among scholars in technology-related disciplines, but have yet to be assimilated into the art historical canon. One reason is that no single methodology currently employed by art historians (including post-structuralist, feminist and revisionist strategies) can sufficiently address issues posed by computer-mediated art forms such as telepresence and scripted art works.[1] Both 'visual' and 'technological' literacy depend on scholarly investigation into the social implications of these cultural forms. The canon of art history has come under criticism in the past two decades, and methodologies (especially from feminism) have been employed in order to expand it from a traditional domination by white male artists. However, art history could provide, through its traditional structure of analysis, a well-established framework for the analysis and discussion of visual strategies of communication, whether they have been described as 'art' per se, or relegated to visual or popular culture. Along with the expansion into new media, alternative canons can be fostered with a greater consideration of race and gender. Placement of digital and technology-based works into the art historical canon can be accomplished only through the development of a theoretical model for the appreciation and comparative analysis of these works. A methodology can be constructed by merging a variety of theoretical constructs, including iconographical analysis and semiotics.

Traditional methods for the evaluation of painting and sculpture, as well as methods used to gauge the significance of postmodern genres, such as earth art and performance art, cannot be applied equally to art designed for viewing on the web or on DVD. At a most basic level, the evaluation of digital art and its integration into the framework of art history can be accomplished through comparison with existing art forms. Web art, DVD compilations and other new media forms can be tabulated using grids which allow the classification of the technical elements, formal elements, compositional elements, display considerations and the role of the viewer along the horizontal axis.[2] The technical elements consist of the specific materials used to create a work in a particular medium. These might be a brush, paint and stretched canvas in the case of a painting, or pixels in the case of digitally produced art. The formal elements are line, shape, light, colour, space and texture. In the case of colour, for instance, it would be noted that its effect in pigment is substantially different from the coloured light of the computer monitor. The compositional elements are larger considerations created through the manipulation of the formal elements, including unity, harmony and balance. The display considerations consist of the method of presentation to a viewer – in a museum space, outdoors, on a computer monitor. Finally, the role of the viewer might be simply characterised as 'active' or 'passive', or more substantial observations might be made: whether the viewer is standing or seated, and the relative size of the presented work vis-à-vis the viewer. It should be noted that it is necessary to acknowledge the inherent subjectivity of formal analysis and to accept generalisations that are likely to be made as a result.

Nevertheless, some preliminary observations can be made based on the resulting data. The comparison of painting and photography, for instance, reveals the development of technology in both media (when different paints came into use; when specific photographic processes were developed). The creation of implied texture through the manipulation of pigment and the interaction of light can also be compared easily. The development of three-dimensional effects through stereoscopy and holography provides a technological link to contemporary virtual environments. Further comparison might include discussion of computer programs that allow drawing and painting, and that even mimic different types of processes familiar to both studio artists and art historians. Collage and photomontage techniques are also in use in software programs and in web formats. The debate over photography as a 'fine art' medium during the nineteenth and twentieth centuries is relevant to the discussion of new media, which is now being argued for and against in similar ways. In addition, the centuries-old debate over the 'value' of the original versus the multiple (in printmaking, then in photography and sculpture) provides the opportunity to discuss the reproducibility of digital works and implications for the assignment of price in today's market place. Digital printmaking is a new planographic process that can be compared with lithography. Students might also compare the traditional frame found around a painting to that provided by the computer monitor. The role of the viewer as active rather than passive and the setting of the encounter (the psychological implications of the museum as opposed to the home computer) similarly provide avenues for comparison and contrast.

Erwin Panofsky wrote his *Studies in Iconology: Humanistic themes in the art of the Renaissance* in 1939, after having become a member of the Institute for Advanced Study in Princeton, New Jersey.[3] While his method continues to be discussed in books chronicling the development of art history as a discipline, Panofsky's strategy found wide application only in the work of scholars of Renaissance art (which is understandable, for the method was articulated specifically for works of art from that period). For the most part Panofsky's methodology is no longer used in the practice of art history at all, although his work has recently been applied to the design of textual layouts on the Internet.[4] Iconography, as defined by Panofsky, is concerned with subject matter and meaning in a work of art rather than with its form. His method uses three stages that move from simple description to interpretation. In the first stage, Panofsky describes formal elements such as line and colour, as well as common objects and the overall mood. The 'controlling principle' in this phase is the history of style or the use of specific forms to communicate objects or events.[5] The tendency for Renaissance works to use single-point perspective, or the tendency of Impressionist paintings to exhibit what is known as the broken brushstroke technique, are examples of this.

Structuralist, post-structuralist, feminist and other contemporary theories can be embraced in a reconceptualised version of Panofsky's system, resulting in a shift of focus favouring the work of art (as opposed to pure theory).[6] The fact that the system was developed for art history (rather than literature) is a second strong point in favour of its continued use, with significant modifications. In particular, direct extension from the period of the Renaissance to art of the present day is necessary. In stage two, specific research into literary subjects from primary sources from the period under consideration is included, with attention to biases in original documents. The greatest degree of modification is made to the third stage, where the 'intuition' and 'world view' of Panofsky's interpreter is replaced with a more pragmatic approach that embraces the possibility of applying contemporary structuralist and post-structuralist methodologies (semiotics, Marxism, feminism and so on).[7] There is a preference for the use of theories from other disciplines and from other time periods over theories developed concurrently with the date of the work under consideration. Disclosure of which resources were chosen (and which were eliminated from consideration) is encouraged, in alignment with the postmodern belief in no one singular 'truth'.

A restructured version of Panofsky's method has the flexibility to elucidate any work of art, up to and including the predilection for installation art since the 1990s and the current trend in technology-driven media. What Panofsky calls 'equipment for interpretation' includes the experience favoured by modern critics and theorists, the primary sources valued by archivists and the contextual properties of *Weltanschauung*. His 'corrective principle of interpretation' can accommodate the aforementioned theoretical positions adopted by the discipline since the 1970s, yet maintains the primacy of the work of art and a rationale for the viability of art history.[8] This proposed revision does not result in the abandonment of contemporary methodologies but rather reframes their use as a choice made by a particular investigator with a stated purpose. Ideally the reasons for applying a theory developed in a different discipline or from a different time period would be disclosed and rationalised on a case-by-case basis.

An example of a strategy of interpretation borrowed from another discipline, and currently favoured by art historians, is semiotics, which similarly can be applied to technology-influenced artworks. The term 'digital semiotics' indicates interest in how meaning occurs in the digital realm.[9] Terminology from Ferdinand de Saussure and Charles Sanders Peirce can be applied to digital media, as can Roland Barthes' description of a text as a plural, unclosed process with no clearly identifiable origin created expressly for play (a process that indefinitely defers meaning).[10] This approach, which resists the idea of a single original meaning, rather considers meaning as invested by the scriptor, with layers of subsequent socially constructed meanings added by viewers/users, and is particularly appropriate in digital media. Saussure described a signifier as the sound/image with which meaning is made, signified as the 'concept' produced in the brain, and the sign as a combination of both signifier and signified. Peirce used the terms 'icon', 'index' and 'symbol' to describe three types of signs which can be approximated in the digital realm. Peirce's icon is a sign by virtue of its resemblance to its object (such as objects on the graphical user interface). An index points to its object by virtue of a physical connection (such as a hyperlink).[11] A symbol is a type of sign connected to its object by habit, and is the result of culturally produced meaning. The 'browser' and 'web' are among many examples of symbols in the digital realm; these terms have been appropriated because their meaning in their original contexts help to foster an understanding among the general public of processes and structures in the digital environment.[12] Semiology, as expanded by Roland Barthes, can similarly be adapted to the digital. The web functions like Barthes' text, as an example of a plural unclosed process 'with no clearly identifiable origin' created for play.[13] In this sense semiology is useful, for it describes an active viewer, and allows for multiple interpretations.

Carolyn Speranza's 1995 'Hole Poem' uses two icons – the heart and the brain – to explore mind/body disorientation in general and the artist's battle with alopecia and heart disease in particular, the equivalent of what art historians have termed 'body art'.[14] The relationship between the human body and the computer is a logical subject for artists working with digital media, because it is a physical, bodily interaction that takes place in the viewing of such artworks. This multimedia presentation uses sound, text, images and interaction. The user/viewer decides the sequence of presentation and may not even see the entire site. Clicking on Speranza's poem results in its being read aloud, presumably by the author/artist. It incorporates hyperlinks that pull up images related to the poem, such as tubs and woods; in the latter case the viewer sees documentation of environmental works of art mimicking the shape of enlarged alopecia patches. The chance to see different sets of images while hearing the poem recited encourages a variety of associations to happen between the verbal, visual and auditory functions, allowing individual visitors to the site to derive personalised meaning. Speranza's self-designed icons on the top of the window range from easily identifiable symbols to abstract forms. These link to pages about heart disease and alopecia, as well as the artist's biography and an abstract of the project. The question mark on the right directs users to a page where they are instructed to resize the format of their browser window to best view the art. In the museum, curators design the presentation of an artwork, either with or without the artist's input, while in the digital realm the artist might provide instructions giving the viewer a form of curatorial responsibility.

Jay Bolter and Richard Grusin have commented upon how the artist/programmer/designer draws upon the 'logic of hypermediacy' to call attention to the medium as a medium by redefining 'visual and conceptual relationships among spaces' ranging from 'simple juxtaposition to complete absorption'. Ultimately the viewer/user should not only recognise the role played by this new medium, but 'delight in that acknowledgement'.[15] Artworks can be produced using script (HTML, XML, Lingo), programming languages (Java, C/C++, Perl) or software programs (Flash, Director). The primary distinction among these processes is the relative

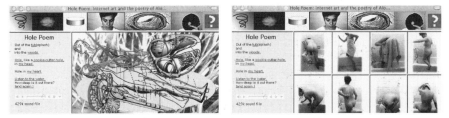

Carolyn P. Speranza, 'Hole Poem', 1995 (screenshots). Copyright Carolyn P. Speranza.

amount of control the artist/programmer/designer has in the creative process. Programming languages provide the greatest amount of control and flexibility, and are the most difficult to master. Script consists of language-based commands as opposed to the mostly numerical basis of code. Software programs are object-oriented, automatically producing the scripts that will control actions and appearance on the Internet as a result of the user's manipulation of text and image. Each method of creation results in the production of a set of textual commands invisible to the viewer/user. As in a theatre setting, the viewer/user watches a performance played out by actors (visually manifest individuals or objects) based on a script that controls the action and physically exists, although it is not literally visible.

When artists utilise HTML, scripting or software programs such as Macromedia Flash, they are using a digital language that can also become content to be reflected upon. Jim Johnson uses typography in which the lines between the verbal and the visual are blurred, and the multimedia environment of the web can further enhance this effect. A devotee of the concrete poetry of the late 1960s, Johnson has created works that embrace both verbal and visual structures. His 'Index', for instance, is an artist's book displayed digitally.[16] In the 'Index', the letters of the alphabet are paired with images that do not relate in the traditional way, in which the object pictured begins with a letter of the alphabet; 'a' with a clock instead of an apple, for instance, or 'b' with a pipe. Johnson calls attention to the play between the verbal and the visual by disconnecting this expectation and embracing a certain level of randomness. The result is clearly influenced by René Magritte's surrealist paintings, such as the *Key of Dreams* (1930), which also paired pictures with unrelated words, but is nonetheless powerful because of the viewer's interaction with the piece. Johnson states that he 'wanted to "see" what pictures would result from the arbitrary associations and, in that sense reveal, rather than impose meaning'.[17] Johnson's works are structured in a one-way distribution. The physical participation of the viewer/user is limited to the ability to choose the direction and sequence of the presentation of images. The fracturing of the semiotic link between word and image that occurs in Johnson's 'Index' encourages the viewer to construct personal meaning, and thus facilitates a high level of intellectual interactivity.

The space of the web installation can be understood as extending from the illusionistic space created on the computer screen to the space where the viewer sits. In these contexts, 'installation' refers specifically to the material that appears on the screen rather than the initial act of setting up the computer program. The range of interaction possible between the web installation and its audience is expressed with the combined term 'viewer/user' (with more limited or traditional contemplation expressed by the former, and a highly physical or intellectual engagement suggested by the latter). When the viewer/user looks at art on the web they control the sequence of viewing and make choices that result in of the creation of personal meaning. In some instances viewers/users add contributions to the art within these web installations, which result not only in the ways such personal meanings are expressed, but in the ability to participate in the creation of meaning among other viewers/participants. As Roy Ascott explained in the 1960s, the basic principle underlying what he terms 'participational' art is feedback – 'it is this loop which makes the triad artist/artwork/observer an integral art'.[18] Therefore the production of a public, cybernetic art depends on the creation of flexible structures to house images capable of producing multiple meanings. This type of artwork exists in a constant state of transition; any possible 'final' resolution must be determined by the viewer/user. The artist is responsible for the 'general context of the art-experience' while its evolution is 'unpredictable and dependent on the total involvement of the spectator'.[19]

The particular program or software used by each artist/designer affects both the appearance and the performance of the resulting interface. In the examples considered here, the most standard of input devices (keyboard and mouse) are required for viewer/user interaction within the art/design environments. The communication systems present within these examples exist at one of two possible levels. Some exist at a 'multilogue' level (with multiple participants or users contributing to the eventual shape and size of the permanently 'unfinished' work), while others function in 'one-way distribution' (viewers/users choose a viewing sequence but do not transform the original work for future viewers/users).[20]

Brenda Laurel, in *Computers as Theater*, describes the conceptualisation of human–computer interaction through comparison to elements of the dramatic arts, using six qualitative elements of drama described in Aristotle's *Poetics*: action, character, thought, language, melody (pattern)

Jim Johnson, 'Index', Internet version of original artist's book, 1992. Copyright Jim Johnson.

and spectacle (enactment).[21] These elements exist in a hierarchy in which each successive element is shaped by that which precedes it. While in a theatrical play the action is theoretically the same in every performance, in the computer–human realm the action is 'collaboratively shaped by system and user', leading to the possibility of a different set of actions in each session.[22] The high probability of variance in connection rate (for example dial-up modem versus high-speed digital), along with the processor speed, the platform type, the nature of the software owned by individual viewers/users and their level of computer literacy, determine the range of experiences that are available to the viewer/user, in addition to factors such as educational and cultural background, age, race or gender.

Laurel determines that in the computer realm Aristotle's elements of character (inferred predispositions) and thought (inferred internal processes) are identical to those manifest in drama, but are the results of agents and processes, respectively, 'of both human and computer origin'.[23] Language is shaped by semiotics in human–computer activity, defined by Laurel as 'the selection and arrangement of signs, including verbal, visual, auditory, and other nonverbal phenomenon when used semiotically'.[24] What is heard (melody) in the realm of drama is replaced with pattern, defined as 'the pleasurable perception of pattern in sensory phenomena', while what is seen (spectacle) is replaced with enactment, 'the sensory dimensions of the actions being represented: visual, auditory, kinesthetic and tactile'.[25] The connection of these dramatic elements to the realm of human–computer interaction is important to this discussion, since it is the level of engagement defined as an emotional, not strictly cognitive, process.

But where do the aesthetics of the machine end and those of the artist who controls the machine begin? In 'Golem', Jason Salavon automated the production of 100,000 abstract paintings using code that he consistently modified during a five-month process to 'direct' the aesthetics. The Golem legend – a post-biblical, Jewish story of an automaton (a machine/man hybrid) – has been linked to everything from Mary Shelley's *Frankenstein* to cybernetics and the development of test-tube babies.[26] The legend makes important distinctions between man and God: while man has the inherent ability to become creators (in God's image), the level of creativity (and imitation) is limited by sin; whereas the creations of God are distinguished from the artificial creations of man by the presence of a soul. The Golem, who received its life through language – the correct placement of letter forms on its body – presents a challenge to its human creator to acknowledge his primordial origins as soulless matter. In each of the many variations of the story the Golem develops dangerous powers, and what was created as a servant becomes a threat to its human creator/master. Only through the removal of certain letters from the Golem can man regain control of what has become a powerful monster. Like the medieval alchemist, the human responsible for the Golem's life is ultimately filling the role of a transformer of matter, rather than a 'creator' as such. The significance of the language used to control the Golem can be interpreted in terms of DNA, computer code and art (as a visual language with identifiable formal components that can be rearranged ad infinitum).

Salavon analysed paintings by Abstract Expressionists (including Mark Rothko and Gerhard Richter) for plane subdivision and colour relationships. Code was then written to replicate these characteristics. Salavon's purpose in 'Golem' was to utilise what he terms 'relentless' computer automation to create works that read as man-made rather than machine-produced. In fact they exist as more of a collaboration, since the artist compulsively oversaw the production process, 'harvesting' images from the bank of computers daily and making changes to the code as a result of the output. The 100,000 paintings produced, which are numbered chronologically, demonstrate both the evolution of the code and the artist's increasing ability to manipulate the aesthetic result.

In addition to the stylistic mimicry of Abstract Expressionists, Salavon's 'Golem' appropriates a number of other art historical issues, not the least

Jason Salavon, 'Golem (printer)' (top left), 'Golem (browser)' (top right), 'Golem (#00321)' (bottom left) and 'Golem (#95155)' (bottom right), 2002. Copyright Jason Salavon.

of which is the very nature of art and the artist's role in its creation, first demonstrated (if not completely theorised) by Marcel Duchamp's readymades. The question of whether a machine can produce 'art' was posed first by Jean Tinguely, who has been developing 'meta-matic' drawing machines since 1955.[27] His initial intent was to declare a work of art itself as capable of a creative action that was always in process and thus never complete. But in fact the 'meta-matics' were collaborations between humans and machines capable of producing something without function (art).

Tinguely's 'meta-matics' have been rightly identified as preludes to the later-twentieth-century angst caused by computers, as well as debates about the level of creativity made manifest in works produced with the aid of computer technology.[28] Salavon extends, twists and complicates these notions in 'Golem'. The computer is both a tool and a collaborator; the artist farms the images from an assembled field of printers in a merging of technological and natural processes; parallels between computer code and DNA are reinforced. The printed nature of Salavon's resulting paintings turn abstract expressionist works into a Pop Art format (comparable to Andy Warhol's silkscreens on canvas). They doubly question the exact nature of high art while parodying Warhol's famous desire to be a machine.

While Salavon's aesthetic and mechanised process has precedents in the history of art, the underlying concept references the history of computer science. Each painting/print produced in the sequence conforms to the Turing test, developed to determine whether or not a computer program is successful at modelling human ability to think (as proof of intelligence). While Tinguely wondered whether machines could make art, the Turing test asks whether machines can think. In its modern manifestation, the Turing test pits a human interrogator against two unknowns: one human and one computer. If, during the course of asking questions of each, the interrogator misidentifies the machine as human, the machine passes the intelligence test. Salavon's project turns the audience of these artworks into Turing's interrogator. Three versions (entitled 'Projection', 'Browser', and 'Printer', respectively) challenge viewers to consider the works as man-made in various time–space formats. The digital projection displays each painting for 6.5 seconds in short sequences, taking more than a week to display the entire collection of works. The browser displays the works as a database that can be perused by viewers, who can manipulate the size of the individual images (from micro to macro) and navigate through them using a dual-panel monitor and trackball interface designed by the artist. One hundred of the works became unique objects when they were printed onto canvas using a large-format Hewlett Packard printer. This latter enterprise reveals the digital nature of the 'brushstrokes' – as pixelation evident in the printed paintings is not visible in either of the other formats.

Techno-aesthetics can be described in a general sense as a 'taste for technology' which has had a tremendous impact on the style, form and content of much postmodern art. Elements of techno-aesthetics embodied in the works mentioned in this chapter include not only the formal appearance of technology-driven art forms (such as a 'pixelated' texture, or the appearance of a computer monitor as sculpture) but also systems, concepts and objects specific to new media. Systems include script (such as HTML, XML and Lingo), programming languages or code (Java, C/C++, Perl) and software programs (Flash, Director) that can be used to create artworks. Perhaps the most obvious concept associated with techno-aesthetics falls in the realm of language – the computer language that finds an equivalent with semiotics, especially when works make use of signs, symbols and icons associated with the computer desktop, such as the work of Jim Johnson and Carolyn Speranza. Another concept associated with techno-aesthetics involves investigation of the relationship between the human body and the computer, as in Speranza's 'Hole Poem'. A third major concept addressed by digital artists examines one of the most basic formal elements – colour – as it is produced and displayed in digital media. Salavon's 'Golem' addresses this particular concept associated with new media. The final component of techno-aesthetics can be summarised using the term 'objects' or the appearance of formal elements associated with both the hardware (the monitor, for instance) and software (the pixelised characteristics of screen display) of computer and other technology-driven art forms. The transformation and filtering of reality (the creation of metafictions) provided by digital technologies have fundamentally altered viewers' experiences. Technology-driven art forms might exist on the Internet or in a museum-sponsored 'virtual gallery' with open access. Whether they use HTML, scripting or software such as Macromedia Flash or Director, the examples cited above present human/computer activity as a designed experience.

12 Real Photography

Damian Sutton

The history of photography is replete with attempts to define what the photograph *is* or to define what photography *does*. Yet, despite the fact that this is a common approach in writing, and in spite of many writers' good intentions and intellectual rigour, in criticism photography always seems to resist precise definition; a type of photograph always seems to slip under the net and escape capture. Roland Barthes' affective photograph, for example, evocative of memory and always signifying death, has been the touchstone for a majority of critical writing on the photograph since the 1980s, at the same time gathering up the earlier writings of Walter Benjamin and André Bazin.[1] Yet this long-held definition seems to be the antithesis of so much commercial photography, and even of much of the domestic or studio portraiture to which it is often applied. It seems to oppose the enthusiasm in early photography for its conveyance of the lifelike, whilst the connection of memory to the photograph as a memorialisation seems brittle in explaining the proliferation of 'objectless' photography, such as is represented by the digital photograph and its emergent culture. This problem of parsing the photograph and its 'attesting that the object has been real' seems especially problematic when the definition relies in particular on the embodiment in a specific type of photograph or technology of ideas intended to pertain to all photographs and all technologies.[2] Given the diversity of photographic practice and media, it seems that when a particular kind of photograph is expected to represent all photography it will always be inadequate. In short, it seems that any attempt to define photography, or to explain what the photograph 'is', is *always asking for trouble*. However, it is a common approach, perhaps because the matter always seems to be so pressing: the invention or discovery of photography necessitated definitions – Oliver

Wendell Holmes' 'mirror with a memory' is perhaps the most evocative – whilst the arrival of cinema and more recently the technological ambiguities of the digital image have appeared to put the photographic image's established ontology under threat.[3] Perhaps 'established' should be read as 'taken for granted'.

The two ideal definitions at stake here are, firstly, the photograph as an object in itself and, secondly, the photograph as a transparent record of something. Put another way, one might argue that a photograph 'just is', and the 'real' is in the object recorded by it, whilst one might also argue that the photograph was taken for a reason, and that it is with the photograph as a representation that we have a 'real' relationship. Furthermore, representation itself is independent of any particular medium and easily translated across photographic technologies (print, slide, screen etc.). This apparently paradoxical relationship continues to exercise critical writing on photography, yet an obvious question might be: do we not have a 'real' relationship with photography, one that involves the material culture of the photograph as an object, as well as the immanent culture of the image? How can any one definition capture all these forces and tensions?

Any useable or valuable definitions of photography rely on two things: an equivalence of forms to allow for the identification of a common ontology or 'essence', and the observable embodiment of this in any chosen photographic image. Notions of the photographic must be levelled out in order to identify a particular characteristic of all photography which is evident in the photograph itself. Even if two conflicting ontologies appear – the photograph-as-transparent, and the photograph-as-object, for example – they need only be apparent within one image to demonstrate how photographic theory is rooted in its practical base. The public dangers of forfeiting such 'roots' are clear: a suggestion by Peter Osborne, speaking at a conference in 2002, that photography criticism should leave 'The Photograph' behind, drew a collective gasp from his audience, made up of some of the mandarins of UK photography education. Despite the strength of Osborne's argument the reaction was clearly significant, as the statement was excised from his essay in the conference proceedings.[4] In that essay, Osborne's description of photography as a 'distributive unity', developed from Kant, suggests that photography's many technologies and forms appear to demand organisation based on equivalence. Any physical embodiment is in 'The Photograph' as an ideal historical or mythological unity. Yet, crucially, it seems that the desire for a mythical unity has never been stronger, as the technological foundations of photography around which its rich history and cultural heritage is based seem to be crumbling. At the time of this writing, Bronica, Kodak and Leica have all announced a curtailing of their manufacture of celluloid-based equipment. For the UK company Ilford the digital revolution nearly meant the end.[5]

Embodiment and equivalence are still crucial to understanding the photographic image, even in an historical period marked by the absence of the object of photography – the paper print has been replaced by the computer screen, the negative by the coded jpeg. The homogeneous environment of photographic representation in advertising and popular use has changed little in the move from analogue to digital, whilst a technical equivalence is imposed by remediation in the studio or archive. As noted by Scott McQuire, many analogue formats (35mm still, 8mm movie film for example) can now be archived and manipulated as one digital standard.[6] The characteristic appearance of these analogue forms remains only as an historical signature, an embodiment of cultural memory. Yet, despite this technological 'levelling', the fact that photography resists definition provides a continued challenge for theory. Furthermore, to the twin characteristics of *equivalence* and *embodiment* can be added a third: *immanence*. This philosophical notion, drawn from the work of Gilles Deleuze and Deleuze's collaboration with Félix Guattari, goes some way to provide an understanding of the relationship between photography's many unique forms and objects (embodiment) and the necessity of 'levelling' required in both theory and practice (equivalence). Following Deleuze and Guattari's lead, the photographic image can be understood as a plane of immanence, an intersection of critical or cultural evaluations and practical or technological forms.

Richard Beard, 'Charles John Canning, Earl Canning', c.1840. Photograph courtesy of the National Portrait Gallery, London.

Samsung SCH-a790 (corporate material). Courtesy of Samsung.

Transparency and Objecthood: photography and the photograph

The classic paradox of photography theory is that of the apparent contradiction between the photograph as transparent and the photograph as representation. Thierry de Duve has described this paradox in the development of Modernist photographic art as between the photograph's 'referential series' (its attestation of the real) and its 'superficial series' (the effect of the artist's hands on the record of the object).[7] The paradox itself is seductive for critics: André Bazin has described the photograph as an 'hallucination that is also a fact', for Kendall Walton it is 'a mixture of fictions', for Victor Burgin 'a record of reality refracted through a sensibility'.[8]

The argument behind the photograph's transparency – that the photograph has a causal relationship with the object and thus simply 'is' the object – has its roots in Bazin's 'Ontology of the Photographic Image', in which he argues that the photograph 'shares' existence with the object photographed: 'The photographic image is the object itself... it shares, by virtue of the very process of its becoming, the being of the model of which it is the reproduction; it is the model.'[9]

This Bazinian causal connection still has considerable critical weight. In the 1980s, founded on this connection, Roger Scruton invoked Bazin in order to relegate the photographer's creative action to a mere 'gesturing finger'.[10] More recently, Bazin's 'common-sense' approach has helped provide a foundation for the semiotic theory first developed by Burgin and others in the 1980s (itself modelled after the work of Charles Sanders Peirce and Ferdinand de Saussure).[11] This has in turn been crucial to our early understanding of the place of the digital image in photographic theory. The apparent break in the indexical link between object and image, the 'causal connection', has been the focus of early criticism of the digital image. Digital photography, and especially its apparently invisible manipulability, destroyed the photograph's privileged connection to the object. Without this anchor to reality, the semiotic relationship seemed over-balanced towards the iconic and the symbolic – i.e. representation.[12] Yet the concerns expressed in the 1990s, that the digital image equates photography with fallibility and distrust, now seem caught up in the historical moment of the digital technology's first real flourishing; photography has always been 'dubitative' (a word that Peter Lunenfeld borrows from Hollis Frampton), and this characteristic is not the province of the digital image alone.[13] The act of photography, 'gesturing finger' though it may be, ensures that photography cannot be defined merely by transparency.

The *object* that is the photograph has its own dual history in the Modernist contingency of the art photograph and in the social contingency of the document. The photograph in art relies upon its uniqueness in time and space, often demonstrated by the visible intervention of the photographer (de Duve's superficial series), and often made in dialogue with the technologies of reproduction which are perceived to threaten the unique work of art. The art print is at once a singular object, created by the artist's own hands, and an indelible record of their sensibility. Walter Benjamin saw, in his analysis of photographs, the aura of the sitters transfixed by the camera's gaze – Dauthendey's wife, Kafka's 'immeasurably sad eyes'.[14] Yet his belief in the power of the process to convey their presence was transcended in his own lifetime by the foregrounding of the unique art print by Alfred Stieglitz and others. This was to overpower Benjamin's ideas, even as his attack on bourgeois artistic ritual (the aura of the work of art) continued to influence critics and photographers alike. The aura of the photograph in art is now conveyed in the *vision* of the photographer as much as in the limited or unique print.

In comparison, the establishment of the Internet and the gradual proliferation of digital photography online can challenge only the mechanics of photography, with photography now essentially 'object-less'. Images are often circulated electronically, and the decision to make hard copy often made by exception. It seems almost an afterthought to produce printout technology for digital photographs. Whilst this offers for many the possibility of art-without-walls, the photography-without-objects that appears online is, as John Roberts has noted, less of a break with past technologies than it initially appears.[15] The 'extended contextual space' offered online merely enlarges or repackages the same extended contextual space offered by the distribution of other copying technologies – slide, photocopy, bookplates. In a discussion of the photograph's relationship with the aura of the work of art, this is Benjamin's formulation writ large and in multimedia, but also one that emphasises the life of an image across media and not linked to a unique object. The photographer's eye remains paramount.

The 'other' history of the photograph as object involves its role as a document recorded by or on behalf of society. As the mainspring of the public archive, the social or cultural value of the photograph is tied to its use as an object. Photographs are collected in the museum, the library or by the state because of what they record, yet the object's value is not only in what it records but also in *why* – reasons that are often inscribed on the object via the framing of the image or the continuity of the collection. This social contingency has been linked to class and power by John Tagg as a demonstration of its 'currency', whilst Allan Sekula has argued that it was the creation of the archive as a collection of quantifiable objects that has been instrumental in the development of a modern society of surveillance.[16] It was the idea that power relations – especially those of class, race and state – were invested in the object of the photograph that led scholars to appreciate the vernacular photograph as being similarly invested. Tagg's own history of quotidian portraiture in the nineteenth century is neatly paralleled by studies of the contemporary family portrait.[17] Both see the personal photograph, and the personal photograph collection, as tell-tale inscriptions of society's mores, anxieties and fantasies.

Ultimately, the photograph-as-object tends to find its apogee in either the artwork or the family image. At this point, photographic transparency is often taken as read. In the psychological studies of objects by Mihalyi Csikszentmihalyi and Eugene Rochberg-Holton the family photograph is a 'tangible artefact' contrasting with the 'fragility of the material world we create around us'.[18] Photographs hang around. At other times, transparency confounds this tangibility, as suggested in Barthes' *Camera Lucida*. Much of Barthes' post-semiologic reappraisal of the photograph comes from his trying to explain the paralysis caused by the clash of the photograph's referential and practical ontologies. His self-confessed intellectual collapse comes after he finds a photograph of his recently deceased mother, and its transparency (it is of his mother before he was born) presents him with a moment that escapes his own testimony. Since it represents one of the clearest attempts to give photographs a conceptual equivalence that relies on both the photograph-as-object and the photograph-as-transparent, it is perhaps unsurprising that Barthes' attempt to define photography has had such extraordinary influence since it was published.

Equivalence

The notion of 'equivalence' has been put forward by Elizabeth Edwards, curator of the Pitt Rivers Museum, University of Oxford, as a way of conceptualising the cataloguing of the diverse types of object which can be understood by the term 'The Photograph'. As an ethnographer, Edwards made use of equivalence as scientific, enabling the creation of continuity within an archive – for example, in the mounting of photographs of various sizes on identical record cards: 'The archive effect is achieved only through the creation of a new material object'.[19] Thus a practical equivalence imposes a conceptual equivalence through a material translation. Material culture is seen as chaotic by Edwards, but nonetheless relevant, and so the 'plasticity of the photographic object' must be reined in by the filing cabinet. Since Edwards notes that an equivalence already exists in the material culture of photography, such as in the photographic album – or its historical predecessor, the carte-de-visite – she suggests giving equal weight to representation and use in photographs, since these are often equally responsible for their social as well as ethnographic value. Edwards' preference is for a 'social biography' of the photograph as a method of combining its material and representational forms. Social biography can be applied to the photograph as an individual and unique object moving through space and time, thus appreciating either the historical trajectory of the modernist artwork, the photograph as social evidence, or simply the photographic memento mori. The same social biography, however, can be used to trace the image across technologies and forms, one image followed through various media. This becomes a biography based on distribution, and a history of the technology involved. It is also the strongest connection that a study of the photograph has with the study of photography's 'illegitimate' forms. Cinema, the Internet, and now cellphone technologies all extend John Roberts' 'contextual space of the photograph'. This suggests that definitions of photography rely on theories of these new media and their formation in culture as much as they do the philosophies of realism or the psychology of objects. A photograph might be a print or a jpeg, but its distribution has the same representational effect as the card mounts used to create an archive in Edwards' example: an equivalence between variations of the same image is achieved only through the creation of *each* new material object.

Yet with this passage across media, Edwards' scientific equivalence parallels the cultural equivalence of the image as representation. Technologies may change, but the images stay the same. Advertisements for photo-messaging that appeared in 2003 might emphasise the fleeting transience of life 'on the go' with a cellphone, yet the images are drawn from a wider archive of representations. That cellphones can take the same quality of picture as a 'regular' digital camera is shown by their taking the types of photographs for which regular cameras are used – or to which the users of regular cameras aspire. Cellphones that take photographs join the 'mass culture of cameras adjusted to the norm', as Vilém Flusser has stated.[20] For Flusser, the camera itself was the embodiment of the social apparatus of representation, an abstraction of the cultural condition of image-making. Flusser's argument was essentially political (post-Marxist), drawn from, amongst others, Louis Althusser and Deleuze/Guattari. Flusser's anger was directed at photographers who are not prepared to question the representations that their medium makes it so easy to replicate. But throughout, the regular use that Flusser makes of embodiment – the camera, the photograph, 'the distribution' apparatuses that repeat the cultural programme – suggests that theories of representation are still attracted to these objects of photography.

Immanence

Since theories of photography suggest so many conflicting notions of objecthood and transparency, it is possible that the principles of difference themselves need to be rethought. There is undoubtedly an immanence of photography, and of the photograph – something that connects all thoughts of photography – but an immanence of such complexity as to present itself to each of us differently. 'Conflicting' notions of photography, for example, appear to conflict only because we expect all photographs to naturally embody transparency and objecthood in precisely the same way. For example, whilst there are many forms of photography, and many types of photograph that appear to be different from each other, an alternative view might be to see a continuity between all photographs – an immanence which they share and which is indivisible. The aim is not to impose an arbitrary equivalence on all photography – our ideal definition – since 'aberrant' forms are always likely to appear.

Immanence has been used by Gilles Deleuze, and by Deleuze and Félix Guattari, to conceptualise a substantial link between apparently multiple forms. Deleuze's book on Leibniz, *The Fold*, and the collaborative project of *A Thousand Plateaus* both attempt to demonstrate how a continuous world appears with variation and apparent multiplicity. The authors' *plane of immanence* can be understood as a coalescing of continuity into consistent, apparently discontinuous forms – objects – through inference or use. It is conceived as a plane, perhaps, because it is both a superficial connection yet depthless, suggesting a surface that both reflects (or illuminates?) and refracts its depth. The plane is a 'formless elastic membrane', a screen.[21]

To develop this explanation of photography's unifying ontology, we might conclude that the treatment of 'The Photograph' as a singular, reified object encourages its continued treatment as such. Furthermore, rather than seeing photography as the evolution of ideal form, individual photographs are always imitations attracted to an imagined unity. That this is an historical unity, as Peter Osborne has described, suggests that such notions 'harden' and 'soften' over time, and that they become object-ideals with a temporal significance: Deleuze called such things 'objectiles'.[22] Immanence is thus 'viscous', Gregg Lambert suggests, or 'sticky' (suggesting also 'bonding').[23] Ideal photographs are 'sticky' notions made so by repetition across media. The photograph that appears on cellphone advertisements is a 'sticky' one. This would seem to oppose the notion of the 'essence' of photography. There is no *eidos*, as in Barthes. There is nothing innate in a photograph. Photographic immanence, as Deleuze and Guattari suggest, can 'only be inferred, induced, concluded from that to which it gives rise…'.[24] Essences are only virtual inclusions of form.[25]

From a general plane of immanence Deleuze and Guattari draw two particular and distinctive notions. The first, the 'plane of organisation', more closely resembles the 'sticky' forms of photography, which coalesce as types, styles or particular examples of embodiment: the melancholic emptiness of black-and-white street scenes, the haloed glamour model in a gesture of mock modesty. These ideal photographs coalesce into 'strata', suggesting fossilisation, immobility and stasis. However, an alternative, the 'plane of consistency', is suggested, as one of 'material proliferation' or collective assemblages. Here, the collection of forms is a 'peopling', connected by 'contagion' rather than linear development or evolution.[26] It is this plane that more closely approximates the multiple technologies of photography bound together by singular representations. Furthermore, it suggests that it is the immanence of representation that stimulates and conjures the appearance of new practical forms.

Embodiment

These two 'planes' are, of course, offered as opposing poles by Deleuze and Guattari, and, rather like the poles of transparency and objecthood, we might see the general immanence of photography as an exchange or circuit between the two. This is a feature characteristic of Deleuze's approach to binary oppositions. A political argument might suggest that it is organisations of class power that create the singular forms and representations, the sticky ideal photographs, whilst the radical employment of technology disperses them. However, there remains a tendency to seek an embodiment of this exchange that is common to all photography, and, since the advent of digital photography, the negative/print hardly suffices as such an embodiment.

If there is an object of photography, an ideal embodiment, it has to be the screen. For Flusser, images are screens because they simultaneously represent and obscure, a barrier and a window.[27] The photographic act is the throwing up of a screen that simultaneously frames and obscures the world, which in turn exists only as a 'pretext for the states of things'.[28] The screen is therefore a 'teleological plane' (Deleuze and Guattari), the condition for the event (Deleuze).[29] The surface of the image exists, and is often prized in the photograph as artwork when it reveals the hand of the artist, yet the surface should also never give itself away. The surface of a photograph may crack, stain or fade, but the raster of the pixel screen refuses that tangibility. Whilst embodiment in 'the screen' outwardly suggests a reference to digital photography and the electronic screen, it must be remembered that photography is full of screens and always has been. Slides are screens, as much as the surfaces upon which they are projected. The plate of the camera is a screen for light entering through the lens, and then a screen for the light projected through the negative. Even the daguerreotype, with its mirrored ground, presented viewers with their own reflection behind the sensitised silver, the one image screening the other. The object of the cellphone may seem an anathema to photography purists when placed alongside the velvet-lined daguerreotype case, yet both cradle like a jewel a screen presenting, at the same time, depth and surface. Photography's equivalence is a genus or species embodied in the screen. The screen contains, frames or unifies the world (transparency), or reveals itself by reflecting the expectations of culture (objecthood). Photography cannot escape its technology, although that technology may change so much as to appear fundamentally different. The 'real' always exists in photography. There is a world out there, a camera records it, a photograph of it is created, touched, manipulated, distributed. Yet the mechanics of photography act on behalf of an eye, a window, a *screen*, and representation, acting as a virtual equivalence, clings to the surface of the screen like a patina, an immanence of the thought of photography.

13 Virtual Cinematography and the Digital Real: (dis)placing the moving image between reality and simulacra

Jenna Ng

Introduction

'We awaken to the real, which discards emotions for the image.' In this manner, Alfian, all art is the dissolving of a dream.

Alfian Sa'at [1]

That the objective world might be merely an illusion is not an original proposition. One of the most famous figurations of this delusion is, of course, the timeworn allegory of Plato's cave – the ensconcing of our blindness in a confining interiority, seeing 'literally nothing but the shadows of the images',[2] while truth resided outside as a world of sunlight, water and spangled heavens. This idea, albeit in variations, has been further hosted upon many different conceptual platforms: religion,[3] mysticism,[4] academic philosophy,[5] postmodernism,[6] popular culture,[7] and even twentieth-century physics.[8]

The polemics, however, are taking on a subtly different slant today. Animated to a large extent (abashedly or otherwise) by the blockbuster success of *The Matrix* (US, Andy and Larry Wachowski, Warner Bros, 1999), the imaginations of millions were captured by the film's diegetic philosophy of the reality/illusion dialectic, whereby the 'real' world is a machine-generated simulation/experience within the Matrix while reality takes place in an apocalyptic, war-ravaged landscape and the enlightened living are decked out in grey robes and inhabit austere caverns.[9] The film's direct allusion to Jean Baudrillard's *Simulacra and Simulation* easily launched in popular consciousness the new idea on the block: reality understood not in terms of its delusion, but, rather, its more sinister simulacrum and the attendant spectres of technological domination and copy/image creation.[10] The world does not exist as objective truth, but as image and likeness. Our metaphysical ambivalences today thus teeter not between reality and illusion, but between real and hyperreal, original and copy, reality and simulation.

A little uncannily, discourse surrounding the moving image has also been traversing a similar theoretical trajectory. The film medium has traditionally asserted its particular relationship with reality by virtue of the *indexical* function of the photographic image, as posited in the context of Charles Sanders Peirce's triadic sign categories of icon, index and symbol. These sign relations are characterised (broadly) by similarity, contiguity and convention respectively.[11] By dint of its inherent operation – the mechanical impression of light on film – the camera is thus commonly asserted to have assured in the image the unique capture of its sliver of reality.

However, the advent of digital applications in filmmaking today, particularly in the use of computer-generated imagery, potentially threatens to unravel the ontology of the moving image: unlike the case for its filmic counterpart, the creation of CGI on a computer, entailing its independence of an indexical engagement with the object, dispossesses the digital image of any connection to the reality of its referent.[12] Like a copy plaguing the Baudrillardian hyperreal, CGI is construed as an *iconic* simulation – immaculate in its photographic credibility, yet always lacking an existential relation to the real.

The issues surrounding the interfacing of digitality, image and reality are explored here, and in particular the dichotomous positions within which film and digital imaging have been placed alongside the dialectical discourse of real and virtual. An argument is made against the excessive simplicity of the split construct as well as its unsound correspondence within the discourse of digitality. Finally, citing virtual cinematography as the prime example of cinema's unique engagement with digitality, an alternative framework is proposed – the digital real – in which to analyse the image–object relation, and ultimately to reconsider the digital moving image.

This chapter explores these issues surrounding the interfacing of digitality, image and reality. In particular, it critiques the dichotomous positions within which film and digital imaging have been placed along the dialectical discourse of real and virtual, and argues against the excessive simplicity of the split construct as well as its unsound correspondence within the discourse of digitality. Finally, citing virtual cinematography as the prime example of cinema's unique engagement with digitality, an alternative framework is proposed – the digital real – in which to analyse the image–object relation, and ultimately to reconsider the digital moving image.

Seeking the Real: deconstructing the image–object relation

The photograph has been variously theorised as possessing aspects of all three semiotic categories.[13] Nonetheless, its indexical strategy – what Lars Kiel Bertelsen calls 'the indexical drive' – is primarily the supposition for which the photographic image (and, by extension, celluloid cinema) is most celebrated and the theoretical basis upon which its extraordinary bond with reality most emphatically asserted.[14] The touchstone of the photograph's indexicality lies in the *physical connection* between image and object inherent in the chemical operation of the photographic process: the exposure of film to light, resulting in an imprint of the image on film which is subsequently developed into the photograph. In characterising the semiotic status of the photograph, Peirce specifically highlights this physical correspondence between image and object:

> Photographs, especially instantaneous photographs, are very instructive, because we know that they are in certain respects exactly like the objects they represent. But this resemblance is due to the photographs having been produced *under such circumstances that they were physically forced to correspond point by point to nature*. In that aspect, then, they belong to the second class of signs [indices], those by physical connection.[15]

This notion, in turn, is consistently invoked as a tribute to the wonder of the photographed image, in whose creation process, as Bill Nichols puts it, 'something of reality itself seems to pass through the lens and remain embedded in the photographic emulsion'.[16] Susan Sontag describes a photograph as 'not only an image (as a painting is an image), an interpretation of the real; *it is also a trace, something directly stenciled off the real, like a footprint or a death mask.*'[17] Roland Barthes characterises the connection between image and object as almost tautologous: 'It is as if the Photograph always carries its referent with itself, both affected by the same amorous or funeral immobility, at the heart of the moving world: they are glued together, limb by limb…'[18]

When related to as an historical witness or an attested document, it is ultimately the indexicality of the photograph which is appealed to, as 'a trace of something which has been'.[19] Thus, the sign function of the photograph as an index – on the basis of the image as a trace relinquished by object qua referent – becomes effectively a ready affirmation of the unqualified connection between the filmic image and the real. Stanley Cavell proclaims: 'A photograph does not present us with "likenesses" of things; it presents us, we want to say, *with things themselves*'.[20] Bazin's oft-quoted declaration sums this up most memorably: 'The photographic image is the object itself, the object freed from the conditions of time and space that govern it…[the image] shares, by the very process of its becoming, the being of the model of which it is the reproduction; *it is the model.'*[21]

In contrast, digitisation and digital image creation processes such as CGI and computer animation are characterised dominantly by their pictorial qualities, implying the digital image's semiotic significance as an *icon* which, in turn, problematises the connection to its referent. In his analysis of digital cinema, Lev Manovich explicitly denotes digital cinema as a function of the graphic and the painterly:

> [Digital cinema] is no longer an indexical media technology, but, rather, *a subgenre of painting...* No longer strictly locked in the photographic, *cinema opens itself toward the painterly...* Cinema becomes a particular branch of painting – painting in time. No longer a kino-eye, but a kino-brush.[22]

Specifically, Manovich posits a 'distinct logic of a digital moving image' which *'subordinates the photographic and the cinematic to the painterly and the graphic*, destroying cinema's identity as a media art'.[23] Such emphasis on digital cinema as a mode of the graphic, *particularly in opposition to a depiction of cinema as being previously a recording process*, forcefully portrays the digital image as being simply a pictorial representation of fantasy and imagination, whose manual construction on a computer is signified as the modus operandi of copy and simulation, whereby, unlike the filming of a camera, there is no direct, physical path between image and object. Even if a referent was involved (for example, where a model is used, as in the case of creating Yoda in the *Star Wars* prequels), the digital image is only a function of mimesis – an icon in the Peircean sense, a representation of likeness and no more.[24]

Thus poised, celluloid faces off digital in an almost confrontational set-up: the indexicality of film placed against the iconic status of the digital image, creating a theme of divergence which, it is argued, runs as a persistent, if implicit, thread throughout the discourse of digitality. Take, for example, the inherent mutability of the digital format, which increasingly assumes a shade of unease in the interpretation of innovation as an unstoppable nightmare of metamorphosis: William Mitchell describes an art world today 'that recognizes continual mutation and proliferation of variants';[25] *The Sunday Times* reports an indignant outcry over the 'deception' of a digitally altered picture of Kate Winslet.[26] Reactions of nostalgia, loss and concern over historical realities permeate with the increasing sense of lack of permanence and reliance: 'No longer do we posit such a code of digital image encryptment [sic] through verifying codes than we imagine how easy it would be to counterfeit them.'[27] Filmmakers mourn a certain loss in the enduring solidity of the old tools, as expressed by Carlo Rambaldi, 'creature designer' for *Alien* (US, Ridley Scott, 20th Century Fox, 1979):

everything [in the past] was made by hand, you know, in a down-to-earth way, just rubber-suits and mechanics. That was the power of it… *It is a physical thing, and that is extremely important, because when you start to make it on the computer it ceases to become real.* You lose all sense of feeling and reality regarding to the creature.[28]

However (in an unabashed play on Newtonian physics as metaphor), reaction is underpinned by action; elemental to the reflex against the digital world of effortless change is ultimately the defence of truth and permanence entrenched in the film image, grounded fundamentally in the indexicality of the photograph, which informs the reliability of the connection between between image and reality. For example, Maureen Turim writes: 'Digitalization disturbs the capturing of an image on a photographic plate as an elemental gathering of visual proof'.[29] Her assertion of digitality as confounder of 'visual proof', however, is effectively propped against an implied immutability of film: she could not have made one charge without the premise of the other. Her statement assumes the sense of truth in film that is recalled in Jean-Luc Godard's *Le Petit soldat*: 'Photography is truth. And the cinema is truth 24 times a second.'[30] Or, as Jean Cocteau similarly proclaims, the 'greatest power of a film is to be *indisputable* with respect to the actions it determines and which *are carried out before our eyes*'.[31] The sense of permanence in the referent is also invoked by Barthes when he writes: 'Discourse combines signs which have referents, of course, but these referents can be and are most often "chimeras". Contrary to these imitations, in Photography I can never deny that *the thing has been there*.'[32] Film imagery is thus, misguidedly or otherwise, assigned an almost irrevocable conceit of authenticity, trustworthiness and integrity beyond the fallibilities of human mediation – conditions which digitality, set in its contrasted iconic groove, invariably countervails. Like an equal and opposite reaction, in contrast with film the contexts of digital imagery take the adverse poles of trickery, unreliability, deception, deceit and distrust.

Yet, such an antagonistic set-up, explicit or otherwise, is inaccurate and fallacious, for the following reasons.

Firstly, the antagonism forces the object–image relation into a dichotomy between index/icon and film/digital which is broad-brushed and simplistic. Where, for example, would digital video (DV) fit in? The DV image is akin to an indexical sign in that it is 'filmed off' a physical referent. In contrast with CGI, which is created from scratch with graphics software, computer-simulated textures and lighting and so on, in digital video there can be no image without the object. To that extent, there is indeed a certain 'physical and direct' connection as described by Peirce, in the sense of light from the object passing through camera lens (and filters) onto a photosensitive surface as an integral and quintessential part of its creation process. Yet, taken further, that connection fails, for while the light signals ultimately do result in producing the image (albeit via conversion from analogue to digital through an analogue-to-digital-converter (ADC)), the digital camera is capable of processing only a limited amount of information, even as that runs into vast numbers of bytes. The DV image is thus constantly being adjusted and modified through various compensating features – for example, interpolation, whereby complex algorithms analyse neighbouring pixels, thus altering colour boundaries, or anti-aliasing (anti-pixelising) filters, which control chrominance and luminance levels so as to prevent pixelation. Hence, whereas the film image appears explicitly 'stamped' on the celluloid strip by the direct impact of light, the digital video image is a hybrid progeny, delivered equally from the passing of light as well as the machinic crunching of zeros and ones. The peculiarities of digital technology thus cannot be fully borne out in the prevailing iconicity/indexical divide.

Secondly, the status of the indexicality of the film image is essentially problematic. While not completely refuted, the indexicality of the photograph has, however, been qualified in a number of ways. For example, Göran Sonesson argues that the photograph's indexicality is merely 'an open potentiality': 'indexicality cannot be the primary sign relation of photographs'.[33] The premise of his theory is that 'the photographic signifier, like that of the verbal sign, is omni-temporal and omni-spatial…apt to be instantiated at any time and place'. Sonesson's conclusion, therefore, is that 'the photograph must originally be seen as an icon, before its indexical properties can be discovered'.[34] A stronger qualification is the assertion of an absence of a *truth relation* between the image and the world *an sich* – the breakdown of what Michael Charlesworth has termed 'the "white mythology" of photography': the idea that photography is free of value judgements and rhetoric.[35] In other words, the image is but a coded artificiality, a visual construct, an ideological end, whose significance is to be produced only 'in the act of *looking at the image*, by a way of talking'.[36] The photograph has no meaning in itself: its indexical sign function ultimately counts for little. In this sense, as Bertelsen concludes, '[n]ot even the indexicality of the photographic image can overcome the fundamental limitation of perspective representation'.[37] To that extent, the condemnation of the digital image's relation to the real in terms of its mutability is no more than 'the breakdown of naïve trust in photographic transparency'.[38] Hence, in view of the qualified status of the relationship between referent and image, the truth relation of film, so vitally contrary to the discourse of digitality, becomes questionable, both in terms of the basis of the photograph's indexicality and the episteme of its ontological significance.

Virtual Cinematography and the Digital Real

> The cinema does not just present images; it surrounds them with a world.
>
> Gilles Deleuze[39]

The final argument against the digital/film divide is that digital special effects technology in cinema has advanced to a level at which a superficial analysis of digitality against film is ultimately irrelevant. That stage in question is the development of virtual cinematography, a technology first widely heralded in big-budget, spectacular blockbuster films such as *The Matrix Reloaded* (US, Andy and Larry Wachowski, Warner Bros, 2003), *The Matrix Revolutions* (US, Andy and Larry Wachowski, Warner Bros, 2003), *Hulk* (US, Ang Lee, Universal Pictures, 2003) and *The Fast and the Furious* (US, Rob Cohen, Universal Pictures, 2001).[40]

Briefly described, virtual cinematography is the process of creating images from virtual reality – a depository of digitised, three-dimensional depictions – where, as a *Wired* journalist enthused, 'everything and everyone' in the real world is rendered into virtuality, 'a zone where skyscrapers, skin, flames, and marauding machines are all re-created equal', whose reality can be 'tweaked as easily as a CAD file'.[41] There are essentially two stages to the process. The first involves real-world data acquisition, where relevant subjects are captured as film images. The techniques for achieving this vary depending on the nature of the information required: for example, buildings, streets, locations and backgrounds are taken by photographing the locations and architecture from multiple angles, while movement is recorded by motion capture, a process whereby motion-analysis cameras record movement data from reflective bodysuits worn by actors executing the required actions. The *Matrix* sequels used a much-publicised procedure, universal capture (or u-cap), in which five synchronised high-resolution, high-definition video cameras are placed in an array around the human actors, digitising at the rate of one gigabyte per second, solely to capture every specification of their skin texture, hair movement, human expression and facial nuance.[42]

The second stage is the digitisation – the virtualisation – of this real-world data as virtual reality for the purposes of the film. Scanned into digital format, the visual information is triangulated with algorithms to interpolate any position not captured in the original stills. Three-dimensional models of the images are then generated from the photographs[43] and perfected in texture and appearance by being 'wrapped' using rendering software (for example Mental Ray[44]) in order to '[transform] the chosen photographs into the surface geometry of the models'.[45] Thus, virtual cinematography becomes 'the first real-world application of virtual reality':[46] the virtually cinematographed image is ultimately a product not of the physical real world (as a recording of it), but conceived from this photorealistic image matrix. Each is a scrap of VR, trumped up first by 'master performances' culled from photographs, then interpolated, generated into 3D, wrapped and fused with other layers of visual elements such as computer-generated enhancements (like glistening glass, bullet wakes and blood). If the world has disappeared into image – the real 'that which is always already reproduced' – then, indeed, image today is birthed from image.[47]

This break posed by virtual cinematography has to be distinguished from previous conventional uses of digitality in cinema. The application of digital technology to rework film is not new: it is common for filmed images to be scanned and digitised for manipulation, such as wire removal or filter effects, as well as the incorporation of pure CGI (such as the dinosaurs in *Jurassic Park*). Even the groundbreaking 'bullet-time' effects of *The Matrix*, a sequence of dynamic camera movement around a slow-motion event, such as that of Trinity hovering in mid-air while the camera swirls around her, is fundamentally based on the same principle. The special effect is created from a composition of photographic images of Trinity's movement, taken from an array of still cameras rigged on a trajectory mirroring the camera movements that will ultimately capture the final scene, against a photorealistic computer-generated background.

However, in all these cases the filmed images remain the cardinal foundation and component of the cinematic image. Digital technology is used simply to work over film; the fundamental premise of the filmed image as the terminal product is never compromised. Virtual cinematography, on the other hand, operates along a very different vector. The film images involved in its process are not for the purpose of being embellished for the screen but to be, when translated into digital data, pieced together as an alternative virtual reality from which the image is ultimately produced. In that sense, the virtually cinematographed image does not engage with the physical world in the way that the filmed image does (as a recording or through the physical relationship of an indexical sign). Created from the VR of digitised images, its affiliation, rather, is with the characterisations of a digitised, virtual (hyper)reality.

Thus, the mutability of digitality, its desubstantialisation,[48] its spatio-temporal incoherence, its immateriality and so on are argued here to be the natural conceits of the digital image. In this way, digitality maintains its unique vectors to reality, rather than merely traversing the advocacy of adverse positions taken in analyses positing digitality against film along an icon/index divide which inform the discourse of images taken from our physical reality.

Conclusion

To that end, it is argued that the true dissociation between the digital image and its referent does not lie in terms of its iconic status but in the recognition that the image is engaged on an entirely different platform, one on which it may abandon (as opposed to overcome) the limitations of being posited within its semiotic function. As technology brings with it different worlds, different concepts and different paradigms, our understanding of the real is constantly in flux. Divisions between the real and the illusion, the simulacrum or the unreal are constantly renewed, reassessed and re-understood; it is a negotiation which never ends. The challenge, then, is to understand the relationship on its own terms. Alfian Sa'at's ghazal is thus wise in this sense: perhaps what is needed to tell us the truth is neither theory nor argument, but the soul of the artist.

14 Science of Appearances, Politics of the Real

Slavoj Žižek

Copernicus, Darwin, Freud ... and many others

The story of three successive humiliations of man, the three 'narcissistic illnesses' ('Copernicus–Darwin–Freud'), is more complex than it may appear. The first thing to say is that the latest scientific breakthroughs seem to add to it a whole series of further 'humiliations' which radicalise the first three, so that, as Peter Sloterdijk has perspicuously noted, with regard to today's 'brain sciences', psychoanalysis rather seems to belong to the traditional 'humanist' field threatened by the latest humiliations. Is the proof of it not the predominant reaction of psychoanalysts to the latest advances in brain sciences? Their defence of psychoanalysis often reads as just another variation of the standard philosophico-transcendental gesture of pointing out how a positive science can never encompass and account for the very horizon of meaning within which it is operative ...

There are, however, some complications to this image. The first one: from the very beginning of modernity, humiliation, 'narcissistic illness', seems to generate a sense of superiority paradoxically grounded in the very awareness of the miserable character of our existence. As Blaise Pascal put it several centuries ago, in an unsurpassable way, man is a mere insignificant speck of dust in the infinite universe, but he KNOWS about his nullity, and that makes all the difference. Paradigmatically modern is this notion of greatness not as simply opposed to misery, but as a misery aware of itself. The second complication concerns the precise status of this knowledge: it is not only the knowledge about our own vanity, but also its inherent obverse, the technological savoir-faire, knowledge which is power. Strictly correlative to the 'humiliation' of man is the exponential growth of humankind's technological domination over nature in modernity.

These two features combined give us the basic paradox of the modern philosophy of subjectivity: the couplet of the humiliation of empirical man and the elevation of transcendental subject. René Descartes, who asserted 'cogito' as the starting point of philosophy, simultaneously reduced all reality, life included, to *res extensa*, the field of matter obeying mechanical laws. In this precise sense, the thought of modern subjectivity is NOT a 'humanism', but, from the very outset, 'anti-humanist': humanism characterises Renaissance thought, which celebrated man as the crown of creation, the highest component of the chain of created beings, while modernity proper occurs only when mankind loses its privileged place and is reduced to just another element of reality – and correlative to this loss of privilege is the emergence of subject as the pure immaterial void, not as a substantial part of reality. The Kantian sublime itself is grounded in this gap: it is the very experience of the impotence and nullity of man (as a part of nature) when he is exposed to a powerful display of natural forces that evokes in a negative way his greatness as a numenal ethical subject.

These two complications, however, are part of the standard narrative of modernity; it is only the third one which effectively disturbs the received image: the fact that the twentieth-century 'humiliations' are much more ambiguous than they may appear – and, retroactively, render visible the ambiguity of the classic humiliations. That is to say, in a first approach, Marx, Nietzsche and Freud all share the same 'desublimating' hermeneutics of suspicion: a 'higher' capacity (ideology and politics, morality, consciousness) is unmasked as a shadow-theatre which is effectively run by the conflict of forces that takes place on another 'lower' scene (economic process, conflict of unconscious desires). And, today, things go much further: in cognitivism, human thinking itself is conceived of as being modelled after the functioning of a computer, so that the very gap between understanding (the experience of meaning, of the openness of a world) and the 'mute' functioning of a machine potentially disappears; in neo-Darwinism, (not only) human individuals are conceived of as mere instruments of, or rather vehicles for, the reproduction of 'their' genes, and, in a homologous way, human culture, the cultural activity of mankind, as a vehicle for the proliferation of 'memes'…However, one is tempted to say that, insofar as the nineteenth century 'demystification' is a reduction of the noble appearance to some 'lower' reality (Marx–Nietzsche–Freud), then the twentieth century adds to it another turn of the screw by rehabilitating (a weird, previously unheard-of) appearance itself. Indicative here is the Husserlian *phenomenology*, the first true event of twentieth-century philosophy, with its attitude of 'reduction', which aims at observing phenomena 'as such', in their autonomy, not as attributes/expressions/effects of some underlying 'real entities'. A line is opened up here which leads to figures as different as Henri Bergson, Gilles Deleuze, Ludwig Wittgenstein and quantum physics, all of them focusing on the autonomy of the pure flux-event of becoming with regard to real entities ('things').

In short, is the shift from substantial Reality to (different forms of) Event not one of the defining features of modern sciences? Quantum physics posits as the ultimate reality not some primordial elements but, rather, some kind of string 'vibrations', entities that can be described only as desubstantialised processes; cognitivism and systems theory focus on the mystery of 'emerging properties', which also designate purely processual self-organisations and so on. No wonder, then, that the three crucial contemporary philosophers – Martin Heidegger, Deleuze, Alain Badiou – deploy three thoughts of the Event: in Heidegger, it is the Event as the epochal disclosure of a configuration of Being; in Deleuze, it is the Event as the desubstantialised pure becoming of Sense; in Badiou, the reference to an Event grounds a Truth-process. For all three of them, the Event is irreducible to the order of being (in the sense of positive reality), to the set of its material (pre)conditions. For Heidegger, the Event is the ultimate horizon of thought, and it is meaningless to try to think 'behind' it and to render thematic the process that generated it – such an attempt equals an ontic account of the ontological horizon; for Deleuze, one cannot reduce the emergence of a new artistic form (*film noir*, Italian neo-realism and others) to its historical circumstances, or account for it in these terms; for Badiou, a Truth-event is totally hetero-geneous with regard to the order of Being (positive reality). Although, in all three cases, Event stands for historicity proper (the explosion of the New) versus historicism, differences between the three philosophers are crucial, of course. For Heidegger, Event has nothing to do with ontic processes; it designates the 'event' of a new epochal disclosure of Being, the emergence of a new 'world' (as the horizon of meaning within which all entities appear). Deleuze is a vitalist, insisting on the absolute imma-nence of the Event to the order of Being, conceiving Event as the One–All of the proliferating differences of Life. Badiou, on the contrary, asserts the radical 'dualism' between Event and the order of Being. It is here, in this terrain, that one should locate today's struggle between idealism and materialism: idealism posits an ideal Event which cannot be accounted for in the terms of its material (pre)conditions, while the materialist wager is that one CAN get 'behind' the event and explore how Event explodes out of the gap in/of the order of Being. The first to formulate this unheard-of task was Friedrich Schelling, who, in his *Weltalter* fragments, outlined the dark territory of the 'pre-history of *logos*', of what had to occur in the pre-ontological proto-reality so that the openness of logos and temporality could take place. With regard to Heidegger, one should risk a step behind the Event, naming/outlining the cut, the terrifying seizure/contraction, which enables any ontological disclosure.[1] The problem with Heidegger is not only (as John Caputo argues) that he dismisses ontic pain with regard to ontological essence, but that he dismisses the proper (pre)ontological pain of the Real ('symbolic castration').

Is the ontology of cartoons not that of pure becoming in Deleuze's precise sense of the term? Cartoons take place in a universe of radical plasticity, in which all entities are deprived of all substance and reduced to pure surface. They literally possess no depth, there is nothing beneath their surface skin, no meat, bones and blood inside, which is why they all act and react like balloons – they can be blown up; when they are pricked by a needle, they lose air and shrink like an exploded balloon. Recall the nightmarish fantasy of triggering by mistake a trickle which then never stops: in *Alice in Wonderland*, when Alice starts to cry, her tears gradually flood the entire room; Freud reports in his *Interpretation of Dreams* the scene of a small child who starts to urinate on the edge of a street, and his flow grows into a river and then an ocean with a large ship; and, closer to our ordinary daily experience, when witnessing torrential rainfall, who among us does not get the 'irrational' fear that the rain will simply never stop? What happens in such moments of anxiety is that the flow of becoming acquires autonomy, loses its mooring in substantial reality.

The Quasi-autonomy of Appearances

What is even more crucial is that this insight into the autonomy of the phenomena enables us to approach in a new way the classic 'demystifiers' themselves. What we find in Marx is not only the 'reduction' of ideology to economic base and, within this base, of exchange to production, but a much more ambiguous and mysterious phenomenon of 'commodity fetishism', which designates a kind of proto-'ideology' inherent in the reality of 'economic base' itself. Freud accomplishes a strictly homologous breakthrough with regard to the paradoxical status of fantasy: the ontological paradox, scandal even, of the notion of fantasy resides in the fact that it subverts the standard opposition of 'subjective' and 'objective'. Of course, fantasy is by definition not 'objective' (in the naïve sense of 'existing independently of the subject's perceptions'); however, it is also not 'subjective' (in the sense of being reducible to the subject's consciously experienced intuitions). Fantasy belongs, rather, to the 'bizarre category of the objectively subjective – the way things actually, objectively seem to you even if they don't seem that way to you' (as Daniel Dennett put it in his acerbic, critical remark against the notion of qualia). When, for example, we claim that someone who is consciously well disposed towards Jews nonetheless harbours profound anti-Semitic prejudices that he is not consciously aware of, do we not claim that (insofar as these prejudices do not render the way Jews really are, but the way they appear to him) he is not aware how Jews really seem to him?

Apropos commodity fetishism, Marx himself used the term 'objectively-necessary appearance'. So, when a critical Marxist encounters a bourgeois subject immersed in commodity fetishism, the Marxist's reproach to him is not: 'Commodity may seem to you a magical object endowed with special powers, but it really is just a reified expression of relations between people'. The actual Marxist's reproach is, rather, 'You may think that the commodity appears to you as a simple embodiment of social relations (that, for example, money is just a kind of voucher entitling you to a part of the social product), but this is not how things really seem to you; in your social reality, by means of your participation in social exchange, you bear witness to the uncanny fact that a commodity really appears to you as a magical object endowed with special powers.' This difference between the two appearances (the way things really appear to us rather than the way they appear to appear to us) is linked to the structure of the well-known Freudian joke about a Jew who complains to his friend, 'Why are you telling me you are going to Lemberg when you are really going to Lemberg?' Say, in the case of commodity fetishism, when I immediately perceive money as just a knot of social relations, not any kind of magic object, and I treat it like a fetish only in my practice, so that the site of fetishism is my actual social practice, I could effectively be reproached: 'Why are you saying that money is just a knot of social relations, when money really IS just a knot of social relations?' Jean Laplanche wrote about the hysteric's 'primordial lie' which articulates the original fantasy: '…the term "*proton pseudos*" aims at something different from a subjective lie; it renders a kind of passage from the subjective to the founding, even, one could say, to the transcendental; in any case, a kind of objective lie, inscribed into the facts'.[2] Is this not also the status of the Marxian commodity fetishism? – not simply a subjective illusion, but an 'objective' illusion, an illusion inscribed into facts (social reality) themselves? Let us read carefully the famous first sentence of chapter one of *Capital*: 'A commodity appears, at *first sight*, a very trivial thing, and easily understood. Its analysis shows that it is, *in reality*, a very queer thing, abounding in metaphysical subtleties and theological niceties.'[3]

Kojin Karatani[4] is right to link this passage to the starting point of the Marxian critique, the famous lines from 1843 about how 'the criticism of religion is the premise of all criticism'.[5] With it, the circle is in a way closed upon itself – that is to say, at the very bottom of the critique of actual life (of the economic process), we again encounter the theological dimension inscribed into social REALITY itself. Karatani refers here to the Freudian notion of 'drive' (*Trieb*), as opposed to the multitude of human desires: capitalism is grounded in the Real of a certain quasi-theological impersonal 'drive', the drive to reproduce and grow, to expand and accumulate profit.[6]

This is also one of the ways of specifying the meaning of Jacques Lacan's assertion of the subject's constitutive 'decentrement': its point is not that my subjective experience is regulated by objective unconscious mechanisms that are 'decentred' with regard to my self-experience and, as such, beyond my control (a point asserted by every materialist), but rather something much more unsettling. I am deprived of even my most intimate 'subjective' experience, the way things 'really seem to me', that of the fundamental fantasy that constitutes and guarantees the core of my being, since I can never consciously experience it and assume it... According to the standard view, the dimension that is constitutive of subjectivity is that of the phenomenal (self)experience. I am a subject the moment I can say to myself: 'No matter what unknown mechanism governs my acts, perceptions and thoughts, nobody can take from me what I see and feel now'. Say, when I am passionately in love, and a biochemist informs me that all my intense sentiments are just the result of biochemical processes in my body, I can answer him by clinging to the appearance: 'All that you're saying may be true, but, nonetheless, nothing can take from me the intensity of the passion that I am experiencing now...' Lacan's point, however, is that the psychoanalyst is the one who, precisely, CAN take this from the subject – i.e. his ultimate aim is to deprive the subject of the very fundamental fantasy that regulates the universe of his (self)experience. The Freudian 'subject of the Unconscious' emerges only when a key aspect of the subject's phenomenal (self)experience (his 'fundamental fantasy') becomes inaccessible to him, is 'primordially repressed'. At its most radical, the Unconscious is the inaccessible phenomenon, not the objective mechanism that regulates my phenomenal experience. So, in contrast to the commonplace that we are dealing with as a subject the moment an entity displays signs of 'inner life' (of a fantasmatic self-experience that cannot be reduced to external behaviour), one should claim that what characterises human subjectivity proper is, rather, the gap that separates the two, the fact that fantasy, at its most elementary, becomes inaccessible to the subject. It is this inaccessibility that makes the subject 'empty'. We thus obtain a relationship that totally subverts the standard notion of the subject who directly experiences himself, his 'inner states': an 'impossible' relationship between the empty, non-phenomenal subject and the phenomena that remain inaccessible to the subject. When David Chalmers opposes phenomenal and psychological concepts of mind (conscious awareness/experience and what mind effectively does), he quotes the Freudian unconscious as the exemplary case of psychological mind external to phenomenal mind: what Freud describes as the work of the unconscious is a complex network of mental causality and behavioural control which takes place 'on the other scene', without being experienced.[7] However, is it really like that? Is not the status of the unconscious fantasy nonetheless, in an unheard-of sense, PHENOMENAL? Is not THIS the ultimate paradox of the Freudian unconscious – that it designates the way things 'really appear' to us, beyond their conscious appearance? Far from being overrun by the later brain sciences' decentrement, the Freudian decentrement is thus much more unsettling and radical. The later one remains within the confines of a simple naturalisation: it opens up a new domain of weird 'asubjective phenomena', of appearances with no subject to whom they can appear – it is only here that the subject is 'no longer a master in his own house' – in the very house of his (self)appearances themselves.

And even the evolution of 'hard' sciences in the twentieth century generated the same paradox: in quantum physics, the 'appearance' (perception) of a particle determines its reality. The very emergence of 'hard reality' out of the fluctuation through the collapse of the wave function is the outcome of observation – that is to say, of the intervention of consciousness. Consciousness is thus not the domain of potentiality, multiple options and so on, opposed to hard, single reality; reality prior to its perception is fluid-multiple-open, and conscious perception reduces this spectral, pre-ontological multiplicity to one ontologically fully constituted reality. This gives us the way that quantum physics conceives of the relationship between particles and their interactions. In an initial moment, it appears as if, first (ontologically, at least), there are particles interacting in the mode of waves, oscillations and so on; then, in a second moment, we are forced to enact a radical shift of perspective: the primordial ontological fact is the waves themselves (trajectories, oscillations) and particles are nothing but the nodal points in which different waves intersect.

Consequently, quantum physics confronts us with the gap between the Real and reality at its most radical: what we get in it is the mathematised Real of formulas which cannot be translated into ontologically consistent reality, or, to put it in Kantian terms, they remain pure concepts which cannot be 'schematised', translated/transposed into objects of experience. This is also how, after the crisis of the 1920s, quantum physics in practice resolved the crisis of its ontological interpretation: by renouncing the very effort to provide such an interpretation. Quantum physics is scientific formalisation at its most radical – formalisation without interpretation. Is it, then, not accurate to say that quantum physics involves a kind of reversal of the Kantian transcendental ontology?[8] In Kant, we have access to ordinary experiential reality, while the moment we try to apply our transcendental categories to the numenal

Real itself, we get involved in contradictions; in quantum physics, it is the numenal Real which can be grasped and formulated in a consistent theory, while the moment we try to translate this theory into the terms of our experience of phenomenal reality, we get involved in senseless contradictions (time runs backwards, the same object is at two places simultaneously, an entity is both a particle and a wave). (However, it can still be claimed that these contradictions emerge only when we try to transpose into our experiential reality the 'Real' of the quantum processes; in itself, this reality remains the same as before: a consistent realm with which we are well acquainted.)

So not only is appearance inherent in reality; what we get beyond this is a weird split in appearance itself, an unheard-of mode designating 'the way things really appear to us' as opposed to both their reality and their (direct) appearance to us. This shift from the split between appearance and reality to the split, inherent in appearance itself, between 'true' and 'false' appearance is to be linked to its obverse, to a split inherent in reality itself. If, then, there is appearance (as distinct from reality) because there is a (logically) prior split inherent in reality itself, is it also that 'reality' itself is ultimately nothing but a (self-)split of the appearance?

Resistances to Disenchantment

Today's achievements of the brain sciences seem to fulfil the prospect envisaged by Freud of science supplanting psychoanalysis: once the biological mechanisms of pain, pleasure, trauma, repression and so on are known, psychoanalysis will no longer be needed, since, instead of intervening at the level of interpretation, one will be able to regulate directly the biological processes that generate pathological psychic phenomena. Hitherto there were two ways psychoanalysts replied to this challenge.

1. They took recourse in the standard philosophico-transcendental gesture of pointing out how a positive science can never encompass and account for the very horizon of meaning within which it is operative ('even if brain sciences will succeed in totally objectivising a symptom, formulating its bioneuronal equivalent, the patient will still have to adopt a subjective stance towards this objectivity...'). In his debate with Etchegoyan, even Jacques-Alain Miller had recourse to this move: when science fully objectivises our thought, achieving the goal of translating mental processes into their neuronal counterparts, the subject will still have to subjectivise this fact, assume it, integrate it into his/her universe of meaning – and this excess of symbolic integration, what this discovery will 'mean to us and for us', escapes science... However,

this self-complacent answer is all too short: the success of the brain sciences, if really subjectively assumed, would undermine our very status as subjects of meaning. (Its *mauvaise foi* is already clear from the oscillation of the critics of brain sciences between two extremes. As a rule they combine the quick 'transcendental' answer ('science a priori cannot objectivise our subjective attitude towards objectivity') with empirical arguments against – and rejoicing in – the specific failures of scientific accounts of the brain: this very form of specific argumentation is meaningful only against the background of its possible success.)

2. They clung desperately to the parallels or structural homologies between psychoanalysis and brain sciences ('see, we were right, there is a neuronal process that corresponds to repression').

Both these approaches – which supplement each other in their two respective excesses, the first with its abstract arrogance, the second with its subservient modesty – fall short of the challenge of the brain sciences: the only proper reply to this challenge is to meet the brain sciences' neuronal Real with another Real, not only to ground the Freudian *semblant* within the neuronal Real. In other words, if psychoanalysis is to survive and retain its key status, one has to find a place for it within the brain sciences themselves, from their inherent blanks and impossibilities. However, within the cognitive sciences themselves, things are no less confused when one tries to account for the emergence of consciousness – whence consciousness? The surprising thing is how 'everything goes', all possible answers co-exist, from dismissing the question as meaningless through evolutionist accounts of it up to declaring it an insoluble mystery and proposing that consciousness has no (evolutionary) function at all, that it is a by-product – not a central phenomenon, but an epiphenomenon. What strikes the eye is how evolutionist or cognitivist accounts always seem to end up in the same deadlock: after we construct an artificial intelligence machine which can solve even very complex problems, the question pops up: 'But it can do it precisely as a machine, as a blind operating entity – why does it need (self)awareness to do it?' So the more consciousness is demonstrated to be marginal, unnecessary, non-functional, the more it becomes enigmatic – it is consciousness itself which is here the Real of an indivisible remainder. Generally, this multitude can be reduced to four main positions.

1. Radical/reductive materialism (Patricia and Paul Churchland): there simply are no qualia, there is no 'consciousness', they exist only as a kind of 'naturalised' cognitive mistake. The anti-intuitional beauty of this position is that it turns subjectivist phenomenalism around (we are only aware of phenomena, there is no absolute certainty that anything beyond them exists); here, it is pure phenomenality itself that does not exist!

2. Anti-materialism (Chalmers): consciousness-awareness cannot be accounted for in terms of other natural processes, it has to be conceived of as a primordial dimension of nature, like gravity or magnetism.

3. The position of 'cognitive closure', which asserts the inherent unknowability of consciousness (Colin McGinn, even Steven Pinker): although consciousness emerged out of material reality, it is necessarily unknowable.

4. Non-reductive materialism (Dennett): consciousness exists, but it is the result of natural processes and has a clear evolutionary function.

These four positions obviously form a Greimasian semiotic square: the main opposition is the one between 2 and 4, idealism and materialism; 1 and 3 each give to materialism or idealism a cognitive twist. That is to say, both 2 and 4 believe in the possibility of the scientific explanation of consciousness: there is an object ('consciousness') and its explanation, either accounting for it in terms of non-conscious natural processes (materialism) or conceiving of it as an irreducible dimension of its own (idealism). For 1, however, the scientific explanation of consciousness leads to the result that the object-to-be-explained itself does not exist, that it is an epistemological mistake like old notions of phlogiston; 3 inverts this position: what disappears here is not the object but explanation itself (although materialism is true, it a priori cannot explain consciousness).

Perhaps the problem of consciousness should be formulated in Badiou's terms: what if the emergence of THOUGHT is the ultimate Event? Does the zombie problem (how to differentiate a zombie who acts like a human from a 'real' human with inner life?) not directly point to the INDISCERNIBILITY of the emergence of consciousness – that there are no 'objective' criteria enabling us to differentiate a zombie from a 'real' human, and that this difference can be perceived only FROM WITHIN, from the standpoint of a conscious subject? In Kierkegaard's terms, the problem is here to grasp 'mind-in-becoming': not the already constituted mind opposed to bodily reality, but the way mind is 'for the body' – that is to say, the break (the vanishing mediator) as such.

It is a standard philosophical observation that one should distinguish between knowing a phenomenon and acknowledging it, accepting it, treating it as existing – we do not 'really know' if other people around us have minds or are just robots programmed to act blindly. However, this observation misses the point: if I were to 'really know' the mind of my interlocutor, intersubjectivity proper would disappear, they would lose their subjective status and turn – for me – into a transparent machine. In other words, not-being-knowable to others is a crucial feature of subjectivity, of what we mean when we impute to our interlocutors a 'mind': you only 'truly have a mind' insofar as this is opaque to me.

These cognitivist impasses bear witness to the fact that today's sciences shatter the basic presuppositions of our everyday life-world notion of reality. There are three main attitudes one can adopt towards this breakthrough. The first is simply to insist on radical naturalism – to pursue heroically the logic of the scientific 'disenchantment of reality' whatever the cost, even if the very fundamental coordinates of our horizon of meaningful experience are shattered. (In the brain sciences, Patricia and Paul Churchland most radically opted for this attitude.) The second attitude is the attempt at some kind of New Age 'synthesis' between the scientific Truth and the pre-modern world of Meaning: the claim is that new scientific results themselves (say, quantum physics) compel us to abandon materialism and point towards some new (gnostic or Eastern) spirituality. The third option is that of a neo-Kantian state philosophy, whose exemplary representative today is Jürgen Habermas. It is a rather sad spectacle to see Habermas trying to control the explosive results of biogenetics, to curtail the philosophical consequences of biogenetics; his entire effort betrays the fear that something may effectively happen, that a new dimension of the 'human' would emerge, that the old image of human dignity and autonomy would survive unscathed. The excessive reactions are symptomatic here, such as the ridiculous overreaction to Sloterdijk's Elmau speech on biogenetics and Heidegger, discerning echoes of the Nazi eugenics in his (quite reasonable) proposal that biogenetics compels us to formulate new rules of ethics. What this attitude towards scientific progress amounts to is a kind of 'temptation of (resisting) temptation': the temptation to be resisted is precisely the pseudo-ethical attitude of presenting scientific exploration as a temptation which can lead us into 'going too far' – entering the forbidden territory (of biogenetic manipulations, amongst other things) and thus endangering the very core of our humanity.

The latest ethical 'crisis' apropos biogenetics effectively created the need for what one is fully justified in calling a 'state philosophy': a philosophy that would, on the one hand, condone scientific research and technical process, and, on the other hand, contain its full socio-symbolic impact – that is to say, prevent it from posing a threat to the existing theologico-ethical constellation. No wonder those who come closest to meeting these demands are neo-Kantians: Kant himself was focused on the problem of how to guarantee, while fully taking into account Newtonian science, that there is a space of ethical responsibility exempted from the reach of science. As he himself put it, he limited the scope of knowledge in order to create the space for faith and morality. And are today's state philosophers not facing the same task? Is their effort not focused on how, through different versions of transcendental reflection, to restrict science to its preordained horizon of meaning and thus to denounce as 'illegitimate' its consequences for the ethico-religious sphere? It is interesting to note how, although Sloterdijk was the target of a violent Habermasian attack, his proposed solution, a 'humanist' synthesis of the new scientific Truth and the old horizon of Meaning, although much more refined and ironically sceptical than the Habermasian 'state philosophy', is ultimately separated from it by an almost invisible line of separation (more precisely, it seems to persist in the ambiguity between the Habermasian compromise and the New Age obscurantist synthesis). According to Sloterdijk, 'humanism' always involves such a reconciliation, a bridge between the New and the Old: when scientific results undermine the old universe of meaning, one should find a way to reintegrate them into the universe of Meaning – or, rather, to meta-phorically expand the old universe of Meaning so that it can 'cover' new scientific propositions as well. If we fail in this mediating task, we remain stuck in the brutal choice: either a reactionary refusal to accept scientific results, or the shattering loss of the very domain of meaning. Today, we confront the same challenge: 'Mathematicians will have to become poets, cyberneticists, philosophers of religion, [medical] doctors, composers, information-workers, shamans'.[9] Is this solution, however, not that of *obscurantism*, in the precise sense, in the attempt to keep meaning and truth harnessed together?

> the simplest definition of God and of religion lies in the idea that truth and meaning are one and the same thing. The death of God is the end of the idea that posits truth and meaning as the same thing. And I would add that the death of Communism also implies the separation between meaning and truth as far as history is concerned. 'The meaning of history' has two meanings: on the one hand 'orientation', history goes somewhere; and then history has a meaning, which is the history of human emancipation by way of the proletariat, etc. In fact, the entire age of Communism was a period where the conviction that it was possible to take rightful political decisions existed; we were, at that moment, driven by the meaning of history [....] Then the death of Communism becomes the second death of God but in the territory of history. There is a connection between the two events and the consequence is, so to speak, that we should be aware that to produce truthful effects that are primarily local (be them psychoanalytical, scientific, etc.) is always an effect of local truth, never of global truth. [...] Today we may call 'obscurantism' the intention of keeping them harnessed together – meaning and truth.[10]

Badiou is right here in emphasising the gap between meaning and truth – the non-hermeneutic status of truth – as the minimal difference that separates religious idealism from materialism. This is also the difference between Freud and Jung: while Jung remains within the horizon of meaning, Freudian interpretation aims at articulating a truth which is no longer grounded in meaning. Badiou is also right in formulating the ultimate alternative that confronts us today, when the impossibility of the conjunction of meaning and truth is imposed on us: either we endorse the 'postmodern' stance and renounce altogether the dimension of truth, constraining ourselves to the interplay of multiple meanings, or we engage in the effort to discern a dimension of truth outside meaning – in short, the dimension of truth as REAL.

However, what rings false is the parallel between the death of God and the death of Communism, implicitly referring to the boring old anti-Communist cliché of Communism being a 'secular religion'; and linked to this falsity is also the all-too-quick acceptance of the 'postmodern' notion that, in today's politics, we are limited to 'local' truths, since, without a grounding in global meaning, it is no longer possible to formulate an all-encompassing truth. The fact that renders this conclusion problematic is the very fact of capitalist globalisation. Of course, the predominant religious strategy today is that of trying to contain the scientific real within the confines of meaning – it is as an answer to the scientific real (materialised in the biogenetic threats) that religion is finding its new *raison d'être*.

> Far from being effaced by science, religion, and even the syndicate of religions, in the process of formation, is progressing every day. Lacan said that ecumenism was for the poor of spirit. There is a marvelous agreement on these questions between the secular and all the religious authorities, in which they tell themselves they should agree somewhere in order to make echoes equally marvelous, even saying that finally the secular is a religion like the others. We see this because it is revealed in effect that the discourse of science has partly connected with the death drive. Religion is planted in the position of unconditional defense of the living, of life in mankind, as guardian of life, making life an absolute. And that extends to the protection of human nature. [...] This is ... what gives a future to religion through meaning, namely by erecting barriers – to cloning, to the exploitation of human cells – and to inscribe science in a tempered progress. We see a marvelous effort, a new youthful vigor of religion in its effort to flood the real with meaning.[11]

This simple, but salient, diagnosis ends up in a surprising paraphrase of Heidegger, defining the analyst as the 'shepherd of the real'. However, it leaves some key questions open. Is the death-drive for which science stands, which it mobilises in its activity, not simultaneously an EXCESS OF OBSCENE LIFE, of life as real, exempted from and external to meaning (life that we find embodied in Franz Kafka's 'odradek' as well as in the 'alien' from the film of the same name)? One should not forget that death-drive is a Freudian name for immortality, for a pressure, a compulsion, that insists beyond death (and let us also not forget that immortality is also implicitly promised by science). One should therefore also assert a gap between life and meaning, homologous to that between truth and meaning; life and meaning in no way fully overlap. Furthermore, can all religious experiences and practices themselves effectively be contained within the dimension of the conjunction of truth and meaning? Does not Judaism, with its imposition of a traumatic Law, point towards a dimension of truth outside meaning (which is why Judaism is the mortal enemy of any Gnostic obscurantism)? And does not, at a different level, the same go for the early Christian Paul himself?[12]

The Real of Politics

This is why Badiou has recently started to elaborate the 'logic of worlds': the impetus came from his deeper insight into capitalism; the concept of 'world' was necessitated by the need to think the unique status of the capitalist universe as 'world-less'. Badiou recently claimed that our time is *devoid of world* – how are we to grasp this strange thesis?[13] The problem with today's superego injunction to enjoy is that, in contrast to previous modes of ideological interpellation, it opens up no 'world' proper – it just refers to an obscure Unnameable. Even Nazi anti-Semitism opened up a world: by way of describing the present critical situation, naming the enemy (the 'Jewish conspiracy') and specifying the goal and the means to achieve it, Nazism disclosed reality in a way which allowed its subjects to acquire a global 'cognitive mapping', inclusive of the space for their meaningful engagement. Arguably, it is here that one should locate the 'danger' of capitalism: although it is global, encompassing the whole world, it sustains a *stricto sensu* 'worldless' ideological constellation, depriving the large majority of people of any meaningful 'cognitive mapping'. The universality of capitalism resides in the fact that capitalism is not a name for a 'civilisation', for a specific cultural-symbolic world, but the name for a truly neutral economico-symbolic machine, which operates with Asian values as well as with others, so that Europe's worldwide triumph is its defeat, its self-obliteration, the cutting of the umbilical link to Europe. The critics of 'Eurocentrism' who endeavour to unearth the secret European bias of capitalism fall short here: the problem with capitalism is not its secret Eurocentric bias, but the fact that it REALLY IS UNIVERSAL, a neutral matrix of social relations – a REAL, in Lacanian terms. (Of course, to avoid misunderstanding, this does not mean that the entire empirical reality of capitalism is 'real' – what is 'real' is the underlying matrix of its functioning, its 'matheme'.)

What is capitalist globalisation? Capitalism is the first socio-economic order which *de-totalises meaning*: it is not global at the level of meaning (there is no global 'capitalist world-view', no 'capitalist civilisation' proper – the fundamental lesson of globalisation is precisely that capitalism can accommodate itself to all civilisations, from Christian to Hindu to Buddhist); its global dimension can be formulated only at the level of truth-without-meaning, as the 'real' of the global market mechanism. Consequently, insofar as capitalism already enacts the rupture between meaning and truth, it can be opposed at two levels: either at the level of meaning (conservative reactions to re-enframe capitalism into some social field of meaning, to contain its self-propelling movement within the confines of a system of shared 'values' which cement a 'community' in its 'organic unity'), or to question the real of capitalism with regard to its truth-outside-meaning (what, basically, Marx did). Badiou, of course, is here referring to Marx's well-known passage from *The Communist Manifesto* about the 'de-territorialising' force of capitalism which dissolves all fixed social forms:

> The passage where Marx speaks of the desacralisation of all sacred bonds in the icy waters of capitalism has an enthusiastic tone; it is Marx's enthusiasm for the dissolving power of Capital. The fact that Capital revealed itself to be the material power capable of disencumbering us of the 'superego' figures of the One and the sacred bonds that accompany it effectively represents its positively progressive character, and it is something that continues to unfold to the present day. Having said that, the generalized atomism, the recurrent individualism and, finally, the abasement of thought into mere practices of administration, of the government of things or of technical manipulation, could never satisfy me as a philosopher. I simply think that it is in the very element of desacralisation that we must reconnect to the vocation of thinking.[14]

Badiou thus recognises the exceptional *ontological* status of capitalism, whose dynamics undermines every stable frame of re-presentation; what is usually the task to be performed by the critico-political activity (namely, the task of undermining the re-presentational frame of the state) is already performed by capitalism itself. This poses a problem for Badiou's notion of 'evental' politics. In pre-capitalist formations, every state, every re-presentational totalisation, implies a founding exclusion, a point of 'symptomal torsion', a 'part of no-part', an element which, although part of the system, did not have a proper place within it – and the emancipatory politics had to intervene from this excessive ('surnumerary') element which, although part of the situation, cannot be *accounted for* in its terms. However, what happens when the system no longer excludes the excess, but directly posits it as its driving force – as is the case in capitalism, which can reproduce itself only through its constant self-revolutionising, through the constant overcoming of its own limit? To put it in a simplified way: if a political event, a revolutionary emanci-patory intervention into a determinate historical world, is always linked to the excessive point of its 'symptomal torsion', if it by definition undermines the contours of this world, how, then, are we to define the emancipatory political intervention into a universe which is already in itself world-less, which, for its reproduction, no longer needs to be contained by the constraints of a 'world'? As Alberto Toscano has noted in his perspicuous analysis, Badiou gets caught here in an inconsistency: he draws the 'logical' conclusion that, in a 'worldless' universe (which is today's universe of global capitalism), the aim of emancipatory politics should be the precise opposite of its 'traditional' modus operandi – the task today is to form a new world, to propose new Master-Signifiers to provide 'cognitive mapping'.

> … whilst in Badiou's theoretical writings on the appearance of worlds he cogently argues that events engender the *dysfunction* of worlds and their transcendental regimes, in his 'ontology of the present' Badiou advocates the necessity, in our 'intervallic' or world-less times, of *constructing* a world, such that those now excluded can come to invent new names, names capable of sustaining new truth procedures. As he writes, 'I hold that we are at a very special moment, a moment *at which there is not any world*' [...] As a result: 'Philosophy has no other legitimate aim except to help find the new names that will bring into existence the unknown world that is only waiting for us because we are waiting for it.' In a peculiar inversion of some of the key traits of his doctrine, it seems that Badiou is here advocating, to some extent, an 'ordering' task, one that will inevitably, if perhaps mistakenly, resonate for some with the now ubiquitous slogan 'Another World is Possible'.[15]

And the same problem arises apropos truth: if, for Badiou, the truth-event is always local, the truth of a determinate historical world, how are we to formulate the truth of a world-less universe? Is this the reason why, as Toscano seems to indicate, Badiou, in spite of his acknow-ledgement of the 'ontological' break introduced by capitalism, avoids the topic of anti-capitalist struggle, even ridiculing its main form today (the anti-globalisation movement), and continues to define the emancipatory struggle in strictly political terms, as the struggle against (liberal) demo-cracy as today's predominant ideologico-political form? 'Today the enemy is not called Empire or Capital. It's called Democracy.' Toscano's critique of Badiou at this point nonetheless falls short:

> In this respect, we disagree with Badiou's strong claim … This is emphatically not because we think that Badiou's attack on the fetishism of democracy is problematic, but rather because we contend that – despite chattering battalions of smug idolaters and renegade ideologues

– Badiou overestimates the inhibiting force, as an 'ideological, or subjective, formalisation,' of the liberal-democratic notion of equality. It is not the principle of democratic representation that hampers the political emancipation of subjects, but rather the deep-seated conviction that there is no alternative to the rule of profit. The cynicism of today's 'democratic' subjects, who know full well that they play a negligible role in the management of the commons and are entirely aware of the sham nature of the apparatuses of representation, is founded on the perceived inevitability of capitalism, not *vice versa*.[16]

What one should add here, in defence of Badiou, is that it is not specifically 'the deep-seated conviction that there is no alternative to the rule of profit' which 'hampers the political emancipation of subjects'; what prevents the radical questioning of capitalism itself is precisely *the belief in the democratic form of the struggle against capitalism*. Here, Lenin's stance against 'economism' as well as against 'pure' politics is crucial today, apropos the split attitude towards economy in (what remains of) the Left: on the one hand, the 'pure politicians', who abandon economy as the site of struggle and intervention; on the other hand, the economists, fascinated by the functioning of today's global economy, who preclude any possibility of a political intervention proper. Today, more than ever, we should here return to Lenin: yes, economy is the key domain, the battle will be decided there, one has to break the spell of the global capitalism – BUT the intervention should be properly POLITICAL, not economic. Today, when everyone is 'anti-capitalist', up to the Hollywood 'socio-critical' conspiracy movies (from *The Enemy of the State* to *The Insider*) in which 'the enemy' is the big corporations with their ruthless pursuit of profit, the signifier 'anti-capitalism' has lost its subversive sting. What one should problematise is rather the self-evident opposite of this 'anti-capitalism': trust in the democratic substance of the honest Americans to break up the conspiracy. THIS is the hard kernel of today's global capitalist universe, its true Master-Signifier: democracy. And are the latest statements of Antonio Negri and Michael Hardt not a kind of unexpected confirmation of Badiou's insight? Following a paradoxical necessity, their very (focusing on) anti-capitalism led them to acknowledge the revolutionary force of capitalism, so that, as they put it recently, one no longer needs to fight capitalism, because capitalism is already in itself generating communist potentials – the 'becoming-communist of capitalism', to put it in Deleuzian terms…

What we are dealing with here is another version of the Lacanian '*il n'y a pas de rapport*…': if, for Lacan, there is no sexual relationship, then, for Marxism proper, there is *no relationship between economy and politics*, no 'meta-language' enabling us to grasp from the same neutral standpoint the two levels, although – or, rather, BECAUSE – these two levels are inextricably intertwined. The 'political' class struggle takes place in the midst of economy (recall that the very last paragraph of *Capital*, volume III, where the texts abruptly stops, tackles the class struggle), while, at the same time, the domain of economy serves as the key enabling us to decode political struggles. No wonder that the structure of this impossible relationship is that of the Möbius strip: first, we have to progress from the political spectacle to its economic infrastructure; then, in the second step, we have to confront the irreducible dimension of the political struggle in the very heart of the economy.

It is this parallax that also accounts for the two irreducible dimensions of modernity: 'political' is the logic of domination, of regulative control ('biopolitics', 'administered world'); 'economic' is the logic of the incessant integration of the surplus, of constant 'deterritorialisation'. The resistance to the political domination refers to the 'surnumerary' element which cannot be accounted for in terms of the political order – but how are we to formulate resistance to the economic logic of reproduction-through-excess? (And, let us not forget, this excess is strictly correlative to the excess of power itself over its 'official' representative function.) The Leftist dream throughout the twentieth century was: through the subordination of the economic to the political (state control of the process of production). In their last works, Negri and Hardt seem to succumb to the opposite temptation, to shifting the focus on economic struggle, in which one can rely on the state.

And therein resides the deadlock of Badiou's politics, after he proclaimed the end of the Jacobinian revolutionary paradigm: while he is aware that the anti-statist revolutionary party politics which aimed at taking over and demolishing the state apparatus is exhausted, he refuses to explore the revolutionary potentials of the 'economic' sphere (since, for him, this sphere belongs to the order of Being and does not contain potential 'evental sites'); for this reason, the only way left is that of a 'pure' political organisation which operates outside the constraints of the state and, basically, limits itself to mobilisatory declarations… The only way out of this deadlock is to *restore to the 'economic' domain the dignity of Truth*, the potential for Events.

Notes on the Text

Notes on Introduction

1   Susan Greenfield, *Tomorrow's People: How 21st-century technology is changing the way we think and feel* (London: Penguin, 2003).

2   Ibid., p.15.

3   John Russell, *Geniess*, Norwich Gallery, Norwich, 21 April–28 May 2005, publicity brochure.

4   J.L. Austin, *Sense and Sensibilia*, ed. by G.J. Warnock (London: Oxford University Press, 1962 and 1964).

5   A.J. Ayer, *The Foundations of Empirical Knowledge* (London: Macmillan, 1940).

6   Austin, *Sense and Sensibilia*, p.68.

7   Ibid., p.70.

8   Ibid.

9   A particularly interesting case is offered by the adverbial form, 'really'. When we ask: 'Did you *really* shoot that tiger?' we are inviting a simple confirmation that we are not being lied to. This is very different from Slavoj Žižek's use of the word when he distinguishes between the claim that we know something and the claim that we 'really know' it (p.190). The latter suggests a form of knowledge that is definitive, conclusive, in some crucial sense *terminal*. Apart from analytical statements, can there be such knowledge?

10 Elizabeth C. Holt, ed., *A Documentary History of Art*, vol.1, *The Middle Ages & the Renaissance* (New York: Doubleday, 1957), p.172.

11 For the full text of Manetti's account, see ibid., pp.170–173.

12 Leon Battista Alberti, *Della pittura* (MS, Florence, 1435–1436). See John R. Spencer, ed. and trans., *Leon Battista Alberti on Painting* (New Haven, CT, and London: Yale University Press, 1956, rev. and repr. 1970).

13 Spencer, *Leon Battista Alberti on Painting*, p.40.

14 Ibid., p.56.

15 This panel is sometimes attributed to Piero della Francesca. Interestingly, an acrylic reconstruction of 'the Urbino panel', entitled *Footfalls echo in the memory down the passage we did not take towards the door we never opened*, was produced by the contemporary photo-realist painter Ben Johnson in 1993. See: http://www.benjohnsonartist.com/benjohnsonartist.htm [10 July 2005].

16 G.H. Lewes, 1858, quoted in Andrea Rose, *The Pre-Raphaelites* (Oxford: Phaidon, 1981), p.10.

17 Henry D. Thoreau, quoted in John Updike, 'A sage for all seasons', *The Guardian*, 'G2' supplement, 26 June 2004, p.6.

18 Tim Barringer, 'Rethinking Delaroche/Recovering Leighton', *Victorian Studies*, vol.44, no.1 (2001). Available online. URL: http://iupjournals.org/victorian/vic44-1.html [16 June 2005].

19 André Bazin, 'The Ontology of the Photographic Image', in André Bazin, *What is Cinema?*, vol.1, trans. by Hugh Grey (Berkeley, CA: University of California Press, 1967), pp.9–16.

20 'Bertillonage' (named after its inventor, Alphonse Bertillon) was a French method of making criminal records using photography to record measurements of the criminal body, thus providing a relatively foolproof archival record to be used in early profiling and identification. It was developed in the 1880s. See Allan Sekula, 'The Body and the Archive', in *The Contest of Meaning*, ed. by Roger Bolton (Cambridge, MA: MIT Press, 1989), pp.343–389.

21 Roland Barthes, *Camera Lucida: Reflections on photography* [1980], trans. by Richard Howard, 3rd edn. (London: Vintage, 1993), p.115.

22 Lewis Hine, 'Social Photography' [1920], in *Classic Essays on Photography*, ed. by Alan Trachtenberg (New Haven, CT: Leete's Island, 1980), pp.109–113 (p.111).

23 A good example of a critical analysis of the role of photography, in terms of optics, chemistry and physics, in being an unacknowledged manipulation of vision can be found in Joel Snyder and Neil Walsh Allen, 'Photography, Vision and Representation', *Critical Inquiry* vol.2, no.1 (1975), pp.143–169.

24 See, for example, the exhibition catalogue and anthology *Photography After Photography: Memory and representation in the digital age*, ed. by Hubertus von Amelunxen, Stefan Iglhaut and Florian Rotzer (Munich: G&B Arts, 1996). See also William J Mitchell, *The Reconfigured Eye: Visual truth in the post-photographic era* (Cambridge, MA: MIT Press, 1994).

25 Plato, *The Republic*, trans. by Desmond Lee, 2nd edn. (London: Penguin, 1987), p.422.

26 Mark J. Jones, 'Char Davies: VR through osmosis', *Cyberstage*, vol.2, no.1 (1995). Available online. URL: http://www.cyberstage.org/archive/cstage21/osmose21.html [16 June 2005].

27 Char Davies, cited in ibid.

28 Gilles Deleuze, *Cinema 2: The Time-image*, trans. by Hugh Tomlinson and Robert Galeta, 2nd edn. (London: Athlone, 1994), p.83.

29 Mimi Sheller and John Urry, 'Mobile transformations of "public" and "private" life', *Theory, Culture & Society*, vol.20, no.3 (2003), pp.107–125 (p.116); John Urry, 'Connections', *Environment and Planning D: Society and Space*, vol.22, no.1, (2004), pp.27–37 (p.35).

30 Frederic Jameson, 'Postmodernism and Consumer Society', in *Postmodern Culture*, ed. by Hal Foster (London: Pluto Press, 1985, repr. 1993), pp.111–125.

31 William J. Richardson, 'Lacan and Non-Philosophy', in *Philosophy and Non-Philosophy since Merleau-Ponty*, ed. by Hugh J. Silverman (New York and London: Routledge, 1988), p.121.

32 Parveen Adams, 'I. A Little Object – Sleep', in *In the Place of an Object*, ed. by Sharon Kivland and Marc du Ry (London: Centre for Freudian Analysis and Research, 2000), p.10.

33 Mog Johnstone, 'Mirror Phase', in *Guide to Human Thought*, ed. by Kenneth McLeish (London: Bloomsbury, 1993), p.478.

34 Danuza Machado, 'III. The Impossible', in Kivland and du Ry (eds.), *In the Place of an Object*, p.42.

35 Bertrand Russell, *A History of Western Philosophy* (1946), 2nd edn. (London: George Allen & Unwin, 1983), pp.123, 166.

36 Plato, *The Republic*, pp.240–248. See also Russell, *A History of Western Philosophy*, pp.140–141, for an interpretation.

37 Bertrand Russell, *The Problems of Philosophy* (1912), 2nd edn. (Oxford: Oxford University Press, 2001), p.40.

38 Charles Rycroft, 'Sigmund Freud: Austrian psychoanalyst', in *Dictionary of Modern Culture*, ed. by Justin Wintle (London, Boston, Melbourne and Henley: Routledge & Kegan Paul – Ark Paperbacks, 1984), p.126. See also Sigmund Freud, *Beyond the Pleasure Principle*, trans. by C.J.M. Hubback, (London: Hogarth Press and Institute of Psycho-Analysis, 2nd edn., 1942), pp.46–53.

39 Russell, *A History of Western Philosophy*, p.568.

40 The initial state being *an-nafs al-ammārah*, 'the commanding self – [that] incites human beings towards fulfillment of their basest desires and tendencies…the first of seven stages of self that may be achieved through progressive refinement'. Shaykh al-Tariqat Hazrat Azad Rasool, *Turning Toward the Heart: Awakening to the Sufi way* (Louisville, KY: Fons Vitae, 2002), pp.36, 132.

41 Reza Shah-Kazemi, 'The Metaphysics of Interfaith Dialogue: Sufi perspectives on the universality of the Quranic message', in *Paths to the Heart: Sufism and the Christian East*, ed. by James S. Cutsinger (Bloomington, IN: World Wisdom, 2002), pp.140–189 (p.147).

42 Vincent Rossi, 'Presence, Participation, Performance', in ibid., p.68.

43 Victor Burgin, *In/Different Spaces: Place and memory in visual culture* (Berkeley CA, and Los Angeles: University of California Press, 1996), p.273.

44 Plato, *The Republic*, p.247.

45 Machado, 'The Impossible', p.41.

46 Julia Kristeva, 'The True Real', in *The Kristeva Reader*, ed. by Toril Moi, trans. by Seán Hand (Oxford: Basil Blackwell, 1989), pp.214–237.

47 Jean Baudrillard, 'Consumer Society', in *Jean Baudrillard: Selected writings*, ed. by Mark Poster (Cambridge and Stanford, CA, Polity Press and Stanford University Press, 1989), pp.29–56.

48 See, for example, George Monbiot, *The Age of Consent: A manifesto for a new world order* (London: Flamingo, 2003), pp.51–66.

49   Russell, *The Problems of Philosophy*, p.40.

50   Michael Le Page, 'Orgasms: a real "turn-off" for women', *New Scientist* news service, 20 June 2005. Available online. URL: http://www.newscientist.com/article.ns?id=dn7548 [22 July 2005].

51   René Descartes, quoted in Frederick Copleston, *A History of Philosophy*, vol.4, *Modern Philosophy: Descartes to Leibniz* (New York: Image Books, 1963), pp.130–131.

52   Ibid. p.131.

53   Henry Gray, *Anatomy, Descriptive and Surgical* (Philadelphia: Running Press, 1901 edn., repr. 1974), pp.672–673.

54   See Julia Kristeva interviewed by Catherine Flancbin, 'On New Maladies of the Soul', in *Julia Kristeva Interviews*, ed. by Ross Mitchell Guberman (New York: Columbia University Press, 1996), p.86.

55   Russell, *The Problems of Philosophy*, p.40.

Notes on Chapter 1

1   Jean Baudrillard, 'I don't belong to the club, to the Seraglio', from an interview with Mike Gane and Monique Arnaud, November 1991, in *Baudrillard Live: Selected interviews*, ed. by Mike Gane (London and New York: Routledge, 1993), p.23.

2   David Bate, 'After Thought', *Source*, vol.40 (2004), pp.30–33, asks whether it is 'another "ism", fading into the background'. He also asks: 'Is an end to the discussion of postmodernism the end of ideology?' and suggests the current era to be one of 'neo-realism'. Jürgen Habermas prefers to label reaction as 'anti-modernism'; see his 'Modernity – an Incomplete Project', in *The Anti-Aesthetic: Essays in postmodern culture*, ed. by Hal Foster (Port Townsend, WA: Bay Press, 1983).

3   Jean-François Lyotard, *The Postmodern Condition: A report on knowledge*, trans. by Geoffrey Bennington and Brian Massumi (Manchester: Manchester University Press, 1984).

4   Foster, *The Anti-Aesthetic*.

5   Jean Baudrillard, *Simulations*, trans. by Paul Foss, Paul Patton and Philip Beitchman (New York: Semiotext(e), 1983), p.13.

6   Paul Graham, 'I blame Elvis', an interview with Jennifer Winters, in Jennifer Winters, ed., *End of an Age* (Zurich, Berlin and New York: Scalo, 1999), n.p.

7   Nick Waplington, *Indecisive Memento* (London: Booth Clibborn Editions, 1998).

8   Jean Baudrillard, 'When Reality merges with the Idea', interview with Mike Gane and Monique Arnaud, November 1991 in Gane, ed., *Baudrillard Live: Selected interviews*, p.205.

9   Baudrillard, *Simulations*, p.11.

10   Annelies Strba, *Annelies Strba: Shades of Time* (Baden: Lars Muller Publishers, 1997) – pictures of her family over a 20-year period.

11   Bettina von Zwehl , *Untitled* series, 1998 – subjects hold their breath whilst the photograph is taken; Marjaana Kella, *Hypnosis* series, 1997–2000 (Amsterdam, Van Zoetendaal Publishers, 2000) – subjects are photographed when under hypnosis.

12   Shizuka Yokomizo, *Stranger* series, 2002 – subjects are encountered via the filter of an illuminated window, anonymously; Beat Streuli uses a telephoto lens, e.g. *New York* series, 2000.

13   Nikki S. Lee, *Project* series – Lee infiltrates an identifiable group and 'becomes' one with them, adopting an appropriate persona. Her 'projects' include *The Yuppie Project*, *The Lesbian Project* and *The Senior Project*, 1999.

14   See, for example, Jean Baudrillard, *Fatal Strategies*, trans. by Philip Beitchman and W.G.J. Niessluchowski (London: Pluto Press, 1999).

15   Jean Baudrillard, 'The Art of Disappearance', in *Jean Baudrillard: Art & artefact*, ed. by Nicholas Zurbrugg (London: Sage Publications, 1997), pp.28–31.

16   Jean Baudrillard, 'For Illusion Isn't the Opposite of Reality…', in *Photographies 1985–1998*, ed. by Peter Weibel (Ostfilern [Ruit], Germany: Hatje Cantz Publishers, 1999), pp.128–142. Andy Grundberg refers to the 'masking quality' of postmodernist practice in the more literal sense in 'The Crisis of the Real, Photography and Postmodernism' [1987] in *The Photography Reader*, ed. by Liz Wells (London and New York: Routledge, 2003), p.171.

17   Jean Baudrillard, 'The Ecstasy of Photography', interview with Nicholas Zurbrugg, June 1993, in Zurbrugg, ed., *Jean Baudrillard: Art & artefact*, p.34.

18   Ulf Lundin, series of photographs entitled *Pictures of a Family*, 1996.

19   Speaking at the 'Siting the Photograph' conference, Victoria and Albert Museum, London, May 2003.

20   See, for example, the eclectic collection in Wolfgang Tillmans, *If One Thing Matters, Everything Matters* (London: Tate Britain, 2003), and the 'realism' of Richard Billingham, *Ray's a Laugh* (Zurich, Berlin and New York: Scalo, 2000), or Boris Mikhailov, *Case History* (Zurich, Berlin and New York: Scalo, 1999).

21   Thomas Ruff's portrait series from 1983. Mark Durden discusses Ruff's work with reference to Baudrillard's 'Transparency of Evil' and asserts that it 'accords with Baudrillard's idea of the photograph's capacity to "disincarnate" the things it represents – a fundamental discord between image and reality'. See Mark Durden, 'An Aesthetics of Detachment', *Portfolio*, no.35, June 2002.

22   Roland Barthes, 'The Reality Effect', in *French Literary Theory Today*, ed. by Tzvetan Todorov, trans. by R. Carter (Cambridge: Cambridge University Press, 1982), pp.13–16.

23   'Contemporary photography, operating as it does in the name of forced signification, knows only how to capture banality, the absence of destiny, insignificance, humanity's confusion with its environment' – Baudrillard in Weibel, ed., *Photographies 1985–1998*, p.140.

24 Jean Baudrillard, *For a Critique of the Political Economy of the Sign* [1972] (St Louis: Telos, 1981), cited in Mike Gane, *Baudrillard's Bestiary* (London: Routledge, 1991), p.3.

25 Baudrillard in Weibel, ed., *Photographies 1985–1998*, p.139.

26 Roland Barthes, 'The Great Family of Man' [1957], in *Mythologies* (London: Vintage, 1983), pp.100–102.

27 See quotation cited by Shawcross as her translation of 'Photo-chocs', a commentary by Barthes on an exhibition, in Nancy Shawcross, *Roland Barthes on Photography: The critical translation in perspective* (Gainesville, FL: University Press of Florida, 1997), pp.3–4.

28 Roland Barthes: 'The Great Family of Man', pp.100–102.

29 Roland Barthes, *Camera Lucida: Reflections on photography* [1980] trans by Richard Howard, 3rd edn. (London: Vintage, 1993), pp.32–38.

30 Ibid., p.38.

31 Boris Mikhailov, see note 20.

32 Margarite Tupitsyn, 'Photography as a Remedy for Stammering', in Boris Mikhailov, *Unfinished Dissertation* (Zurich: Scalo, 1998), p.219.

33 Ibid.

34 Jean Baudrillard, 'Forget Baudrillard', interview with Sylvere Lotringer, 1984–1985, in Gane, ed., *Baudrillard Live: Selected interviews*, p.100.

35 Barthes: *Camera Lucida*, p.7. See also Baudrillard's discussion of 'allergy to culture' in 'I don't belong to the club, to the Seraglio' and 'Forget Baudrillard', Gane, *Baudrillard Live: Selected interviews*, pp.24, 100.

36 Jean Baudrillard, 'Aesthetic Illusion and Virtual Reality', in Zurbrugg, ed., *Jean Baudrillard: Art & artefact*, p.22.

37 Jean-François Lyotard, *The Postmodern Explained* [1988], (Minneapolis: University of Minnesota Press, 1997).

38 See 'Parergon' in Jacques Derrida, *The Truth in Painting*, trans. by Geoff Bennington and Ian McLeod (Chicago: University of Chicago Press, 1987).

39 Baudrillard, 'The Ecstasy of Photography', p.35.

40 Steven Skopik, 'Contemporary Photography and the Recuperation of the Aesthetic Mode', *Exposure*, vol.36, no.1 (2003), pp.4–9.

41 Olga Sviblova, 'Sergey Chilikov', *Imago*, vol.14 (Summer 2002), p.25. Chilikov calls his method 'provocation'.

Notes on Chapter 2

1 Hilla Becher in Daniel Sausset, 'La photo objective des Becher', *L'Oeil*, no.526 (2001), p.42.

2 Ibid., p.40.

3 Hilla Becher, interview with James Lingwood, *Art Press*, no.209 (1996), p.25.

4 Becher in Sausset, 'La photo objective des Becher', p.41.

5 Anne Wauters, 'Photographie réaliste/Architecture ordinaire', *Art Press*, no.209, January 1996, p.41.

6   Desa Philippi, 'Moments of Interpretation', *October*, no.62, (1992), p.120.

7   Régis Durand, 'The Secular Imagery of Thomas Ruff', in *Thomas Ruff* (ex. cat., Centre National de la Photographie, Paris, Éditions Actes Sud, Arles, 1997), p.20.

8   Régis Durand, cited in Alexandre Castant, 'Thomas Ruff: atlases, fictions, nights', *Art Press*, no.227 (1997), p.49.

9   See, for example, Sven Lütticken, 'Thomas Ruff: the art of anachronism', *Camera Austria*, no.70 (2000), pp.29–30.

10   For examples, see Robert Storr, *Gerhard Richter: October 18 1977* (ex. cat., Museum of Modern Art, New York, 2000).

11   Matthias Winzen, 'A Credible Invention of Reality', in Winzen, *Thomas Ruff: 1979 to the present* (Cologne: Verlag der Buchhandlung Walther König, 2001), p.142.

12   Thomas Ruff, interview with Régis Durand, in Durand, 'The Secular Imagery of Thomas Ruff', p.31.

13   Ralph Flores, *A Study of Allegory in its Historical Context and Relationship to Contemporary Theory* (Lewiston, NY: Edwin Mellen Press, 1996), p.1. See also Deborah L. Madsen, *Rereading Allegory: A Narrative Approach to Genre* (Basingstoke: Macmillan, 1995).

14   Paul de Man, cited in Flores, *A Study of Allegory*, p.6.

15   Craig Owens, 'The Allegorical Impulse: towards a theory of postmodernism', in Owens, *Beyond Recognition: Representation, power, and culture* (Berkeley, CA, Los Angeles and Oxford: University of California Press, 1992), p.54.

16   Ibid., p.52.

17   Walter Benjamin, *The Origin of German Tragic Drama* [1928], trans. by John Osborne (London: NLB, 1977), p.165.

18   Ibid., p.166.

19   Ibid., p.178.

20   Owens, 'The Allegorical Impulse', p.57.

21   Thomas Demand, interview with Ruedi Widmer, 'Building the Scene of the Crime', *Camera Austria*, no.66 (1999), p.11.

22   Stephen Horne, 'Thomas Demand: catastrophic space', *Parachute*, no.96 (1999), p.24; see also Jason Oddy, 'Thomas Demand: the photographer as sculptor', *Modern Painters*, vol.14, no.1 (2001), p.41.

23   Wauters, 'Photographie réaliste/Architecture ordinaire', p.42.

24   See Dietrich Klose, *Multi-Storey Car Parks and Garages* (London: Architectural Press, 1965; orig. pub. by Verlag Gerd Hatje, Stuttgart), p.167.

25   W.G. Sebald, *On the Natural History of Destruction* (London and New York: Hamish Hamilton, 2003), pp.76–77.

26   See Klose, *Multi-Storey Car Parks and Garages*, pp.198–201.

27   Régis Durand, 'Tracings', in Francesco Bonami, Régis Durand and François Quintin, *Thomas Demand* (ex. cat., Fondation Cartier pour l'art contemporain, Paris, 2000), p.80.

28   Thomas Demand, interview with Ruedi Widmer in Widmer, 'Building the Scene of the Crime', p.15.

29   'Stasi assassin holds murder clues', the *Telegraph*, filed 27 September 2003, URL: http://www.telegraph.co.uk/news/2003/09/27/wstasi27.xml [12 November 2003].

30   Benjamin, *The Origin of German Tragic Drama*, p.217.

31   See Helmut Gernsheim, *The Origins of Photography* (London: Thames & Hudson, 1982), p.69.

32   Sebald, *On the Natural History of Destruction*, p.10.

33   Jörg Friedrich, cited in Luke Harding, 'Germany's forgotten victims', 22 October 2003, *Guardian Unlimited*, http://www.guardian.co.uk/elsewhere/journalist/story/0,7792,1068437,00.html [12 November 2003].

34   Sebald, *On the Natural History of Destruction*, p.98.

35   Susan Buck-Morss, *The Dialectics of Seeing: Walter Benjamin and the Arcades Project* (Cambridge, MA, and London: MIT Press, 1989), pp.182–183.

Notes on Chapter 3

1   The term 'photography-based articulations' is used here to refer to what Martin Lister has categorised as 'images originated in a camera of some kind, subject to processing by other graphic and reprographic technologies than the strictly chemical'. See Martin Lister, *The Photographic Image in Digital Culture* (London and New York: Routledge, 1995), p.4. As it is not limited strictly to photochemically produced images, but also includes 'images which share some of the mechanical, lens-based and analogue features of the chemical photographic process but which are registered by electromagnetic means: broadcast television and video' (ibid.), the term implies a stretched conceptualisation of photography. However, where Lister reserves the term for a spectrum of non-digital-camera-generated images, I will stretch it even further to include digitally recorded and reproduced images.

2   William J. Mitchell, *The Reconfigured Eye: Visual truth in the post-photographic era* (Cambridge, MA: MIT Press, 1992); Geoffrey Batchen, *Burning with Desire: The conception of photography* (Cambridge, MA: MIT Press, 1997).

3   W.J.T. Mitchell, 'Representation', in *Critical Terms for Literary Study*, ed. by Frank Lentricchia and Thomas McLaughlin (Chicago, IL: University of Chicago Press, 1995) pp.16–17.

4   Johan Grimonprez, 'Beware! In playing the phantom you become one', interview in *Saving the Image: Art after film*, ed. by Tanya Leighton and Pavel Büchler (Glasgow: Centre for Contemporary Art, in collaboration with Manchester Metropolitan University, 2003), p.122. The passages of text appearing in *Dial H-I-S-T-O-R-Y* are slightly modified from their original appearance in DeLillo's novels. They are paraphrases rather than quotes or excerpts.

5   In his other compositions, David Shea works consistently with the interface between digital samplers and analogue sound; his work in *Dial H-I-S-T-O-R-Y* is thus in line with his general oeuvre as a composer.

6   Thierry de Duve, *Kant after Duchamp* (Cambridge, MA: MIT Press, 1998), p.389.

7   Quoted in Annik Wiik, *Förebild film: Panoreringar över den samtida konstscenen* (Stockholm: Aura förlag, 2001), p.29.

8   Walter Benjamin, 'The Work of Art in the Age of Mechanical Reproduction' [1936], in *Video Culture: A Critical investigation*, ed. by John G. Hanhardt (New York: Visual Studies Workshop Press, 1986).

9   See Wiik, *Förebild film*, p.30.

10   Thom Holmes, *Electronic and Experimental Music* (London: Routledge, 2002), p.212.

11   An often used term for sampled sounds is 'found sounds', with 'found footage' as its equivalent in the visual media.

12   Ulf Poschardt, *DJ Culture* (London: Quartet Books, 1998), pp.361–363.

13   Lev Manovich, *The Language of New Media* (Cambridge, MA: MIT Press, 200), p.118.

14   W.J.T. Mitchell, 'Representation', pp.16–17.

15   Jean Baudrillard, 'The Hyperrealism of Simulation' [1976], in *Art in Theory 1900-1990: An anthology of changing ideas*, ed. by Charles Harrison and Paul Wood, (Oxford: Blackwell, 1992), p.1049.

16   Grimonprez, 'Beware! In playing the phantom you become one', p.126.

17   Marit Paasche, 'In the Name of Truth', in *An Eye for Time: Video, art and reality*, ed. by Stian Grøgaard et al. (Oslo: Unipax, 2004), p.25.

18   John Durham Peters, 'Witnessing', *Media, Culture & Society*, vol.23, no.6 (2001), pp.707–723 (p.717).

19   *Moonlighting* was a mystery television series that was aired on ABC in the United States from 1985 to 1989. The series included frequent breaks with the conventions for fictional realism and continuity editing, such as addressing the audience with direct reference to the scriptwriters, the network and the series itself. *Moonlighting* is considered the first prime-time television series that extensively employed self-reflexive textual devices.

20   Hal Foster, *The Return of the Real* (Cambridge, MA: MIT Press, 1996).

21   Ibid., pp.190–191.

22   Ibid., p.128.

23   Hal Foster, 'An Archival Impulse', *October*, vol.110 (2004), pp.3–22.

24   Ibid., pp.4, 5.

25   Ibid., p.5.

26   Grimonprez, 'Beware! In playing the phantom you become one', p.125.

27   Manovich, *The Language of New Media*, p.218.

28   Foster, 'An Archival Impulse', p.4.

29   Ibid., p.5.

30   Manovich, *The Language of New Media*, pp.218, 225.

31   Manovich contradicts this when he proposes that databases and narratives are two competing, if unequal cultural forms, but concludes that 'a database can support a narrative, but there is nothing in the logic of the medium

itself that would foster its generation' (*The Language of New Media*, p.228). Rather than the two forms being contradictory, he thus sees that the one form, the database, can contain or 'support' the other, the narrative.

32   Ibid, p.225.
33   Simon Waters, 'Beyond the Acousmatic: Hybrid tendencies in electroacoustic music', in *Music, Electronic Media and Culture*, ed. by Simon Emmerson (Aldershot: Ashgate, 2000), p.56.
34   Benjamin, 'The Work of Art in the Age of Mechanical Reproduction', p.29.
35   Peters, 'Witnessing', pp.719–721.
36   Foster, *The Return of the Real*, pp.130–136.
37   Mette Sandbye, 'Avantgarde, hverdagsliv og fotografisk realisme', in *Virkelighed, virkelighed! Avantgardens realisme*, ed. by Karin Petersen and Mette Sandbye (Copenhagen: Tiderne Skifter, 2003), p.186.
38   Ibid., p.202.
39   Manovich, *The Language of New Media*, p.218.
40   Foster, *The Return of the Real*, p.128.
41   Sandbye, 'Avantgarde, hverdagsliv og fotografisk realisme', p.202.

Notes on Chapter 4

1   Adding to the confusion is a tendency to use words such as 'real', 'true' and 'authentic' as largely interchangeable.
2   Robert Drew, Richard Leacock, Donn Pennebaker and Fred Wiseman were the main proponents of a group of highly self-publicising documentary makers who claimed to have developed a way of filmmaking that amounted to an unmediated, 'objective' reflection of reality, known as Direct Cinema, but often (wrongly) referred to as cinema verité (which was the term used by their French counterparts, who had nonetheless a very different approach). Their style is now generally seen as the extreme form of observational documentary. See Richard Leacock in *Imagining Reality*, ed. by Kevin MacDonald and Mark Cousins (London: Faber & Faber, 1996), pp.251–254; Stella Bruzzi, *New Documentary: A critical introduction*, (London: Routledge, 2000), pp.67–74.
3   Jean Baudrillard describes the simulacrum as the end result of four successive phases of the image from representation to simulation, in *Simulations*, trans. by Paul Foss, Paul Patton and Philip Beitchman (New York: Semiotext(e), 1983), pp.11–12.
4   Brian Winston, *Claiming the Real: The documentary film revisited* (London: BFI Publishing, 1995), pp.127–129.
5   Ibid., pp.138–142.
6   André Bazin, *What is Cinema?*, vol.1, trans. by Hugh Grey (Berkeley, CA: University of California Press, 1967), p.13.
7   Bill Nichols, *Introduction to Documentary* (Bloomington, IN: Indiana University Press, 2000), p.1.

8   However, Nichols confuses the matter somewhat by claiming documentary as a 'discourse of sobriety' insofar as it addresses itself to the historical world that we live in, before qualifying this claim by saying that documentary necessarily 'fails to identify any structure or purpose of its own entirely absent from fiction or narrative. See Bill Nichols, *Representing Reality: Issues and concepts in documentary* (Bloomington, IN: Indiana University Press, 1991), p.6.

9   Jon Dovey, *Freakshow: First person media and factual television* (London: Pluto Press, 2000), pp.88–90. Actually, one could argue that he misses Baudrillard's point somewhat, since the empirically established social attitudes cited are *already* mediated by the spectacle of simulacra.

10   Michael Renov, ed., *Theorizing Documentary* (London: Routledge, 1993), p.7.

11   Bruzzi, *New Documentary*, p.3. Aside from this rather reductive statement, I feel there are serious problems with her presentation of her definition of documentary as a radical departure from established documentary theory. Her definition that, to paraphrase, documentary is the result of a dialectical encounter between a real situation and a documentary film crew closely echoes Jean Rouch's pronouncements on documentary 40 years earlier, and her readings of theorists such as Nichols, Renov and Winston appear to be based on a projection of Direct Cinema naïvety and pretensions onto their entire discourse. However, there is no room for a comprehensive critique of her book in this context.

12   See Slavoj Žižek, *Looking Awry: An introduction to Jacques Lacan through popular culture* (Cambridge, MA: MIT Press, 1991), p.120, for an example of the use of (symbolic) reality in opposition to the real. This distinction is based on the Lacanian 'triad' of the symbolic, the imaginary and the real. As a matter of fact, in his keynote address during the 'State of the Real' conference at Glasgow School of Art (21–22 November 2003), Žižek expanded this schema by proposing that each of these three terms could be subdivided into the same three categories, i.e. the real could be subdivided into the 'symbolic real', the 'imaginary real' and the 'real real', etc.

13   Dovey, *Freakshow*, p.57, argues against a technological determinism, citing earlier experiments by artists and documentarists with Sony half-inch equipment, preferring to see the intrusion of 'wobblyscope TV' into the mainstream as a phenomenon whose time had come. However, it seems difficult to deny that the spread of camcorders reached a kind of 'critical mass' that made programmes such as *You've Been Framed* or *Caught on Camera* possible.

14   Dovey, *Freakshow*, pp.81–86.

15   The commodity value of the 'real' footage is such that normally any narrative framing is designed to *accommodate* the spectacular piece of footage, rather than that the footage is used to support an argument made by the narrative, and sometimes the narrative framing is virtually dispensed with altogether. As such it is reminiscent of the earliest film screenings of the Lumière brothers, showing narratively disconnected scenes and events, purely for

their novelty, curiosity and visual stimulation. This has been called the 'cinema of attractions' by the film historian Tom Gunning in 'The Cinema of Attractions: early film, its spectator and the avant-garde', in *Early Cinema: Space, frame, narrative*, ed. by Thomas Elsaesser (London: BFI Publishing, 1990).

16   Dovey, *Freakshow*, pp.65–67.

17   I would argue that even in domestic slapstick there is a certain amount of Schadenfreude at the knowledge that these mishaps are unintentional, and potentially painful.

18   The urgency of the question is reminiscent of those early ambulance-chasing photographers who were determined to capture on film the passing of the soul from a dying person. For them, the most minor smudges, imperfections in the image were of utmost importance, lest it be a trace of the departing soul; similarly, in this kind of reality TV the incidents are almost always replayed in slow motion, allowing us to search for this impossible moment when life (almost) becomes death.

19   Jacques Lacan sets out his structure of the symbolic, the imaginary and the real in 'On a question preliminary to any possible treatment of psychosis', in *Écrits: A selection*, trans. Alan Sheridan (New York and London: W.W. Norton, 1977), pp.179–199.

20   Bill Nichols, *Blurred Boundaries* (Bloomington, IN: Indiana University Press, 1994), p.73.

21   Dovey, *Freakshow*, p.59.

22   Žižek, *Looking Awry*, p.35.

23   Indeed, Dovey himself speaks of 'trauma TV' in his introduction to *Freakshow*, p.22.

24   See Sigmund Freud, 'Beyond the Pleasure Principle' [1920], in *The Penguin Freud Library*, vol.11, *On Metapsychology* (London: Penguin, 1991), pp.308–311.

25   Hal Foster, *The Return of the Real* (Cambridge, MA: MIT Press, 1996), p.132.

26   Jacques Lacan, *The Four Fundamental Concepts of Psychoanalysis* (New York and London: W.W. Norton, 1978), p.55. Elsewhere, Lacan goes so far as to assign to the world the status of 'a fantasy through which thought sustains itself – "reality" no doubt, but to be understood as a grimace of the real'. See Jacques Lacan, *Television: A challenge to the psychoanalytic establishment*, ed. by Joan Copjec, trans. by Denis Hollier, Rosalind Krauss, Annette Michelson and Jeffrey Mehlman (New York and London: W.W. Norton, 1990), p.6.

27   This could be an example of what Žižek recently posited as the 'Imaginary Real': a kind of ever-receding sublime moment that is imagined as awe-inspiring, devastating (and otherwise hyperbolic).

28   Dovey, *Freakshow*, pp.65–70.

29   'Instead of the sublime Thing, we are stuck with vulgar, groaning fornication'; Žižek, *Looking Awry*, p.110.

30   Žižek, *Welcome to the Desert of the Real! Five essays on September 11 and related dates* (London and New York: Verso, 2002), p.6.

31 Ibid., pp. 5–6. We have to keep in mind that Žižek refers here to the Real/reality distinction mentioned above.

32 Dovey, *Freakshow*, pp. 133–135; Bruzzi, *New Documentary: A critical introduction*, pp. 75–80. Dovey credits Stephen Lambert with setting out the parameters of the genre in 1996.

33 I am referring here to the rules of observational documentary introduced by the practitioners of American Direct Cinema (and often broken by themselves), which proscribed narration, interviews, reconstructions, non-incidental lighting and other forms of 'interference' by the filming crew. These rules still form a kind of touchstone of 'pure' observational documentary.

34 Andrew Bethell, a major producer of docusoaps, cited in Richard Kilborn, *Staging the Real: Factual TV programming in the age of Big Brother* (Manchester: Manchester University Press 2003), p. 113.

35 Ibid., pp. 106–108.

36 Brian Winston in *Lies, Damn Lies and Documentaries* (London: BFI Publishing, 2000), p. 25; the entire book makes a comprehensive case against what he sees as the misguided regulation of the documentary form. The effect of this whole episode, and of the resulting new regulations, especially concerning the use of reconstructions, is that certainly for practitioners of 'serious' documentary, despite the much-commented-on blurring of the boundaries between fact and fiction, the delineation of what is to be considered footage that adequately represents the 'real' *is now much stricter than it was before*. Given the fact that, as a result of the popularity of 'witness TV' formats, there is now serious commodity value attached to certain types of 'reality footage', what appears to be at stake here is the protection of that value, and of the existing libraries of such footage, from increasingly sophisticated means to fabricate convincing-looking simulations. Some idea of this newly acquired commodity value can be derived from the news, reported in the *Guardian* (Julian Borger, '$16m for 26-second film of Kennedy killing', 4 April 1999), that when the Zapruder film, an amateur record of the assassination of President John F. Kennedy, and arguably the most famous 'reality film' ever, was surrendered to the American national archives, legal arbitrators ruled that the Zapruder family should be compensated with $16 million, even if the family retains the copyright and have subsequently signed a lucrative deal with MPI home videos to release the film on video. We might say that the 'reality fetish' is also a result of time-honoured Marxist commodity fetishism.

37 In 1969 the sociologist Erving Goffman published a book called *The Presentation of Self in Everyday Life*, cited in Kilborn, *Staging the Real*, p. 23.

38 Jane Roscoe, 'Real Entertainment: new factual hybrid television', in *Media International Australia*, no. 100, August 2001, pp. 13–14 (emphasis added).

39 Winston, *Lies, Damn Lies and Documentaries*, pp. 95–99.

40 Jacques-Alain Miller, 'Microscopia: an introduction to the reading of Television', in Lacan, *Television*, p. xxviii.

41 Judith Butler, *Bodies that Matter* (London: Routledge, 1993), p. 138.

42 Indeed, as Žižek commented during the 'State of the Real' conference, the submission can never be *complete*; in order to work as a subject we have to retain some idiosyncrasy, so, paradoxically, the interpellation of the subject has to fail (somewhat) in order to succeed. It is the *limits* of this idiosyncrasy that are up for contestation, of course.

43 This is also the term Roscoe uses. It is worth pointing out that Endemol Productions, the Dutch company that came up with the *Big Brother* format, was formed in a merger between John de Mol Productions and Joop van de Ende Entertainment, which were both in the business of 'stack-'em-high, sell-'em-cheap' gameshows. John de Mol, especially, made his fortune producing cheap content for the German market via the satellite network RTL, coming up with programmes such as *Es Tut Mir Leid* ('I'm Sorry': punters trying to patch up relationships gone wrong on TV) and *Traumhochzeit* ('Dream Wedding': in the studio!) in the early 1990s, which I believe are the clearest antecedents for the reality gameshow format.

44 I think there is something to be said for Burchill's remark in the *Guardian* (Julie Burchill, 'Chance would be a fine thing', 9 August 2003): 'I like reality shows because I like seeing young working- and lower-middle-class people get a chance, however flimsy, to duck out of the soul-destroying map of life laid out for them'.

45 Roscoe, 'Real Entertainment', pp. 16–17.

46 After all, seeing the footage after the fact does not have the same 'realness value'.

47 'Watch with Brother' (Germaine Greer in *The Observer*, 24 June, 2001), cited in Kilborn, *Staging the Real*, p. 79. Of course, Germaine Greer was 'handpicked' herself for *Celebrity Big Brother 3* in January 2005.

48 When I worked on *Celebrity Big Brother 2* I toured the camera runs which completely envelop the house: the media apparatus is literally *interposed* between the contestants' space and the world outside. It felt like a stage-set version of the reptile house in London Zoo.

49 Jacques Lacan, 'The mirror stage as formative of the I as revealed in psychoanalytic experience', in *Écrits*, p. 2. We have to keep in mind, of course, that in this instance Lacan is speaking of a primordial identification in early childhood.

50 Ibid.

51 It is of course symptomatic that the submission to the language of sexual difference doesn't allow us to speak of the subject in gender-neutral terms.

52 I would argue that this is analogous to the traumatic moment that Žižek has called 'the mark of the world's inconsistency', in *Looking Awry*, p. 8. He refers here to a Dashiell Hammett story in which a man vanishes and starts his life all over again after a falling construction beam narrowly misses his head.

53 In another comment at the 'State of the Real' conference, Žižek claimed that the iceberg that the Titanic hits in the film is a diversion that *stands in* for the symbolic deadlock that occurs when Kate Winslet decides to transgress

her class affiliation: hence his assertion that a big catastrophe like that presents *a lure* for our fascination with the sublime 'imaginary real', which is not the 'real real'.

54   Žižek, *Welcome to the Desert of the Real!*, p.9.

55   This is why Žižek suggests that the attack on the twin towers was to Hollywood catastrophe movies like snuff pornography to S&M porno movies: the 'real thing', but carried out *'for the spectacular effect of it'.* Ibid., p.11 (emphasis in original).

56   'Insensitive show that shot TV in the foot' (Mark Lawson in the *Guardian*, 6 October 2003).

57   Žižek, *Welcome to the Desert of the Real!*, p.19.

58   Come to think of it, what would have been given as the cause of death in the coroner's report? Accident or suicide?

Note on Introduction to Part II

1   In Kant's logic, 'phenomena' are contrasted with 'numena'; that is, respectively, facts or perceptions of the world apparent to the senses or mind are distinguished from objects of purely intellectual intuition (specific examples of the latter being space and time). However, 'numenal' is distinctly different and refers to an understanding of a divine or spiritual world.

Notes on Chapter 5

1   Exhibited at Camden Arts Centre, London, 2001.

2   Nicolas Bourriaud, *Relational Aesthetics* (Dijon: Les Presses du Reel, 2002), p.18.

3   The text messages are presented here in the form in which they were received.

4   Bourriaud, *Relational Aesthetics*, p.21.

5   Jack Burnham, *Great Western Saltworks* (New York: Braziller, 1974), p.15.

6   Jack Burnham, *Beyond Modern Sculpture* (New York: Braziller, 1968), p.363.

7   Burnham, *Great Western Saltworks*, p.22.

8   Jack Burnham, *Framing and Being Framed* (New York: New York University Press, 1975), p.127.

9   Cited in Burnham, *Great Western Saltworks*, p.22.

10   Burnham, *Beyond Modern Sculpture*, p.369.

11   Ibid.

12   Ibid., p.96.

13   Jack Burnham, 'The Panacea that Failed', in *Video Culture*, ed. by J.G. Hanhardt (New York: Peregrine Smith, 1986), p.245.

14   *I, Project's* research team was composed of James Coupe, Hedley Roberts and Rob Saunders. The project was based at the Faculty of Arts and Human Sciences, London South Bank University.

15   John Searle, 'Minds, Brains and Programs', in *The Behavioral and Brain Sciences*, vol.3 (Cambridge: Cambridge University Press, 1980) pp.417–457.

16   Tom Ziemke and Noel Sharkey, 'A stroll through the worlds of robots and animals: applying Jakob von Uexküll's theory of meaning to adaptive robots and artificial life', *Semiotica*, vol.134, no.1–4 (2001), pp.701–746.

17   See *The Nature of Mind*, ed. by David Rosenthal (Oxford: Oxford University Press, 1991), pp.89–136.

18   See also Alan Dunning and Paul Woodrow in this volume.

Notes on Chapter 6

1   Edith Stein, *The Collected Works of Edith Stein*, vol.6, *The Science of the Cross*, trans. by Josephine Koeppel, O.C.D. (Washington, DC: ICS Publications, 2002).

2   Fiona Maddocks, *Hildegard of Bingen* (London: Headline, 2001), p.58.

3   Early editions of his works were published in Venice, 1506, and Paris, 1518. For a modern edition, see Richard of St Victor, *The Book of the Patriarchs, The Mystical Ark, Book Three of the Trinity*, ed. by Grover A Zinn (Mahwah, NJ: Paulist Press, 1979).

4   Louis Dupré and James A. Wiseman, eds., *Light from Light* (Mahwah, NJ: Paulist Press, 1988), p.4. See also Louis Bouyer, *A History of Christian Spirituality*, vol.1, *The Spirituality of the New Testament and the Fathers* (New York: Descleé, 1963).

5   Dupré and Wiseman, *Light from Light*, p.4.

6   Ibid.

7   Ibid., p.6.

8   See, for example, Eugene Gendlin, *Experiencing and the Creation of Meaning: A philosophical and psychological approach to the subjective* (Evanston, IL: Northwestern University Press, 1997).

9   *The Catholic Encyclopedia*, 2004, online copyright K. Knight. Available online. URL: http://www.newadvent.org/cathen/ [6 July 2005].

10   The image of Hildegard has been used as a screen for devotional projections by the left and right wing and points in between. A procession to mark the 750th anniversary of her death, in Bingen in 1929, for example, was rumoured to have attracted 25,000 people. Alternatively, according to a recent account by an American-born nun who lived, for over a quarter of a century, within the community created by Hildegard at Eibingen, '[e]verybody started reading Hildegard' because of the interest stimulated by the ex-Dominican, Matthew Fox: 'they all wanted to make her their own, the esoteric and the New Agers, the feminists, the ecologists and what have you. They all said, "She's our woman." We said Hildegard's task was different.' See Maddocks, *Hildegard of Bingen*, pp.285–299, for this memorable interview.

11 Hildegard of Bingen, from *Liber Scivias*, cited in Maddocks, *Hildegard of Bingen*, p. 49.

12 John Stevens, 'The Musical Individuality of Hildegard's Songs', in *Hildegard of Bingen: The context of her thought and art*, ed. by Charles Burnett, Jill Kraye, and W.F. Ryan (London: Warburg Institute, 1998), p. 188.

13 Alan Beck, 'What is a Fractal? And Who is this Guy Mandelbrot?'. Available online. URL: http://www.glyphs.com/art/fractals/what_is.html [12 July 2005].

14 Ibid.

15 John Stevens, 'The Musical Individuality of Hildegard's Songs', p. 176. As he says, while the 'age of the deliberate "fragment" was a long way off' it was natural that Hildegard's inspiration should find an outlet 'in a form [with which] she was intimate'.

16 Hildegard of Bingen in *Liber Scivias*, quoted in *Hildegard of Bingen*, ed. by Fiona Bowie and Oliver Davies, (London: SPCK, 1990), p. 68. In a letter to Guibert, she says: 'my perception of things depends on the shifting of the clouds and other elements of creation. Still I do not hear these things with bodily ears, nor do I see them with the cogitations of my heart or the evidence of my five senses. I see them only in my spirit, with my eyes wide open...' Her 'science of the heart', it seems, was based on her relationship to 'spirit'. See also *The Letters of Hildegard of Bingen*, vol. 2, trans. by Joseph L. Baird and Radd K. Ehrman (Oxford: Oxford University Press, 1998), pp. 21–25, for the full text of this letter.

17 Oliver Sacks, *Migraine* (London: Picador, 1995), p. 301.

18 Ibid. p. 300.

19 For an interesting discussion of Hildegard's sources, see Peter Dronke, 'The Allegorical World-Picture of Hildegard', in *Hildegard of Bingen: The context of her thought and art*, pp. 1–14.

20 For a discussion of sources see Charles Burnett, 'Hildegard of Bingen and the Science of the Stars', in *Hildegard of Bingen: The context of her thought and art*, pp. 111–120.

21 Titian created images to accompany a copy of Camillo's *L'Idea del Theatro*, but this sadly did not survive a fire at El Escorial in 1671.

22 See Frances Yates, *The Art of Memory* (London: Routledge & Kegan Paul, 1966), pp. 170–172 and map insert; Kate Robinson, *A Search for the Source of the Whirlpool of Artifice* (Edinburgh: Dunedin Academic Press, 2006).

23 Giulio Camillo, *L'Idea del Theatro* (Torrentino, Florence, 1550), pp. 41–42. See also Lu Beery Wenneker's English translation, 'An Examination of *L'Idea Del Theatro* of Giulio Camillo, including an Annotated Translation, with Special Attention to his Influence on Emblem Literature and Iconography' (unpublished PhD thesis, University of Pittsburgh, 1970), pp. 263–265.

24 Camillo, *L'Idea del Theatro*, p. 41.

25 Ibid.

26 The idea of a fluid through which the planets glide has a long history. It can be traced to the Stoics, who said that heaven was filled with *pneuma*, an

animate fluid substance, and to Cicero's *De natura deorum*. The theory was revived by Camillo's hero, Petrarch. Astronomers such as Robertus Anglicus (fl. 1260–1280) and Andalo di Negro (c.1270–1340), and the philosopher Pietro d'Abano (c.1310), had kept the idea alive through the thirteenth and fourteenth centuries. See James M. Lattis, *Between Copernicus and Galileo* (Chicago: University of Chicago Press, 1994), p.94. See also Robinson, *A Search for the Source of the Whirlpool of Artifice*.

27   Psalm 148:4, quoted in Camillo, *L'Idea del Theatro*, p.29. The idea of the waters above the heavens is derived from Genesis 1:7.

28   Camillo, *L'Idea del Theatro*, p.23.

29   The idea of a mystical 'dew' was common parlance in alchemical treatises, and it is appropriate here to mention the probable influence on Camillo of Paracelsus (otherwise known as Theophrastus Bombastus von Hohenheim (1493–1541)), whose alchemical works were widespread.

30   First shown at *The Theatre of Memory*, Collins Gallery, University of Strathclyde, 2001.

31   The VRML was a collaborative work with Carl Smith at the Humanities Advanced Technologies and Information Institute at the University of Glasgow.

32   For more details on the images, see Yates, *The Art of Memory*, pp.129–172, and Robinson, *A Search for the Source of the Whirlpool of Artifice*.

33   Edith Stein, *The Science of the Cross* [1942], trans. by Josephine Koeppel (Washington: ICS Publications, 2002), p.20.

34   Ibid., p.275.

35   Ibid., p.85. Quoting from St John, Stein says: 'all visions, revelations and supernatural feelings...are far less valuable than the slightest act of humility...'

36   Ibid., p.121.

37   Ibid., p.204.

38   Ibid., p.206.

39   Ibid., p.229. From stanza 22 (31).

40   Ibid., p.229. From stanza 21 (30) of 'The Bridal Song'.

Notes on Chapter 8

1   The art and science group the *Einstein's Brain Project* has been collaborating since 1996. The Project's work is featured in Katherine Hayles, 'Flesh and Metal', in *Semiotic Flesh: Information and the human body* (Seattle: University of Washington Press, 2002), Mark Hansen, *New Philosophy for New Media* (Cambridge, MA: MIT, 2004), and in Anna Munster, *Materializing New Media: Embodiment and information aesthetics* (Hanover, NH: University Press of New England, 2006).

2   Antonio R. Damasio, *Descartes' Error* (New York: Avon Books, 1994), p.240.

3   Randall M. Rohrer, David S. Ebert and John L. Sibert, 'The Shape of Shakespeare: visualizing text using implicit surfaces', *Proceedings of the 1998 IEEE Symposium on Information Visualization* (Washington, DC: IEEE Computer Society, 1998).

4   In 1654, Mademoiselle de Scudéry published the first instalment of her ten-volume *Clélie*, a novel of love and courtship. Clélie, her main character, is a walking encyclopaedia of feelings. Such is her knowledge of the human heart that she draws a figurative map of it, under the name 'Carte du Tendre'.

5   And sometimes these reconstructions have startling impact. In an essay entitled 'The Index of the Absent Wound (Monograph on a Stain)', *October*, no.29 (1984), pp.63–81 French art historian Georges Didi-Huberman describes how, in 1894, Secondo Pia tried to produce a clear image of the holy shroud of Turin in his darkroom: '...there in the dark room, the moment the negative image took form (the inaugural glimpse), a face looked out at Pia from the bottom of the tray. A face he had never before seen on the shroud. A face that was, he said, unexpected. And seeing it he almost fainted.'

6   Nigel Kneale, *The Stone Tape*, BBC Television, 25 December 1972.

7   One of a series of maps first exhibited in *Première exposition de psychgéographie*, 1957. Psychographic map by Guy Debord with Asger Jorn, *The Naked City*, 1957, screenprint, Rijksbureau voor Kunsthistorische Documentatie, The Hague.

8   Quoted in Thomas F. McDonough, 'Situationist Space', *October*, no.67 (1994), p.60.

9   Antonio R. Damasio, *The Feeling of What Happens* (New York: Harcourt Brace, 1999), p.171.

10   Donna Haraway, 'A Cyborg Manifesto: science, technology, and socialist feminism in the late twentieth century', in *Simians, Cyborgs and Women: The reinvention of nature* (New York: Routledge, 1991), p.177.

11   Guy Debord, 'Theory of the Dérive', originally published in *Internationale Situationiste*, no.2 (December 1958). Reprinted in *Theory of the Dérive and Other Situationist Writings on the City*, ed. by Libero Andreotti and Xavier Costa (Barcelona: Museu d'Art Contemporani de Barcelona, 1996).

12   Damasio, *The Feeling of What Happens*, p.313.

13   See Drew Leder, *The Absent Body* (Chicago: University of Chicago Press, 1990), for a fascinating discussion of the 'lived body and its cultural elaborations'.

14   'There's a rapt, mindless fascination with these disembodying or ability-augmenting technologies,' says Allucquere Rosanne Stone, Director of the Advanced Communications Technology Lab at the University of Texas. 'I think of it as a kind of cyborg envy...The desire to be wired is part of the larger fantasy of disembodiment, the deep childlike desire to go beyond one's body. This is not necessarily a bad thing. Certainly for the handicapped, it can be very liberating. For others, who have the desire

without the need, there can be problems. Political power still exists inside the body and being out of one's body or extending one's body through technology doesn't change that.' As quoted in Gareth Branwyn, 'The Desire to Be Wired', *Wired*, vol. 1, no. 4 (1993).

15 Thomas J. Csordas, 'Computerized Cadavers: Shades of Being and Representation in Virtual Reality', paper presented at the conference 'After Postmodernism', University of Chicago, 14–16 November, 1997.

16 Haraway, 'A Cyborg Manifesto', p. 1.

17 Kenneth Gergen, *The Saturated Self: Dilemmas of identity in contemporary life* (New York: Basic Books, 1991), p. 7.

Notes on Chapter 9

1 George Gessert, 'Notes sur l'art de la selection végétale', in *L'art biotech*, ed. By Jens Hauser (ex. cat., Le Lieu Unique, Nantes, 2003), p. 47 (authors' translation).

2 Jeremy Rifkin, *The Biotech Century: Harnessing the gene and remaking the world* (New York: Tharcher/Putnam, 1998), p. 236.

3 I. Wilmut, A.E. Schnieke, J. McWhir, A.J. Kind and K.H.S. Campbell, 'Viable offspring derived from fetal and adult mammalian cells', *Nature*, vol. 385, 1997, pp. 810–813.

4 Venter Institute, Press Release, November 2003. Available online. URL: http://www.venterinstitute.org/press/news/news_2003_11_13.php [15 June 2005].

5 Richard Lewontin, *Biology as Ideology: The Doctrine of DNA*, Canadian Broadcasting Corporation, Massey Lecture series (Concord, Ont.: House of Anansi Press, 1991), p. 3.

6 Shawn Bailey and Jennifer Willet, 'Bioteknica: Corporate Art for a Corporeal Public', artists' website. Available online. URL: http://www.bioteknica.org [15 June 2005].

7 Advanced Cell Technology, Press Release: 'Researchers Develop Specialized Cell Types from Embryonic Monkey Stem Cells'. No longer available online. URL: http://www.advancedcell.com/press.htm [5 February 2002].

8 David J. Mooney and Antonios G. Mikos, 'Growing New Organs', *Scientific American*, April 1999. Available online. URL: http://www.sciam.com/search/index.cfm?Q=GrowingNewOrgans [16 June 2006].

9 Anonymous, 'Parkinson's stem cell advance', BBC News, 8 January 2002. Available online. URL: http://news.bbc.co.uk/1/hi/health/1748928.stm [16 June 2006].

10 This work was completed with the assistance of artist/programmers David Jhave Johnston and David Bouchard.

11 A term coined by Oron Catts and Ionat Zurr, 'Growing Semi-Living Sculptures: the Tissue Culture & Art Project', *Leonardo*, vol. 35, no. 4 (2002), pp. 365–370.

12 In private interview with Jens Hauser, curator, *L'art biotech*, Nantes, 2003.

13 Presentation by Joe Davis at the European Media Art Festival Congress, Osnabrück, Germany, 2003.

14 United States Code: Title 18, Part 1, Chapter 10, § 175. 'Prohibitions with respect to biological weapons', as recorded by the Legal Information Institute. Available online. URL: http://www4.law.cornell.edu/uscode/18/175.html [15 June 2005].

15 Critical Art Ensemble, *Critical Art Ensemble*, art collective website. Available online. URL: http://www.critical-art.net [15 June 2005].

16 Critical Art Ensemble, *Critical Art Ensemble Defense Fund*, art collective website. Available online. URL: http://www.caedefensefund.org [15 June 2005].

17 We wish to acknowledge Oron Catts and Ionat Zurr, as well as SymbioticA residents Cynthia Verspaget and Kira O'Reilly, for their patient and knowledgeable training in tissue culture protocols, as well as Guy Ben-Ary for his expert assistance in learning digital optical microscopy.

18 The nucleus of a cell contains a number of chromosomes housing the DNA. On the end of each chromosome is a cap called a telomere. Some researchers believe that telomeres are like a cellular clock, setting the lifespan of the cell. Each time a cell divides its telomeres shorten. When the length of the telomeres becomes too short, cell division stops and the cell soon dies.

19 Anonymous, Culture Collection Cell Biology Catalogue (ATCC). Available online. URL: http://www.atcc.org/common/catalog/numSearch/numResults.cfm?atccNum=CL-173 [15 June 2005].

20 Gessert, 'Notes sur l'art de la selection végétale', p.47.

Notes on Chapter 10

1 Mark Weiser, 'Some Computer Science Issues in Ubiquitous Computing', *Communications of the ACM*, vol.36, no.7 (1993), pp.75–85.

2 William Buxton, 'Living in Augmented Reality: ubiquitous media and reactive environments', in *Video Mediated Communication*, ed. by Kathleen Finn, Abigail Sellen and Sylvia Wilber (Hillsdale, NJ: Erlbaum, 1997), pp.363–384 (370).

3 Hubert L. Dreyfus and Patricia Allen Dreyfus, 'Translator's Introduction', in Maurice Merleau-Ponty, *Sense and Non-Sense* (Evanston, IL: Northwestern University Press, 1964), p.xii.

4 Christopher Tweed, 'The Social Context of CAAD in Practice', in *Proceedings of EUROPIA 98: Cyberdesign – Media, Communication and Design Practice, Paris, France, 25–27 November*, ed. by Cherif Branki and Khaldoun Zreik (Paris: Europia Productions, 1998), pp.177–194.

5 Hiroshi Ishii and Brygg Ullmer, 'Tangible Bits: towards seamless interfaces between people, bits and atoms', in *Proceedings of the CHI '97, Conference on Human Factors in Computing Systems, Atlanta, Georgia*, March 22–27 (New York: ACM Press, 1997), pp.234–241.

6   George Lakoff and Mark Johnson, *Philosophy in the Flesh: The embodied mind and its challenge to Western thought* (New York: Basic Books, 1999).

7   Kent Bloomer and Charles Moore, *Body, Memory and Architecture* (New Haven, CT: Yale University Press, 1977), p.33.

8   Juhani Pallasmaa, *The Eyes of the Skin: Architecture and the senses* (London: Academy Editions, 1996), p.10.

9   Karen Franck, 'It and I: bodies as objects, bodies as subjects', *Architectural Design*, vol.68, no.11/12 (1998), pp.16–19 (p.18).

10   Pallasmaa, *The Eyes of the Skin*, p.13.

11   Ibid., p.18.

12   Walter Benjamin, *Illuminations*, ed. by Hannah Arendt, trans. by Harry Zohn (London: Pimlico, 1999), p.57.

13   Michael Smyth, 'Design Tools as Agents of Disclosure', *Knowledge Based Systems*, vol.13, no.1 (2000), pp.27–35. See also Michael Smyth, 'Supporting Design Exploration' (unpublished PhD thesis, Department of Computer Science, Loughborough University, 2001).

14   Linda Candy and Ernest Edmonds, 'Creative Design of the Lotus bicycle: implications for knowledge support systems research', *Design Studies*, vol.17, no.1 (1996), pp.71–90 (p.78).

15   Robin Roy, 'Case studies of creativity in innovative product development', *Design Studies*, vol.14, no.4 (1993), pp.423–443. See also Donald A Schön, *The Reflective Practitioner: How professionals think in action* (New York: Basic Books, 1983), p.77.

16   Bryan Lawson, *Design in Mind* (Oxford: Butterworth Architecture Press, 1994).

17   Ishii and Ullmer, 'Tangible Bits: towards seamless interfaces between people, bits and atoms', pp.234–235.

18   John Underkoffler and Hiroshi Ishii, 'Urp: a luminous-tangible workbench for urban planning and design', in *Proceedings of the CHI '99 Conference on Human Factors in Computing Systems, Pittsburgh, Pennsylvania, 15–20 May* (New York: ACM Press, 1999).

19   John Frazer, *An Evolutionary Architecture* (London: Architectural Association, 1995).

20   Michael Smyth, 'The Activity of Design as Revealed by Tool Usage', *Journal of Design Sciences*, vol.7, no.1 (1999), pp.11–22.

21   Tom Porter and John Neale, *Architectural Supermodels* (London: Architectural Press, 2000), p.42.

22   Ibid., pp.234–235.

23   Robert Kronenburg, 'Ephemeral Architecture', *Architectural Design*, vol.68, no.9/10 (1998).

24   Robert Kronenburg, *Portable Architecture* (Oxford: Architectural Press, 2000).

25   Anthony Dunne, *Hertzian Tales: Electronic products, aesthetic experience and critical design* (London: RCA/CRD Research Publications, 1999).

26   Ross Lovegrove, cited in Heather Martin, 'The Behaviour of Digital Objects' (unpublished Master's thesis [Computer Related Design], Royal College of Art, 1998), p.17.

27 Angela Chang, Ben Resner, Brad Koerner, XingChen Wang and Hiroshi Ishii, 'LumiTouch: an emotional communication device', in *Extended Abstracts of the CHI '01 Conference on Human Factors in Computing Systems, Seattle, Washington*, March 31–April 5 (New York: ACM Press, 2001).

28 Konrad Tollmar, Stefan Junestrand and Olle Torgny, 'Virtually Living Together: a design framework for new communication media', in *Proceedings of the DIS '00 Conference on Designing Interactive Systems, New York City, New York*, August 17–19 (New York: ACM Press, 2000), pp.83–91.

29 Marion Buchenau and Jane Fulton Suri, 'Experience Prototyping', *Proceedings of the DIS '00*, pp.424–433.

30 Michael Smyth, Bas Raijmakers and Alan Munro, 'Who Am I and Where Am I?: switching and stitching in the digital age', in *Proceedings of the Design 2004, 8th International Design Conference, Dubrovnik, 18–21 May*, ed. by D. Marjanovic (Zagreb: University of Zagreb, 2004), pp.1487–1492.

31 Bill Gaver and Heather Martin, 'Alternatives: exploring information appliances through conceptual design proposals', in *Proceedings of the CHI '00 Conference on Human Factors in Computing Systems, The Hague, Netherlands*, April 1–6 2000 (New York: ACM Press, 2000), pp.209–216.

Notes on Chapter 11

1 These and other contemporary strategies are described in Vernon Hyde Minor, *Art History's History*, 2nd edn. (Englewood Cliffs, NJ: Prentice Hall, 2001). See also Donald Preziosi, ed., *The Art of Art History: A critical anthology* (Oxford: Oxford University Press, 1998), Eric Fernie, *Art History and its Methods: A critical anthology* (London: Phaidon Press, 1995), and Laurie Schneider Adams, *The Methodologies of Art: An introduction*, (Boulder, CO: Westview Press, 1996).

2 I published these grids previously in the article 'Ut Pixel Poesis: strategies for analyzing art in a changing context,' in *Turning Trees: Selected readings of International Visual Literacy Association*, ed. by Robert E. Griffin (Breckenridge, CO: IVLA, 2002), pp.157–164.

3 Erwin Panofsky, *Studies in Iconology: Humanistic themes in the art of the Renaissance* [1939], (New York: Harper & Row, 1962).

4 Salome Schmid-Isler, 'The Language of Digital Genres: a semiotic investigation of style and iconology on the World Wide Web,' in *Proceedings of the 33rd Annual Hawaii International Conference on System Sciences*, ed. by Ralph H. Sprague, Jr. (Los Alamitos CA: IEEE Computer Society 2000); downloaded as a PDF file from the following source: http://www.mediamanagement.org/modules/pub/view.php/mediamanagement-9 [25 June 2005].

5 Panofsky, *Studies in Iconology*, pp.26–30. His original grid appears on pp.40–41.

6   The purpose here is not to describe contemporary methods, rather to show how any method might be included in Panofsky's system. The semiotics of Ferdinand de Saussure and Charles Peirce are considered structuralist, while those of Roman Jakobson, Claude Lévi-Strauss and Maurice Merleau Ponty are post-structuralist. The work of Roland Barthes bridges both areas. Other contemporary practices include the Marxist approach of T.J. Clark and psychoanalytic approaches based on the work of Sigmund Freud (those of Michel Foucault and Jacques Lacan have been the most popular among art historians). Contemporary methodologies in art history have been primarily adapted from other disciplines, such as comparative literature. See note 1 above.

7   I published these grids previously in the article 'Neo-Panofsky: iconography and iconology for the twenty-first century,' in *Changing Tides: Selected readings from the International Visual Literacy Association*, ed. by Robert E. Griffin (Newport, RI: IVLA, 2004), pp. 199–206.

8   Panofsky's 'corrective principle' appears in his grid: *Studies in Iconology*, pp. 40–41. (Other assertions are the author's own).

9   See Elizabeth K. Menon, 'Communicating Vessels: digital semiotics and web installation art,' in *DRH 2001 and 2002: Selected papers from the Digital Resources for the Humanities Conferences at the School of Oriental and African Studies, University of London in September 2001 and at Edinburgh University Library in September 2002*, ed. by Jean Anderson, Alistair Dunning and Michael Fraser (London: Office for Humanities Communication, 2003), pp. 193–202.

10   Ferdinand de Saussure, *Course in General Linguistics*, trans. by Wade Baskin (New York: McGraw Hill, 1966); Charles Sanders Peirce, *Collected Papers* (Cambridge, MA: Harvard University Press, 1931–1958); Roland Barthes, *Elements of Semiology*, trans. by Annette Lavers and Colin Smith (London: Cape, 1967). Peirce's system is summarised by Rosalind Krauss in 'Notes on the Index', *October*, no. 3 (1977), pp. 68–81, and *October*, no. 4 (1977), pp. 58–67.

11   Here I am referring to the use of a colour change and underlining to indicate the hyperlink. While a hyperlink may consist of underlined text (and thus might be interpreted as having a second-order connection through language), a hyperlink need not contain text.

12   Peirce's terms elucidate particular aspects of signs, although there is clearly overlap between the functions of his icon, index and symbol. Nevertheless, his system is being employed to describe the appearance and function of digitally generated objects. See, for instance, Grant Sherson, 'The Relevance of Semiotics to the Internet: how web designers use metaphors in Web Development' (available online. URL: http://www.ucol.ac.nz/~g.sherson/papers/semiotics.htm [28 February 2005] and Gene Callahan, 'Semiotics and GUI Design' (available online. URL: http://gwa.municipia.at/files/semiotics.html [28 February 2005].

13   Roland Barthes, *Image–Music–Text*, trans. by Stephen Heath (New York: Hill and Wang, 1977), p. 144.

14   Carolyn P. Speranza, artist's website. Available online. URL: http://www.speranza.net [28 February 2005].

15   Jay David Bolter and Richard Grusin, *Remediation: Understanding new media* (Cambridge, MA: MIT, 2000), p.42.

16   Artist and educator Jim Johnson's website. Available online. URL: http://spot.colorado.edu/~johnsoja/Index.html [28 February 2005].

17   Jim Johnson's artist's statement. Available online. URL: http://www.altx.com/hyperx/johnson/statement.html [28 February 2005].

18   Roy Ascott, 'Behaviourist Art and the Cybernetic Vision' [1966], in *Multimedia from Wagner to Virtual Reality*, ed. by Randall Packer and Ken Jordan (New York: W.W. Norton, 2001), p.98.

19   Ibid.

20   Pierre Lévy, *Cyberculture*, trans. by Robert Bononno (Minneapolis: University of Minnesota Press, 2001), p.65.

21   Brenda Laurel, *Computers as Theater* (Reading, MA: Addison-Wesley, 1993), p.50.

22   Ibid.

23   Ibid.

24   Ibid.

25   Ibid.

26   Byron L Sherwin, *The Golem Legend: Origins and implications* (London: Lanham, 1985), p.1. See also Mary Wollstonecraft Shelley, *Frankenstein* (New York: Amereon House, 1985); orig. pub. as *Frankenstein, or the Modern Prometheus* (Oxford: Oxford University Press, 1831).

27   Jean Tinguely, Fritz Gerber and Pantus Hulten, *Museum Jean Tinguely Basel: The Collection* (Berne: Benteli Publishers, 1996), p.59.

28   Ibid., p.44.

Notes on Chapter 12

1   See Roland Barthes, *Camera Lucida: Reflections on photography* [1980], trans. by Richard Howard, 3rd edn. (London: Vintage, 1993). See also André Bazin, *What is Cinema?*, vol.1, trans. by Hugh Grey (Berkeley, CA: University of California Press, 1967), and Walter Benjamin, 'A Short History of Photography' [1931], trans. by Stanley Mitchell, in *Screen*, vol.13, no.1 (1972), pp.5–27. Finally, for an extended discussion of the legacy of Barthes' work, see Damian Sutton, *Photography Cinema Time* (Minneapolis: University of Minnesota Press, 2007).

2   Barthes, *Camera Lucida*, p.79.

3   Oliver Wendell Holmes, 'The Stereoscope and the Stereograph', [1859], repr. in *Classic Essays on Photography*, ed. by Alan Trachtenberg, (New Haven, CT: Leete's Island, 1980), p.74.

4   Peter Osborne, 'Photography in an Expanding Field', in *Where is the Photograph?*, ed. by David Green (Brighton: Photoforum and Photoworks, 2003).

5   See 'Leica in Financial Crisis', *Digital Photography Review*, 22 February 2005 (available online). URL: http://www.dpreview.com/news/0502/05022203leica_financialtrouble.asp [15 March 2005]; 'Kodak Confirms Plans to Stop Making Slide Projectors', Kodak Press Release, 26 September 2003, URL: http://www.kodak.com/US/en/corp/pressReleases/pr20030926-01.shtml [15 March 2005]; 'Tamron Announces the Discontinuation of Bronica ETR-Si, SQ-Ai, SQ-B and GS-1 Cameras in the US Market', Tamron Press Release, 1 October 2004. URL: http://www.tamron.com/news/corp/bronica_discontinuation.asp [15 March 2005]. 'Ilford Emerges from Receivership', Ilford Press Release, 21 February 2005, URL: http://www.ilford.com/html/us_english/pr/PRht.html [15 March 2005].

6   Scott McQuire, 'Digital Dialetics: the paradox of cinema in a studio without walls', *Historical Journal of Film, Radio and Television*, vol.19, no.3 (1999), p.384.

7   Thierry de Duve, 'The Photograph as Paradox', *October*, vol.5 (1978), p.114.

8   See Bazin, *What is Cinema?*, p.15, Kendall L Walton, 'Transparent Pictures: on the nature of photographic realism', *Critical Inquiry* vol.11 (1984), pp.246–247, and Victor Burgin, 'Something about Photography Theory', in *The New Art History*, ed. by A.L. Rees and Frank Borzello (Atlantic Highlands, NJ: Humanities Press, 1988), p.46.

9   André Bazin, 'The ontology of the photographic image', in Bazin, *What is Cinema?*, pp.9–16 (p.14.).

10   Roger Scruton, 'Photography and Representation', *Critical Inquiry* vol.7, (1981), p.578.

11   See *Thinking Photography*, ed. by Victor Burgin (London: Macmillan, 1994).

12   See also Jenna Ng's chapter in this volume.

13   Peter Lunenfeld, 'Art Post-History: digital photography and electronic semiotics', in *Photography after Photography: Memory and representation in the digital age*, ed. by Hubertus von Amlunxen (Munich: G&B Arts, 1996), p.95.

14   Benjamin, 'A Short History of Photography', pp.5–18.

15   John Roberts, *The Art of Interruption* (Manchester: Manchester University Press, 1998), pp.220–225.

16   John Tagg, *The Burden of Representation* (London: Macmillan, 1988); Allan Sekula, 'The Body and the Archive', in *The Contest of Meaning*, ed. by Richard Bolton (Cambridge, MA: MIT Press, 1989), pp.343–389.

17   See *Family Snaps: The meaning of domestic photography*, ed. by Patricia Holland and Jo Spence (London: Virago, 1991).

18   Mihalyi Csikszentmihalyi and Eugene Rochberg-Holton, *The Meaning of Things* (Cambridge: Cambridge University Press, 1981), p.224.

19   Elizabeth Edwards, 'Material Beings: objecthood and ethnographic photographs', in *Visual Studies*, vol.17, no.1 (2002), p.71.

20   Vilém Flusser, *Towards a Philosophy of Photography*, trans. by Anthony Mathews (London: Reaktion, 2000), p.34.

21   Gilles Deleuze, *The Fold: Leibniz and the Baroque*, trans. by Tom Conley (London: Athlone, 1993), p.76. Gilles Deleuze and Félix Guattari, *A Thousand*

Plateaus: Capitalism and schizophrenia [1980], trans. by Brian Massumi, 3rd edn. (London: Athlone, 1996).

22   Deleuze, *The Fold*, p.20

23   Gregg Lambert, *The Non-philosophy of Gilles Deleuze*, (London: Continuum, 2002), p.21.

24   Deleuze and Guattari, *A Thousand Plateaus*, p.265.

25   Deleuze, *The Fold*, p.52.

26   Deleuze and Guattari, *A Thousand Plateaus*, pp.266–269.

27   Flusser, *Towards a Philosophy of Photography*, p.10.

28   Ibid, p.37.

29   Deleuze and Guattari, *A Thousand Plateaus*, p.265; Deleuze, *The Fold*, p.76.

Notes on Chapter 13

1   Alfian Sa'at, 'Ghazal of Dreaming', personal weblog on Diaryland. Available online. URL: http://alfian.diaryland.com/ghazal.html [1 March 2005].

2   Plato, *The Republic* (Cambridge: Cambridge University Press, 2000), Book VII.

3   For example, a basic tenet of Buddhism is the concept of the objective world as an illusion, the first fact of existence being the law of change or impermanence. Enlightenment, therefore, is to see this ultimate truth – the limitations of selfhood – and thus transcend the birth–growth–decay–death cycle of existence. See, generally, Christmas Humphreys, *Buddhism*, (Harmondsworth: Penguin, 1962).

4   For example, one of the teachings in Gnosticism is that '[t]he appearance of an objective world distinguishable from a subjective self is but the imaginary form in which Consciousness Perfectly Realizes Itself.' Shankara also wrote: 'All things – from Brahma the creator down to a single blade of grass – are…simply appearances and not real.' See Shankara, *Crest Jewel of Discrimination*, trans. by Swami Prabhavananda and Chris Isherwood (Hollywood, CA: Vedanta Press, 1947), p.97.

5   One of the more prominent examples is the 'brain in a vat' hypothesis posited by Jonathan Dancy, whereby all human beings are brains in a vat and thus perceive reality only as it exists in it: see Jonathan Dancy, *Introduction to Contemporary Epistemology* (Oxford: Blackwell, 1985). Also see Robert Nozick's 'thought experiment' in *Anarchy, State, and Utopia* (Oxford: Blackwell, 1974).

6   See, for instance, Jean Baudrillard, *Simulacra and Simulation*, trans. by Sheila Faria Glaser (Ann Arbor, MI: University of Michigan Press, 1994), and Slavoj Žižek, *Welcome to the Desert of the Real! Five essays on September 11 and related dates* (London and New York: Verso, 2002). The latter posits an interesting division of (and subsequent interaction between) the reality and non-reality of the 11 September attacks.

7   For fiction, see, for example, Philip K. Dick, *The Simulacra* (New York: Vintage Books, 2002), and William Gibson, *Neuromancer* (New York: Ace Books, 2000).

The idea of alternate (non-supernatural) realities beyond that of the real world has also formed the premise of movies such as the *Matrix* films (*The Matrix*, *The Matrix Reloaded* and *The Matrix Revolutions*), as well as *eXistenZ* (gaming realities), *The Truman Show* ('real world' reality as one great manipulation by the media) and *Dark City* (reality as implanted memories).

8   The notion of objective reality being non-existent is one of the paradoxes of quantum mechanics: generally, the paradox states that an object, as a quantum system, will have no definite properties until its wave function is reduced by observation and its state of being properly defined. Without observation, the object will not exist for anybody, and thus will not properly exist. See Martin Gardner, 'Quantum Weirdness', in *The Night Is Large: Collected essays 1938–1995* (New York: Penguin, 1996), pp.22–31.

9   At least two books, focusing exclusively on *The Matrix*'s philosophy and ideas, have been published in the wake of the film. See William Irwin, ed., *The Matrix and Philosophy: Welcome to the desert of the real*, (Chicago: Open Court Publishing, 2002), and Glenn Yeffeth, ed., *Taking the Red Pill: Science, philosophy and religion in The Matrix* (Dallas: BenBella Books, 2003), not to mention various articles in anthologies and the thousands of websites, chatrooms and discussion fora dedicated to it.

10   In the film, Neo (Keanu Reeves) is seen to store his hacker diskettes in a hollowed-out space in the middle of Baudrillard's *Simulacra and Simulation*.

11   See Charles Sanders Peirce, *Philosophical Writings of Peirce*, ed. by Justus Buchler (New York: Dover, 1955).

12   See, for example, Stephen Prince, 'True Lies: perceptual realism, digital images, and film theory' in *Film Quarterly: Forty Years – A Selection*, ed. by Brian Henderson and Ann Martin (Berkeley, CA: University of California Press, 1999), pp.394–401.

13   See Göran Sonesson, 'Post-photography and Beyond (1): from mechanical reproduction to digital production', *Visio: Postphotography*, vol.4, no.1 (2000), pp.11–36, particularly for his account of Philippe Dubois' chronicle of how the photograph was first looked upon as an icon, and then as a symbol by 'that most celebrated generation of iconoclasts', and 'finally' as an index. See also Mette Sandbye, 'Photographic Anamnesia: the past in the present', in *Symbolic Imprints: Essays on photography and visual culture*, ed. by Lars Kiel Bertelsen, Rune Gade and Mette Sandbye (Aarhus: Aarhus University Press, 1998), p.182, on how, depending on the topic of the discussion, 'at various times one aspect [of the photograph's semiotic] has been emphasized in preference to the others'.

14   Lars Kiel Bertelsen, 'It's Only a Paper Moon…Re-reading Apollo photography in the light of digital imagery', in *Symbolic Imprints*, p.88.

15   Peirce, *Philosophical Writings of Peirce*, p.106 (emphasis added.)

16   Bill Nichols, *Representing Reality: Issues and concepts in documentary* (Bloomington, IN: Indiana University Press, 1991), p.5.

17 Susan Sontag, *On Photography*, (New York: Delta, 1978), p.154 (emphasis added).

18 Roland Barthes, *Camera Lucida: Reflections on photography* [1980], trans. by Richard Howard, 5th edn. (London: Vintage, 2000), pp.5–6.

19 Sandbye, 'Photographic Anamnesia: the past in the present', p.182.

20 Stanley Cavell, *The World Viewed* (Cambridge, MA: Harvard University Press, 1979), p.17 (emphasis added).

21 André Bazin, 'The Ontology of the Photographic Image', in *What is Cinema?*, vol.1, trans. by Hugh Grey (Berkeley, CA: University of California Press, 1967), p.14 (emphasis added).

22 Lev Manovich, *The Language of New Media*, (Cambridge, MA: MIT Press, 2001), pp.303–318 (emphasis added).

23 Ibid, p.305 (emphasis added).

24 See 'From Puppets to Pixels: digital characters in Episode II', in DVD featurette, *Star Wars: Episode II – Attack of the Clones*, 20th Century Fox Home Video (2002).

25 William J. Mitchell, *The Reconfigured Eye: Visual truth in the post-photographical era* (Cambridge, MA: MIT Press, 1994), p.52.

26 Richard Woods, 'Does my digitally reduced bum look small in this?', *The Sunday Times*, 'Focus' supplement, 12 January 2003, p.16.

27 Maureen Turim, 'Artisanal Prefigurations of the Digital: animating realities, collage effects, and theories of image manipulation', *Wide Angle*, vol.21, no.1 (1999), p.52.

28 *Alien Evolution*, written and presented by Mark Kermode, FilmFour, 4 January 2003 (emphasis added).

29 Turim, 'Artisanal Prefigurations of the Digital', p.52.

30 *Le Petit soldat* (France, Jean-Luc Godard, Beauregard/SNC, 1963).

31 Jean Cocteau (emphasis added). As cited in Susan Sontag, *Against Interpretation and Other Essays* (New York: Doubleday, 1967), p.197.

32 Barthes, *Camera Lucida*, p.76 (emphasis in original).

33 Göran Sonesson, 'Post-photography and beyond (2): from mechanical reproduction to digital production', Institute of Art History and Musicology of Lund University. Available online. URL: http://www.arthist.lu.se/kultsem/sonesson/VisioPhoto2.html [1 March 2005].

34 Ibid. However, I disagree with Sonesson's theory of subjugating the photograph's indexicality in this way. There is no reason why indexicality should be bound up with specificities of spatio-temporal data; all that is required to establish the basis of the sign function is the physical connection between image and object, which may be ascertained simply by the positive confirmation that the sign is a photograph and that it depicts, say, a horse. For there must have been some physical connection in order for the horse to be photographed – to argue otherwise is to defeat the very mechanism of photography. Since the establishment of that physical connection is sufficient, its details of 'where' and 'when' are thus irrelevant.

35 Michael Charlesworth, 'Fox Talbot and the "White Mythology" of Photography', *Word & Image*, vol.11, no.3 (1995), p.208.

36 Bertelsen, 'Paper Moon...', p. 102. This theory of the film image has also been applied in documentary theory. See for example Linda Williams, 'Mirrors Without Memories: Truth, History, and the New Documentary', *Film Quarterly*, vol.46, no.3 (1993), pp.9–21.

37 Bertelsen, 'It's Only a Paper Moon...', p.97.

38 Ibid, p.89.

39 Gilles Deleuze, *Cinema 2: The Time-image*, trans. by Hugh Tomlinson and Robert Galeta, 4th edn. (London: Continuum, 2005), p.66.

40 Note, however, that elements of the technology had been previously utilised in *The Campanile Movie* (US, Paul Debevec, George Borshukov et al., University of California, Berkeley, 1997), a short film that used photogrammetry (the process of generating three-dimensional models from photographs) to create photorealistic aerial cinematography of the University of California's Berkeley campus. The film's co-creator, George Borshukov, subsequently applied and developed those techniques to create the groundbreaking 'bullet-time' shots in *The Matrix*.

41 Steve Silberman, 'Matrix2', *Wired*, vol.11, no.5 (May 2003). Available online. URL: http://www.wired.com/wired/archive/11.05/ matrix2_pr.html [accessed 6 September 2003].

42 For more on the process of virtual cinematography, see Gordon Devin, 'The Matrix Makers', *Newsweek*, 6 January 2003, pp.80–89, Susan Thomas, '"Matrix" Trilogy Raises the Effects Bar', *Videography*, 1 June 2003 (available online. URL: http://www.highbeam.com/library/doc3.asp?docid= 1G1:105045911 [6 September 2003]; Paula Parisi and Ron Magid, 'Escape All Limits: FX whiz John Gaeta takes the Matrix where no film has been before', *Hollywood Reporter*, 6 May 2003 (available online. URL: http:// www.reevesdrive.com/newsarchive/2003/hr050603b.htm [6 September 2003]) and Simon Gray, 'Simulated Cinema', *American Cinematographer*, vol.84, no.6 (June 2003), p.53.

43 This process, known as photogrammetry, was originally used in the mid-nineteenth century by cartographers, who took multiple exposures of landscape by stringing cameras to kites and subsequently generating topographical maps from the flat images. In the early 1990s, Arnauld Lamorlettem, R&D director for the design firm BUF Compagnie discovered 'digital photogrammetry' by morphing between two photographs to generate the three-dimensional models: Silberman, 'Matrix2'.

44 These are computer programs written by German firm Alias/Wavefront specifically for the technique of image-based rendering. Earlier this year, Alias/Wavefront also won an Academy Award for 'scientific and technical achievement' in its development of Maya software, a 3D animation program. Alias/Wavefront Press Release. Available online. URL:http:// www.alias.com/eng/products-services/announcements/academy_ award/index.shtml [6 September 2003].

45 Christopher Probst, 'Welcome to the Machine', *American Cinematographer*, vol. 79, no. 4 (April 1999), p. 45.

46 Mark Salisbury, 'Rage Against the Machines', *Premiere* (May 2003), p. 11.

47 Jean Baudrillard, *Symbolic Exchange and Death* (London: Sage Publications, 1993), pp. 71–72.

48 D.N. Rodowick, *Reading the Figural, or, Philosophy after the New Media* (Durham, NC: Duke University Press, 2001), p. 212. Rodowick describes this as 'the disappearance of a visible and tactile support for both image and text'.

Notes on Chapter 14

1 Here Sloterdijk is right, although one may disagree with his specific version of the account: Heidegger has to be supplemented with an account of how Clearance itself is generated. See Peter Sloterdijk, *Nicht gerettet* (Frankfurt: Suhrkamp, 2001).

2 Jean Laplanche, *Vie et mort en psychanalyse*, (Paris: Flammarion, 1989), p. 58.

3 Karl Marx, *Capital*, vol. 1 [1867] (New York: International Publishers, 1967), p. 163.

4 See Kojin Karatani, *Transcritique: On Kant and Marx* (Cambridge, MA: MIT Press, 2003).

5 Karl Marx, 'A Contribution to the Critique of Hegel's Philosophy of Right: Introduction' [1844], in Karl Marx, *Collected Works*, vol. 3 (New York: International Publishers, 1970), p. 175.

6 This point – about the theological core of capitalism, which has nothing to do with Max Weber's thesis on Protestant ethic and the rise of capitalism, since it designates a 'theological' character of the very capitalist mechanism – was emphasised by Walter Benjamin: 'Capitalism as Religion', in Walter Benjamin, *Selected Writings*, vol. 1 (Cambridge, MA: Harvard University Press, 1996), pp. 288–291.

7 See David Chalmers, *The Conscious Mind* (Oxford: Oxford University Press, 1996), p. 231.

8 I rely here on the unpublished manuscripts of Adrian Johnston.

9 Sloterdijk, *Nicht gerettet*, p. 365.

10 'A Conversation with Alain Badiou,' *lacanian ink*, vol. 23 (2004), pp. 100–101.

11 Jacques-Alain Miller, 'Religion, Psychoanalysis,' *lacanian ink*, vol. 23 (2004), pp. 18–19.

12 Furthermore, should one not also bear in mind here the key difference between truth and knowledge? Is not, from a certain standard perspective, 'truth' the very name for a conjunction of knowledge and meaning, so that the true materialist task is not primarily to dissociate knowledge from meaning but, rather, to articulate the possibility of asserting a dimension of *truth* outside knowledge?

13   See Alain Badiou, 'The Caesura of Nihilism', lecture delivered at the University of Essex, 10 September 2003.

14   Alain Badiou, 'L'entretien de Bruxelles', *Les Temps Modernes*, vol. 526 (1990), p. 6.

15   Alberto Toscano, 'From the State to the World? Badiou and anti-capitalism', *Communication & Cognition*, vol. 36 (2003), pp. 1–2.

16   Ibid., p. 4

Index

Page numbers in italics refer to illustrations.